W9-ASD-766

FOOTPRINTS ON THE PLANET

FOOTPRINTS ON THE PLANET

A Search for an Environmental Ethic

Robert Cahn

Foreword by Jacques Cousteau

UNIVERSE BOOKS
New York

To all who care enough . . .

Published in the United States of America in 1978
by Universe Books
381 Park Avenue South, New York, N.Y. 10016

© 1978 by Robert Cahn

All rights reserved. No part of this publication
may be reproduced, stored in a retrieval system, or
transmitted, in any form or by any means,
electronic, mechanical, photocopying, recording,
or otherwise, without the prior permission of the publishers

Library of Congress Catalog Card Number: 78-56363
ISBN 0-87663-324-6

Printed in the United States of America

This book is printed on 100% recycled paper.

FOREWORD

Why would the Supreme Court decide to stop the construction of a $120-million dollar dam to save an endangered but useless little fish? Why would hundreds of thousands of concerned citizens protest the slaughter of whales and seals that they have never seen and know very little about? Why would a provincial judge oblige road builders to spend millions of dollars to deviate a planned highway to save a pond in which a few dozen endangered geese come to winter every year?

The answer is simple. Today, the public is realizing that there is an urgent need for an environmental code of conduct.

But today, still, money is the only yardstick used to evaluate projects and make decisions. No planner really cares about the long-range consequences of his enterprises. Nuclear plants are hastily built, while nobody knows what to do with the radioactive waste they generate or how to dismantle the plants themselves when, after thirty years of activity, they will have to be evacuated and will remain atomic threats for tens of thousands of years.

For short-term conveniences, we are taking away from future generations the vital options they would need to exercise in order to survive decently. But there is hope at the horizon: If yesterday, such blind behavior of the decision-makers was not even discussed, today, on the contrary, public opinion is awakening and irresponsible decisions are openly challenged.

Maybe the protection of an endangered, ugly little fish is not worth stopping the construction of a major dam. But if there are no stringent rules, where will we draw the line? After the fish, the birds, the forests, the wolves and foxes and elephants and dolphins? What other victims are we to immolate on the golden calf's altar? What future are we to bequeath to our grandchildren? Bob Cahn's *Footprints on the Planet* will, I hope, be the trail leading to the environmental ethic we urgently need.

Jacques-Yves Cousteau

CONTENTS

How hard to realize that every camp of men or beast has this glorious starry firmament for a roof! In such places standing alone on the mountain-top it is easy to realize that whatever special nests we make—leaves and moss like the marmots and birds, or tents or piled stone—we all dwell in a house of one room—the world with the firmament for its roof—and are sailing the celestial spaces without leaving any track.

John Muir

A SILLY
LITTLE FISH?

Walking up a gentle hill away from the fog-shrouded lake where we had camped on the North Slope of the Brooks Range, I stepped into clear, mistless beauty. The incredible green vastness of Alaska's wilderness enveloped me. The sun cast a golden glow that failed to warm the early morning chill. An Arctic tern circled overhead.

The breeze ruffling the foot-high willows, alders, birches, and berry bushes that emerge in summer from the heavy snows of fall, winter, and spring was the only sound that broke the great silence. I felt awe tinged with uneasiness at the sense of total aloneness in this untamed region hundreds of miles from civilization.

I could almost imagine I was the first white man to set foot on this particular spot, except for the team of scientists back at the base camp. I picked my way through the thick tundra toward the crest of the little hill. What new view would unfold from there?

From the top I looked down on a stark reminder of civilization—a jumble of oil drums, gasoline cans, wooden crates, piles of tin cans and other trash, and a number of bare, ugly gashes cutting across the tundra leading to and from this deserted campsite. The gashes, two-to-three-foot-deep gullies running parallel to each other, had been started years ago by the wheels of a vehicle. Little did the driver know—or care—that his tire tracks would erode into gullies, leaving deepening and damaging imprints on this fragile ground.

Looking at the trash lying just where some oil exploration crew had left it years before in this deep freeze, where things do not readily decay, I could imagine the crew thinking: "What's the harm of some litter in the midst of millions of desolate acres of land? Probably no one will ever come by here again."

I had hitched a ride with David Hickock on one of his inspection runs as senior resource scientist coordinating federal planning activities in Alaska. We had landed in a small float plane on one of Alaska's three million lakes, this one known only as Lake 2900, denoting its elevation. Hickock had come to check on the work of a team of scientists hired by oil companies to conduct ecological studies on soil and wildlife conditions, and for me the trip was part of the research for a series of articles I was writing for *The Christian Science Monitor* on the proposed oil pipeline across Alaska.

On a month-long tour that summer of 1969, I was trying to find out what really was at stake in the controversial decision facing Secretary of the Interior Walter J. Hickel, a decision that could determine the destiny of this last frontier. Actions in the coming months would affect more than the land and the wildlife. It could also change the lives of thousands of rural Alaska Natives. Although many of them welcomed opportunities for employment and improvement in their standard of living, they did not want these benefits at the cost of their centuries-old subsistence way of life and values that allowed them to live in harmony with nature.

The U.S. government was on the verge of giving the go-ahead on the biggest construction project in the nation's history, laying a pipeline to transport oil over 800 miles of fragile arctic vegetation. It would cross mountains, valleys, and seven major earthquake zones, bisect caribou migration routes, dig through permanently frozen ground that erodes badly when disturbed, span the mighty and previously unbridged Yukon River, and all this with the sparsest of ecological research and only a smattering of knowledge about the impact on the environment.

When I'd interviewed Secretary Hickel before I left for Alaska, he told me his department would insist on certain environmental safeguards in advance and would protect the environment as construction proceeded. He had no choice, he said, other than to allow construction once safeguards were assured, because the oil was there and had to be transported to where it could be used. And besides, he said, one 48-inch pipeline and one narrow construction access road were really insignificant in a state of 375 million acres, and would be practically unnoticeable once completed.

As I walked back to camp that summer day in Alaska with the ugly scene of erosion and litter deeply imbedded in thought, I could not help but think of Hickel's comments. After breakfast, one of the scientists, William M. Mitchell, showed me some of the specimens of plants and grasses he was collecting to be test planted later. He was studying what happens when the ground is denuded of its tundra cover, which would occur in pipeline construction. Ordinarily revegetation research of this sort should take place over many years. But Mitchell had been hired only for an eight-week crash study and some follow-up tests at the University of Alaska. This short period was nowhere near adequate to come up with the reliable data needed by the Trans Alaska Pipeline System (TAPS), an amalgam of major U.S. and British oil companies.* Yet the oil companies wanted to start work immediately on the pipeline. When TAPS made its application for a permit to put a pipeline through public lands, little was known of soil conditions, potential wildlife impacts, or earthquake hazards. The oil companies insisted that they would do the needed studies as they went along, making certain not to harm the environment.

When I got to Fairbanks I talked with David R. Klein of the University of Alaska, another of the scientists hired temporarily by the oil companies. He was conducting research on potential harm to the migration of the caribou so necessary to the Natives'

* The Trans Alaska Pipeline System was later reorganized as the Alyeska Pipeline Service Company.

subsistence diet. He, too, warned of the dangers of hasty research. "Engineers estimate the ability to solve a problem by the amount of time and money you put into it," said Klein. "But with ecology you are dealing with cycles, and can't have a rush program. We shouldn't be hurried into such an important decision as the pipeline, and shouldn't have to act fast to meet the pace set by the oil companies. It wouldn't hurt to delay the decision until the basic environmental problems have been solved."

As I continued my travels around this immense and virtually unmolested state, I found other people working on crash research that would become the basis for key decisions in Washington. The oil companies felt that after purchasing leases from the state and now having discovered oil in abundance, they had the right to seek a way to get it to market. However, it was not a simple matter of rights that concerned me, but the methods the companies were using to preempt the orderly decision-making process.

The oil at Prudhoe Bay would feed a part of the gluttonous American fuel appetite for no more than twenty years, if that. It had been under the ground for eons. Where was the public debate about whether this was the time to tap this resource? Where was the consideration of other ways to get the oil out? Where was the consideration of cutting down on energy use so the need for oil would not be so urgent? What about the impact on the Natives' way of life? Was the Natives' right to live off the land and maintain their culture now going to be ended by the introduction of economic and cultural change and potential harm to the physical environment that a multi-billion-dollar construction project would bring? Who was considering the long-term impact on the human environment of these short-term benefits?

I returned to Washington convinced that by rushing into this project—as the government then appeared likely to do—we would repeat many of the same mistakes our nation made in developing the West. In the final article of my *Monitor* series I suggested that President Nixon ought to order Secretary Hickel to delay any go-ahead until thorough studies could be made. "Conservationists are hoping," I wrote, "that for once development will be carried out with proper concern for the environment and that the natural heritage of future generations will not be endangered for a temporary gain during the twenty years it will take to drain this oil pool."

These Alaska experiences impressed upon me as never before that new laws and environmental agitation, while needed and encouraging, would not be sufficient to offset the difficulties ahead. As a nation and as individuals we were finding that our decisions and the steps being taken by leaders in government and business and by average citizens were making footprints on our planet that would scar it perhaps for centuries. And what was being called the advent of the environmental era was really the dawning realization by millions of Americans that we need to consider the impacts of our decisions in our daily activities and try to determine whether we can choose alternative actions that will have less, little, or no harmful effects. It was my first glimmer of an ethical approach to mankind's relation to the earth and its creatures and resources.

This glimpse of what might be called an environmental ethic was a decisive point in my continuing education as a conservationist. It was the beginning of my awareness that the understanding and practice of this ethic in the actions of all of us in all walks of life may be the most important contribution we can make toward a better quality of life.

Another turning point came when, about this time, I first discovered the writings of Aldo Leopold, who defined a land ethic in practical and understandable terms. What John Muir's writings did for preservation of wilderness and parks, what Theodore Roosevelt's speaking and politicking did for protecting natural resources and public lands from avaricious business interests, Leopold accomplished in opening a window to every citizen's individual responsibility.

In an essay, "The Land Ethic," from *A Sand County Almanac and Sketches Here and There* (1949), published the year after his death, Leopold noted the need for an ethic dealing with man's relation to land and to the animals and plants which grow upon it.

The land ethic simply enlarges the boundaries of the community to include soils, waters, plants, and animals, or collectively: the land ... changes the role of Homo sapiens from conqueror of the land-community to plain member and citizen of it. It implies respect for his fellow-members, and also respect for the community as such.

Reading Leopold's essays in the *Almanac* and his *Round River,* I realized for the first time the urgent necessity for every citizen to have a feeling and awareness that the earth is not here for humans to manipulate but that we exist as part of an interrelated world. "We abuse land because we regard it as a commodity belonging to us," he wrote. "When we see land as a community to which we belong, we may begin to use it with love and respect."

It became clear to me that an *environmental* ethic based on a knowledge about our relationship with and impact on nature and natural systems is vital to our everyday life. Ethics do not suddenly bring about a new vision of right and wrong that we did not have before. They help us to understand more clearly what we already sensed or felt but had not yet molded into a clear basis for actions. Ethics are composed of "oughts." They remind us how we ought to think about things, what values we ought to have, what kind of actions we ought to take, and the kind of life we ought to live.

Based on the fact that humankind is part of and inseparably linked to the natural order, my own concept of the environmental ethic is that all of us ought to care about the potential effects of our decisions and actions on the natural systems, on our neighbors, and on all other forms of life, projecting our considerations beyond the immediate, local results to the long-term effects on all peoples in all lands, and even on future generations. The moral ingredients of an environmental ethic are caring about the planet and its inhabitants, allowing unselfishness to control the immediate self-interest that harms others, and living each day so as to leave the lightest possible footprints on the planet.

Interacting with the natural world we are confronted constantly with unknowns. Yet despite uncertainty, we seldom hesitate to forge ahead, with scant concern for the long-term effects of our actions on the earth's natural systems and species, almost as if we were driving in the dark without the lights on. Too often we act not only without *considering* the impacts of our actions, but without the *knowledge* of what these actions might do to the land or our neighbors or the community or, cumulatively, to the planet.

Leopold wrote:

... our grandfathers did not, could not know the origin of their prairie empire. They killed off the prairie fauna and they drove the flora to a last refuge on railroad embankments and roadsides. ... Some day we may need this prairie flora not only to look at but to rebuild the wasting soil of prairie farms. Many species may then be missing.

He maintained that even the scientist is confronted with uncertainty and does not yet recognize how all the pieces fit together.

He tells about a mountain range in Germany, the Spessart, which is the source of the finest oaks in the world, the ones that American cabinetmakers use when they want the last word in quality. But the fine wood comes only from the oaks on the south slope of the Spessart. The north slope, which should be even better, bears an indifferent stand of Scotch pine. Yet both sides are part of the same state forest and have been managed with care for two centuries.

The difference—as ecologists have discovered—is that during the Middle Ages the south slope was preserved in its natural state as a deer forest by a bishop interested in hunting. But the north slope was plowed, pastured, and cut by settlers before being later replanted to pines. During the time of agricultural use the number of species of microscopic flora and fauna in the ground was reduced. The soil thus lost some of its digestive apparatus, and two centuries of conservation practices have not restored these losses.

I didn't have to dip into history to find examples, however. They are happening every day. And frequently the consequences can be recognized before the harm is done, yet are ignored because of our present-day system of values. Our prevailing ethical codes take for granted that the waters, the soils, the trees, and the wildlife can be manipulated at will in the name of progress, even if that progress is short-lived and far outweighed by the loss of the land's long-term ability to benefit mankind.

A case in point is the future of the Little Tennessee River and Valley, an area rich in history, natural beauty, and prime agriculture land. The last 33 miles of river running north toward the mother Tennessee River southwest of Knoxville is unobstructed by dams and has swift-flowing stretches that provide fishing and

canoeing. It is also unique as the last remaining lengthy stretch of
virgin river and high quality water in the entire state.

There are 68 dams on the Tennessee and Cumberland River
systems between their headwaters and the Mississippi River. Only
this segment of the Little Tennessee remains a reminder of the
original river and its tributaries. Yet a dam, the Tellico, has been
virtually completed by the Tennessee Valley Authority (TVA). If—
or when—the last gates are dropped into place and the river is
blocked, this last wild stretch will be transformed into a 30-mile-
long lake that would be mostly mud flats a good part of the year.

The Tellico project was authorized and funded in the autocratic
way in which TVA has been allowed to operate. It received
authorization from Congress in 1966, and initial appropriations in
1967, with no public consideration. (Congress authorizes whatever
projects the TVA Board of Directors submits, and does not require
approval of each project, as it does for Corps of Engineers and
Bureau of Reclamation water projects. Congress appropriates TVA
funds as a lump sum each year, and although the appropriations
committees examine the content of TVA budget requests, they do
not hold hearings on specific proposals.) The project for the Little
Tennessee River promised few of the usual dam benefits except
construction jobs and a possible economic boost for a sparsely
populated, low-income area. The dam would have no generators of
its own, but its stored water would be moved through a small canal
to the nearby Ft. Loudon Reservoir, which had hydroelectric
capability. At its best, however, the project would add less than
one-thousandth to TVA's generating capacity for use during peak
periods. With 26 other dams upstream from the Tellico, flood
control could not be a big benefit. TVA claimed that the new
reservoir would bring huge recreation benefits even though 22
recreation lakes already existed within 60 miles of the area. TVA
also indicated that it would condemn and purchase more than
twice as much land as was needed for the reservoir—38,000 acres—
then sell excess land back to industry for a profit, or to real estate
speculators for shoreline development. And a new town to be
called Timberlake City would be built with federal financing and
with the Boeing Corporation as developer. The project would
create 7,000 permanent jobs and bring in 50,000 residents, according to TVA.

Smoldering public opposition broke out after the first approval from Congress. Many citizens protested the flooding of 16,000 acres of good farmland, the ruining of one of the best fishing and floating rivers in the Southeast, and the destruction of significant cultural, archeological, and historical sites.

Among the places of history that would be inundated were the sites of Echota, where the Cherokee Nation was created; Tennase Town, which gave the river and the state their name; Tuskegee Town, where Chief Sequoia was born; Coytee Springs, an 18th-century treaty site alongside the Little Tennessee River; and Ft. Loudon, part of the Colonial defense perimeter during the French and Indian Wars. Some prehistoric sites on which archeological digs were under way, revealing each year new knowledge of the early residents of this oldest area of continuous use and occupation in the nation—sites with a 10,000-year history—would also be inundated by the reservoir.

Citizens fighting the project said the dam wasn't needed and would be a waste of money and a loss of needed farmland. They suggested that the economic boost the area really needed could be obtained from agriculture and from building up tourist facilities. They also suggested a major push to tap the tourist flow at nearby Great Smoky Mountains National Park, the most heavily used of all national parks, with several million visitors a year. Many of these park-goers could be persuaded to visit the scenic, historic, and recreational sites in the Little Tennessee River Valley.

The public opposition and environmental lawsuits delayed completion of the large earth dam and reservoir, although TVA was able to get money from Congress for the concrete spillway, for buying land, relocating roads, and building bridges.

But in August 1973, University of Tennessee ichthyologist David Etnier, taking the final fish census of the section of the Little Tennessee River about to be flooded, saw a 3-inch-long fish dart in front of his face mask while he swam underwater. Etnier caught the fish with his hands and slipped it into a bottle. On examination he found it to be a tiny member of the perch family which feeds almost exclusively on snails and exists only in clean gravel shoals with cool, swift, low-turbidity water. Scientists believe the rare species—which Etnier named *Percina imostoma tanasi*, or "snail darter"—was once prolific along the eastern Tennessee river system.

The many dams already built on the rivers had altered the species' habitat and caused its disappearance. Etnier notified the Tennessee Valley Authority because the reservoir of Tellico Dam would have destroyed this last known place of survival for the species. The Rare and Endangered Species Act passed by Congress late in 1973 mandated that federal agencies make certain their actions do not jeopardize the continued existence of species or destruction of habitat of the species which have been officially listed by the secretary of the interior as threatened or endangered. The Act does not, however, give the interior secretary veto power over the projects of another agency that disobeys the endangered species law. The only recourse is through citizen lawsuits or political pressure from the president or Congress. Etnier expected TVA to comply voluntarily with the new law. But TVA officials went right ahead with construction of the Tellico Dam, even speeding up the rate of construction, believing that their agency operated under a higher authority—the annual budget appropriation from Congress.

The dam might have been completed then and the snail darter wiped out except for a coincidence. Hiram G. Hill, Jr., an environmental law student at the University of Tennessee, heard about the snail darter from a student of Etnier and rushed to tell his law professor about it and ask for permission to do a term paper on the conflicts between the dam and the Endangered Species Act. The professor, Zygmunt Plater, one of the leading opponents of the Tellico project, not only agreed to the term paper subject but went to TVA officials requesting that they comply with the law. Failing there, Plater urged the Interior Department's Fish and Wildlife Service to take action. Interior also failed to get any cooperation from TVA.

When the secretary of the interior officially listed the snail darter as an endangered species in November 1975, and six months later designated 17 miles of the Little Tennessee River as threatened habitat critical to the snail darter's survival, TVA went on building the dam and started bulldozing trees and vegetation along the river banks and in the areas to be flooded, and knocked down the homes of river valley residents who had been forced to sell to TVA.

When TVA continued to ignore the law, Plater and Knoxville attorney Boone Dougherty, on behalf of law student Hill and other individuals and groups, sought an injunction in the courts. TVA in the meantime started transplanting 710 snail darters from the Little

Tennessee shoals to the nearby Hiwassee River in an experiment it hoped would reestablish the species elsewhere. It also conducted an exhaustive search throughout the region to find snail darters somewhere else and thus prove the species was not really endangered.

A federal district court judge in Knoxville, Robert Taylor, found that TVA had indeed violated the Endangered Species Act. But because construction was so far along, Taylor refused to issue an injunction to stop work on the Tellico Dam. The U.S. Court of Appeals for the Sixth Circuit, however, by a unanimous decision overturned the district court and, in January 1977, issued a permanent injunction against finishing the by-then nearly completed dam.

While the case awaited a Supreme Court hearing, I went to Knoxville to look into the situation. I toured the river valley, guided by Doris Gove, a member of the Tennessee Endangered Species Committee, which had been publicizing the facts all over the nation and raising money for the lawsuit by selling "Save the Snail Darter" tee shirts. Driving along the Little Tennessee River I was unprepared for the scene of devastation that necessarily accompanies preparations for a huge man-made reservoir in which all trees and shrubs on the hills up to the anticipated water level plus most of the vegetation on the river banks have been removed and all buildings demolished. The once prime farmland lay denuded and desolate, the cattle now gone from pastures and hillsides. Having seen the beauty of similar Tennessee valleys some years ago, I could imagine what it had been like before bulldozers swept through. The impact really hit me when we walked down the bank of the Little Tennessee River at Coytee Springs, the place where Etnier had discovered the snail darter. Coytee, according to some historians (there is a dispute as to the exact location), is the site where the colonists' treaty with the Cherokee Nation is said to have been signed. In modern times it had been a favorite picnic, fishing, and trysting spot, shaded by a grove of trees including a giant sycamore, with water from the spring overflowing down the bank to the river. But the Coytee Springs I saw was just weeds and young shrubs trying to blot out the stump of the giant sycamore. The bulldozers and chain saws of TVA had obliterated history and scarred the natural beauty.

While in the valley I also met with attorney Plater, who had come down from Detroit (he now teaches environmental law at Wayne State University) to address a citizen meeting in the nearby town of Madisonville. He had been explaining to the local people, most of whom wanted the dam completed, that other alternatives existed which would in the long run be better for the area than the dam would be. The prime farmland could return to agriculture. The Little Tennessee Valley could be developed for tourism, and the type of industry that would not harm the environment could be brought in.

When I mentioned to Plater the shock I felt at seeing Coytee Springs bulldozed, he told me that immediately after the snail darter had been declared an endangered species, TVA started its land clearing right at that spot even though it already was listed on the national historic sites registry. It was as if the TVA officials were trying to get rid of the historic sites so it would be too late for anyone to argue for their preservation.

I asked Plater (who had been giving his legal services free all during the Tellico Dam fight) about the attitude of some prominent environmentalists who felt he was "playing with fire" in pressing his court case. Winning the battle, they felt, would result in losing the war because it would put overwhelming pressure on Congress to abolish or weaken the Endangered Species Act. Plater said he realized that environmentalists couldn't be absolute about saving all endangered species. In some cases of conflicts between species and projects, compromises might have to be made if a thorough analysis showed public necessity for allowing an almost completed project to be finished if no viable alternative existed. The snail darter, however, represented a principle. TVA had never even considered alternatives. If TVA could successfully ignore the law, the Endangered Species Act wasn't worth much anyway. And to Plater, this case was a test of the linkage between man and nature, an indicator of public values. Species exist because their habitat survives, Plater explained. The habitat for the snail darter requires the same qualities that make the river important for trout fishing, canoeing, and family float trips, for the land as home and farmland to those who live there, and a place with cultural and historic significance for present and future generations. If the habitat is protected, all of these values are protected for the public.

"We decided we had the strongest case in the nation," Plater told me, "if the facts could get through: that a complete species would either survive or be rendered extinct, and that profitable alternatives were available. We had the weakest case in purely political football terms—we could get murdered on the facile theme of that 'silly little worthless fish' versus a big, job-giving, economy-boosting dam project. We took a gamble on the system working."

During my visit to Knoxville I also met with Lynn Seeber, the general manager of TVA (who resigned in the spring of 1978, just before a change in TVA directors). Seeber said that back in 1966 as a TVA lawyer, he had written the original proposal to be considered by Congress, at a time when few people in the Tennessee Valley opposed dams and reservoirs. Seeber defended the Tellico Dam as a necessary part of the TVA system. He lashed out at Secretary of the Interior Cecil D. Andrus for joining with environmentalists "not so much to preserve a species, but to stop a project." The Tellico Dam would provide power for 20,000 additional homes and knock 2 feet off the potential flood crest downstream at Chattanooga, in addition to bringing recreation and industrial income to a depressed economic area around the lower Little Tennessee River, he told me. When I asked why TVA had started bulldozing at Coytee Springs in the middle of the projected reservoir, Seeber answered that it was unfortunate, but that it had not been done out of malice.

On April 18, 1978, shortly after 10 A.M., the attorney general of the United States, Griffin Bell, rose to present the TVA case to the Supreme Court of the United States. Attorneys crowded the lawyers section to hear the hour-long arguments and questions from the bench on this most unusual case, which the press had been publicizing as a battle between a 3-inch-long, practically worthless fish and a $120-million dam. Present in the public section was Hiram Hill, the young man who four years earlier had brought news of the snail darter discovery to his environmental law professor, Plater. It was an eventful week for Hill, who had been admitted to the Tennessee Bar the day before and now was to listen to the case that bore the designation: *Tennessee Valley Authority* v. *Hiram G. Hill, Jr., et al.*

Dressed in the morning coat and striped trousers that the attorney general customarily wears while appearing before the Supreme Court, Bell held a small flask high in the air, stating: "I have in my hand a snail darter. . . . We brought that with us so you could see it," as if to show how ridiculous this whole case was.

After some banter with the court over whether the darter was alive or dead (it was dead), Bell argued against allowing the appellate court's ruling to stand. If an endangered species were discovered in a river the day before an impoundment was scheduled to take place, Bell hypothesized, the new dam would have to be shut down or eliminated. He argued that an injunction had not been warranted. But he seemed to waver on whether the action of TVA in refusing to accept the Endangered Species Act provisions was a violation of law. When one of the justices asked if one of the chief factors to be weighed was that $120 million has been spent, Bell replied, "Exactly." He also pointed out that Senate and House Appropriations Committees had approved in their committee reports continued funding for the Tellico Dam. This, Bell contended, showed an intent by Congress to complete the project and that this intent should override the Endangered Species Act. He said that the two-year-old TVA experiment in the transplanting of snail darters to the Hiwassee River had been a success, so the species was not really endangered. And the law was clear that the secretary of the interior did not have veto power to stop a project. Under questioning, Bell admitted that completing the dam would modify a critical habitat, in violation of the law. And he had no satisfactory answer when Chief Justice Warren E. Burger criticized him for having to attack the position of another cabinet department instead of coming to the court with a unified government position. "It is not easy for me to resolve issues that are of vast importance to our country when two cabinet level departments are at sword's point," said Burger with some irritation. (Bell had tried to get Interior Secretary Andrus to side with the TVA position but did not receive any help from President Carter in resolving the intra-cabinet impasse.)

After Bell's half-hour before the bench, Plater, as attorney for the citizens opposing the Tellico Dam, started his argument. Only a few words into his presentation, Plater was interrupted by Burger's first question about the possible waste of $120 million for an almost completed dam (if it were not now to be used because of the snail darter). Plater replied that the actual concrete dam cost only $5 million and the earth dam $14 million. Most of the $120 million had been spent for things that could still be used—bridges, roads, and 38,000 acres of land which could be sold back to citizens for agricultural and industrial development. TVA had spent most of the money after 1973 when the conflict over the snail darter and the endangered species law arose and alternative development could have been pursued, Plater told the court. TVA had rejected modifications of the project and had not even considered possible alternatives which a 1977 General Accounting Office report indicated would be even better for the area's economy than the dam and reservoir would be.

In reply to questions by Burger and Justices Lewis F. Powell and Thurgood Marshall concerning hypothetical situations in which an endangered species might be discovered at already completed projects, Plater said that the act of finding such a species in a reservoir would indicate that it had not been endangered by the dam. Plater admitted that there might be cases, however, in which the public interest is so intimately involved that a decision would have to be made to render a species extinct. But, he added, "there has never in human history been a conscious extinction of a species." Plater contradicted the attorney general's assertion that the transplant experiment had been successful, saying that scientists feel it would take 5-15 years to determine this. In a check of the Hiwassee shoals where the 710 snail darters had been placed two years earlier, only five fish were found. If the Hiwassee were a healthy habitat for the species, the snail darter would still exist there naturally, Plater said. The most important factor, however, was that "this species turns out to be a highly sensitive indicator of precisely the qualities of the habitat that the citizens have been fighting about in this case for years before the snail darters were known to exist. . . . After 68 dams throughout the TVA river system, 68 of them, one after the other, the range of the snail darter has apparently been destroyed, one by one, until this 33 miles of river is the last place where the species—and human beings as well—still keep the quality of the habitat."

Eight weeks after hearing oral arguments, the Supreme Court handed down its verdict: In a 6-3 decision, with Chief Justice Burger writing the court's opinion, the majority ruled in favor of the Endangered Species Act and against the Tellico Dam. Dissenting Justice Lewis F. Powell, Jr., said: "Today the fish wins 100 percent," and the majority considered that they were upholding the intent of Congress to give endangered species the highest of priorities. But the verdict could not be considered pro-environment, for both majority and dissenters indicated that Congress could change the Endangered Species Act if it wanted to complete the Tellico Dam. The majority opinion, however, did annihilate the argument of Attorney General Bell, who had presented the case in terms of a worthless fish versus "progress" in the form of a nearly completed $120-million dam project.

In emphasizing the limits on judicial power, the majority opinion referred to a key portion of the appellate court decision which had stated:

> Whether a dam is 50 percent or 90 percent completed is irrelevant in calculating the social and scientific costs attributable to the disappearance of a unique form of life. Courts are ill-equipped to calculate how many dollars must be invested before the value of a dam exceeds that of the endangered species. Our responsibility under the Endangered Species Act is merely to preserve the status quo where endangered species are threatened, thereby guaranteeing the legislative or executive branches sufficient opportunity to grapple with the alternatives.

Whereas Chief Justice Burger and five other justices viewed the case as upholding very fundamental principles of the separation of powers, Justice Powell, in a dissent joined by Justice Harry A. Blackmun, sought to go along with the congressional intent and allow the Tellico Dam to be completed, an action "that accords with some modicum of common sense and the public weal." The fate of an endangered species apparently carried no weight in Justice Powell's considerations: "I have little doubt that Congress will amend the Endangered Species Act to prevent the grave consequences made possible by today's decision. . . . There will be little sentiment to leave this dam standing before an empty reservoir, serving no purpose other than a conversation piece for incredulous tourists. . . . If Congress acts expeditiously, as may be anticipated, the Court's decision probably will have no lasting adverse consequences."

Whatever the long-term outcome of the snail darter case—

Congress amending the Endangered Species Act to allow loopholes so that development projects can be carried out by agencies, or TVA redesigning the Tellico project to provide an alternative solution which would avoid destroying the endangered habitat—the fact remains that a civilization that could enact a law protecting endangered species at all must have deep within it the makings of an environmental ethic. Those who were able to sift through the inadequate reporting in the press and on television must have recognized, however, that our value system is woefully out of balance when the only means of gauging the value of a living species is to measure its survival against a multimillion-dollar investment in a pillar of stone. Should provision of a fraction of additional electrical capacity to a mammoth regional system, the promise of a bit more protection for those who have unwisely chosen to build in a flood plain, and one more recreation lake in a region already well supplied with lakes have a higher value than the protection of habitat—both animal and human—for generations to come? Those who have eyes to see may recognize in the snail darter case a reminder that the extermination of a species and of a habitat may be a *warning* that the habitat may soon be unfit for the human species.

Perhaps the most practical lesson offered by the snail darter case is that public officials should seek to determine, *before* they act, the potential impact their decisions may have, and explore alternative courses. TVA officials had the opportunity more than a decade ago to evaluate seriously alternatives to building one more dam on the river. They had an opportunity then to consider what other means were available to help the people in the Little Tennessee River Valley and the region before taking actions that would irreversibly alter a part of the planet, dislocate families, destroy prime farmland and a lovely natural river ecosystem, wipe out historic sites, and possibly endanger wildlife.

In a wider sense, the basic issue (of which the snail darter case is only an illustration) embraces much more than the questionable decision-making process of some former federal officials. It concerns whether or how much all of us in all walks of life build environmental concerns into the decisions we face. It forces us to ask what is the cost to our neighbors, to our surroundings, and to future generations of not adequately considering the impacts of these decisions. And it raises the question: How can we develop new structures or types of institutional organizations through which environmental concerns can be raised and listened to at a high enough decision-making level to make a difference. These are the issues this book explores.

Aldo Leopold once wrote that citizens must "examine each question in terms of what is ethically and esthetically right, as well as what is economically expedient. A thing is right when it tends to preserve the integrity, stability, and beauty of the biotic community. It is wrong when it tends otherwise."

Some may question this attitude as being overly concerned with the biotic community to the neglect of human social needs. Yet man is a part of the biotic community. We cannot judge right and wrong only in terms of immediate consequences and self-interest. We ought to consider whether or not an action is going to disrupt the natural system in some way and how this may affect other people now and in the future.

I wondered when first reading Leopold, and have wondered many times since, how much damage I myself am doing to the environment inadvertently by my daily decisions and actions. What impact are the actions of all citizens having? And what responsibility do we have—whether as writer or banker or government official or corporate president or secretary or homemaker or student or mechanic or architect or scientist—to tread lightly wherever we go and leave footprints that do not mar our planet?

2

A CALL
FROM THE
WHITE HOUSE

The sense of a need for an environmental ethic developed
gradually in my thinking and came into focus when I wrote a series
of articles on national parks for *The Christian Science Monitor* in
1968. At the time I started work on the series I was a Washington-
based correspondent for *The Monitor,* covering urban affairs, the
Supreme Court, and the Interior Department. Although I had
occasionally written about conservation, I had scant knowledge of
the subject.

The route that brought me to *The Monitor* began in Seattle,
where I worked as a sports writer fresh out of the University of
Washington journalism school. After World War II service I
evolved from general newspaper reporter into a nonfiction magazine writer and editor on the staffs of *Life, Colliers,* and *The
Saturday Evening Post,* and White House reporter for the United

States Information Agency's International Press Service, writing on widely varied subjects. I wrote the first national magazine article ever published about Marilyn Monroe (in 1951), did articles on space and the astronauts, nuclear tests, President Kennedy's mail, Disneyland, gold prospecting as a hobby, and children's author Dr. Seuss, and I even co-authored Perle Mesta's life story. On one occasion I collaborated with a National Park Service wildlife expert on an article for *The Saturday Evening Post,* "Wild Animals Have Their Rights," and some of the principles described in that article were very much in my mind when I began to write the 1968 *Monitor* series about problems in the parks.

Traveling 20,000 miles around the country for nearly a year, talking with visitors and park officials at most of the major national parks, I discovered conditions that I soon learned were harbingers of a growing national concern for the environment. Park visitors were encountering traffic jams, crowds, noise, even smog when masses of slow-moving automobiles pumped their exhaust into confined areas such as Yosemite Valley. The sheer numbers of visitors were overburdening some of the parks with sewage and garbage, polluting sparkling streams and lakes, causing erosion of the land, and disturbing the wildlife. The parks' very popularity was damaging the unique environment that attracted the visitors.

Yet despite these problems, I became aware of a rare attitude in the visitors. These were *their* parks, a part of their heritage, and they felt fiercely protective of them. I found that to harm or threaten a national park is to touch a sensitive nerve in the American public. Many visitors as well as park employees seemed to live by a set of values rarely seen elsewhere. They appreciated, even cherished, the natural beauty around them—the land, the plants, the birds, the animals. And what's more, they seemed to have a regard for other people's chance to share the park experience. They seemed to feel they were part of a whole natural system, and most of them behaved as if they did not want to leave that system any worse than they found it, so that others and even future generations could enjoy and share it.

One morning, hiking along May Lake Trail in Yosemite National Park with veteran ranger-naturalist Dave Condon, I asked him why people seem to have this special attitude when they visit the parks.

He was quiet for some moments and then answered: "Coming in contact with the goldenrod, the deer, the giant sequoia, I think we're better able to understand that there's some force, some unseen plan to this whole universe. We're having an experience with eternity. And if we can perceive the beauty here, that ability can enrich our lives no matter where we are—even in the midst of the city—and we can see beauty better than before we had the park experience."

I wondered whether this attitude was really as pervasive as it seemed, so I decided to include a questionnaire in my series and see how readers would react. To my delight—and to my editor's surprise—some 2,000 people cared enough to tear the sheet out of the newspaper, answer the questions, put the sheet in an envelope, and mail it to *The Monitor.*

Their answers were overwhelmingly selfless—they wanted national parks preserved, even at the cost of limiting their own personal use of the parks. Over a third approved the idea of a campground reservations system. They agreed to setting a maximum capacity for each park, with the gates to be closed once the capacity was reached, and opened again when the number of visitors went below the limit. More than half agreed that a 35-mile-per-hour speed limit should be enforced in the parks, that no U.S. highways should pass through parks, and that fees should be charged on those highways that presently cut through parks, to discourage through traffic. Fewer than 10% favored additional visitor services such as stores, restaurants, and coin laundries, and only 5% thought grizzly bears should be eliminated from the parks, even though two campers had been killed by grizzlies the previous year. People in all parts of the nation sent in completed questionnaires. We even got some from soldiers in Vietnam and older folks who never expected to visit a park again, but who still cared deeply about keeping the parks fine for future generations.

The instincts of the people followed the hopes of those early explorers who visited the Yellowstone area in the late 1860s and early 1870s, and who worked to have it protected. "It seems to me that God made this region for all the people and all the world to see and enjoy forever," one of the explorers, Cornelius Hedges, told his colleagues. "It is impossible that any individual should think he can own any of this country for his own in fee. This great wilderness does not belong to us. It belongs to the nation. Let us make a public park of it and set it aside ... never to be changed, but to be kept sacred always."

The feeling for national parks that had come down through the years blended with my own changing values. By the time I had finished the national park series, my sense of priorities had undergone a major shift. Environmental factors seemed to creep into whatever subject I covered. Even my interest in the urban scene took on a new dimension. I was recognizing that the quality of life for city people, as for everyone else, is affected by environmental as well as by political and social influences. And I persuaded the editor of *The Monitor* to let me carve out a full-time beat covering the environment.

My concept of environment broadened beyond U.S. borders when my beat took me to cover a conference on ecological impacts of international development. More than seventy ecologists, economists, social and political scientists, and foreign-assistance officials from twenty countries discussed the environmental damage being done by the introduction of some new technologies.

In the Cañete Valley of Peru, for instance, U.S. development interests had promoted widespread use of insecticides in 1949 to eliminate pests and push cotton yields. Seven years later the cotton crop had gone down 50% and species of destructive insects had doubled. Or the case of the island of Banaba in the Central Pacific: Its inhabitants had to abandon it after phosphate mining destroyed the soil and polluted the water. Or the dam on the Zambezi River on the border between Rhodesia and Zambia. When it was completed in 1958 it formed the largest man-made body of water in the world, the 1,700-square-mile Lake Kariba. Although millions were spent on engineering studies before construction started, very little went into studies of environmental or social impacts. The dam was supposed to enhance the fishing catch. But the catch declined. The newly created expanse of lakeshore encouraged the tsetse fly, which fostered serious outbreaks of disease among cattle. Shifts in the lake level made farming uncertain. And there was severe social unrest when the displaced farmers could not get comparable new land.

On the Washington scene, environment was building as a political issue. One of the events I covered for *The Monitor* late in

1969 was the effort by Congress to pass legislation setting national environmental policy. There had been sporadic attempts to pass this kind of law for almost a decade, but nothing had ever come of them. In 1969, however, with pollution becoming inescapable and environmental concern peaking as a political reality, Congress finally got serious. Of the several environmental bills introduced in 1969, interest centered on one, a National Environmental Policy bill sponsored chiefly in the Senate by Henry M. Jackson of Washington and in the House by John D. Dingell of Michigan.

On April 16, 1969, I sat at the press table in the big Senate Interior Committee room eagerly following the testimony at a public hearing on Jackson's bill. Interior Committee Chairman Jackson reviewed briefly the main provisions of the bill. It sounded like a definition of an environmental ethic. It specified that the federal government had a responsibility to preserve important historic, cultural, and natural aspects of the national heritage, enhance the quality of renewable resources, and approach maximum recycling of depletable resources. Each generation should be a trustee of the environment for succeeding generations. And each citizen had a right to a healthful environment as well as a responsibility to contribute to enhancement of the environment. The bill proposed a council of three members whose principal duties would be to analyze environmental trends, advise the president on national environmental policy, and periodically appraise federal environmental programs.

The most significant witness at the hearing turned out to be Lynton K. Caldwell, a political science professor from Indiana University. An expert on environmental policy, Caldwell had served as a consultant to the Interior Committee in drafting language for the bill. He warned that the proposed law would have little effect unless it included a mechanism to compel implementation of the basic environmental policy. Congress should consider "measures to require the federal agencies, in submitting proposals, to contain within the proposals an evaluation of the effect of these proposals upon the state of the environment."

Jackson responded with enthusiasm, saying he had been concerned that a policy declaration was not enough: "Realistically what is needed in restructuring the governmental side of this problem is to legislatively create those situations that will bring about an action-forcing procedure that departments must comply with. Otherwise, these lofty declarations are nothing more than that."

When the bill went to the floor for a vote it contained—thanks to Caldwell, the Senate committee staff, and further committee deliberations—an added section that was to become the most important part of the act. The section required that for every legislative proposal or other major federal action significantly affecting the quality of the environment, the responsible federal official would have to consider the environmental impacts of the proposed action and any adverse environmental effects that could not be avoided.

Thus was born the revolutionary environmental impact statement requirement of section 102 of the bill that worked its way through Congress in December 1969. While other portions of the bill were important, it was this section 102 that would require federal officials to take cognizance of the environmental implications of their actions. And it provided the *opportunity* for environmental concerns to be applied in their decisions. During the final hours of the 91st Congress, with members rushing to get home for the holidays, the National Environmental Policy Act was passed by Congress without significant debate and with little opposition.

A few days later, on Christmas Eve, I received a phone call from John C. Whitaker, the White House staff man responsible for environmental affairs with whom I had talked frequently as a news source. Whitaker left me almost speechless when he said: "The president wants to nominate you as one of the members of the new Council on Environmental Quality."

When I'd recovered enough to regain my voice, I started rattling off the reasons I didn't think I was right for the job—I wasn't an ecologist, had never even taken a biology course in high school or college, was a comparative newcomer in the environmental arena, and . . .

Whitaker interrupted my protests to remind me that the new law did not require council members to be scientists or ecologists. It stated that a member should be qualified to analyze and interpret environmental trends and information, to appraise federal programs, and to formulate and recommend national policies to promote the improvement of the quality of the environment. That description pretty much matched what I had been doing in the press, Whitaker said. He reminded me that I was one of only two national environmental writers and had received several major awards in that field. I acknowledged that on those terms I probably was as qualified as anyone in this new and rapidly changing field.

My surprise at the presidential offer also stemmed from the fact that I was not a Republican and had, in fact, been critical of President Nixon's environmental efforts—or lack of them. Whitaker did ask how I was registered. To my answer that I was an Independent and had never been active politically, Whitaker responded that my not being a Republican would make the clearance problems a bit more difficult. Yet it should not, he said, block the nomination in the political clearance process.

I asked for time to think it over. That night at home, my wife Pat and I went over the pluses and minuses of the offer. As a journalist I had complete freedom to criticize the powers that be, but as an official part of the bureaucracy I would not be in a position to criticize, at least not publicly. It meant crossing the line between the Fourth Estate and the establishment. Once on the other side, it might not be easy to return, or to be accepted again as an objective reporter.

And I questioned President Nixon's commitment in the environmental area, although Whitaker had assured me the president wanted to comply fully with the new National Environmental Policy Act, and that he would place a high priority on environment.

A presidential appointment, especially to a position as close to power as the Executive Office of the President, was a plum. Potentially I would have some opportunity to influence policy at the highest level of government. And what a unique vantage point I would have from which to see if this budding ethical approach to environment was being practiced in the federal government.

The possibilities outweighed our reservations. Pat and I decided that even though I'd have to accept some decisions with which I disagreed, and would have to be patient enough not to quit if I lost a battle or two, the challenge was just too good to pass up.

Russell E. Train, nominated to be council chairman, and Gordon J. F. MacDonald to be the other member, and I had no difficulties being confirmed by the Senate. But our appointments did not meet with universal approval. Some leading ecologists complained that at least one member ought to have a background in ecological science (MacDonald had served on scientific committees and done research in a wide variety of environmental areas, but was a geophysicist, not an ecologist).

Scientist and author Paul Ehrlich had been quoted soon after the National Environmental Policy Act passed Congress as predicting that there would not be one trained ecologist on the new council. "There'll be a physical scientist of some sort, there'll be somebody who discovered that the dickey-birds disappeared, and there'll be a rabbi, a priest, or a minister, or even God knows what else," Ehrlich said.

After our appointments were announced, the editor of *Motive Magazine* recalled the Ehrlich comment and noted: "The physical scientist appointed by President Nixon is Gordon J. F. MacDonald, former vice-chancellor of the University of California at Santa Barbara. Appointed in the 'dickey-bird' category was Russell Train, past president of the Conservation Foundation and Nixon's former Undersecretary of the Interior. In the 'God knows what else' category is Robert Cahn, a Pulitzer Prize winning reporter for *The Christian Science Monitor.*"

3

POLITICAL
CRASH COURSE

The new status as presidential appointee still pinched like an ill-fitting shoe a few weeks after the swearing in, when I found myself in the White House Cabinet Room, temporarily occupying the secretary of the treasury's big leather chair. The occasion was a meeting of President Nixon with fourteen environmental leaders. Charles Colson, who was responsible for arranging presidential meetings with business, labor, church, professional, and other groups, had decided the time was politically opportune for the president to meet with environmentalists. I was to represent the Council on Environmental Quality.

The Natural Resources Council—a loosely organized group of forty conservation organizations which does not take formal positions on legislation—had been seeking a meeting with the president since he took office a year earlier. The fourteen environmentalists had agreed among themselves beforehand to maintain a conciliatory attitude even though they felt deeply disappointed by Nixon's lack of concern for the environment during the first year of his presidency. They hoped that in an informal meeting they could convince the president of the need to give higher priority to environmental measures.

The president had been making some encouraging statements lately. On signing the National Environmental Policy Act on New Year's Day 1970, he said that "it is now or never" for cleaning up the environment. And in late January he devoted one-third of his state of the union message to the environment. He matched the rhetoric—"clean air, clean water, open spaces should once again be the birthright of every American"—with the announcement of a $10-billion nationwide clean-waters program for municipal waste treatment plants. A special message to Congress on the environment two weeks later included twenty-three legislative proposals and fourteen administrative actions. Its tone signaled that the administration was prepared to crack down on all offenders, even the industry leaders with whom Nixon had been so friendly.

It was in the flush of public applause for the strong message that the White House called this meeting with environmental leaders. When my old colleagues from the White House press corps entered the Cabinet Room for the customary picture-taking, the president started elaborating on his environment message. "This is the year we begin to do the things that have been talked about since the turn of the century, since Theodore Roosevelt's time," Nixon said, gesturing toward TR's portrait on the west wall of the Cabinet Room. He resurrected his "now or never" line from the January 1 bill-signing statement.

After the press left the room, the president asked the Natural Resources Council for help in passing the new environmental measures he had sent to Congress. Richard Stroud, chairman of the group and representing the Sport Fishing Institute, summarized the environmentalists' views and thanked the president for arranging the meeting.

Nixon interrupted to say there would be more and bigger meetings. He turned to National Audubon Society President Elvis Stahr, who had been secretary of the army in the Kennedy adminstration. Audubon members should be interested in clean air and other issues, the president commented. "Smog can kill birds," he said. Dr. Stahr replied that Audubon members were interested not only in clean air and clean water but also in parks, forests, wilderness, rural areas, and even inner-city environmental problems.

For the better part of an hour, the environmental leaders spoke of issues that bothered them, while the president listened intently and made occasional remarks. Most of the environmentalists had said their piece and the meeting was about to end, when Phillip Berry, president of the Sierra Club, broke in to say he had a few remarks to make. The Sierra Club, he said, did not agree with the goals of the administration. The administration was not attacking the root causes of environmental problems. He mentioned population control.

The atmosphere became tense. President Nixon asked if Berry had read the recent population message sent to Congress. "Yes," Berry replied. "But it does not go far enough." He urged the president to support zero population growth.

Nixon suggested that Berry read the message again. He said that the United States does not have a totalitarian form of government and that there are certain limitations to be considered, such as the religious sensitivities of people.

Berry charged on. He questioned the president's emphasis on an ever-increasing gross national product with its wastefulness and dependence on excessive consumption. He mentioned development of Alaska oil as an example of using resources to further a way of life bent only on satisfying excessive consumer demands without considering the needs of the future. Berry urged an environmental bill of rights to make a better quality of life a legally enforceable right.

The president agreed that people don't need electric toothbrushes and a third television set. "But it is very difficult in this society to tell people so," he said. And then he abruptly ended the meeting, irritated at Berry's questioning.

Despite the tense moments with Berry, most of the environment leaders left the meeting believing that the president sincerely was seeking to give some priority to environmental improvement. And even though I had some remaining journalistic skepticism about the depth and strength of environmental concerns at the White

House and throughout government, I dared to hope that the environmental ethic, dormant for many years, was now ready to blossom. All the signs were favorable. Public awareness of the threats to the environment was at an all-time high with Earth Day activities being planned throughout the country. Congress was also warming to the need for new and tougher pollution-control laws. And the president had announced that the new Council on Environmental Quality "will occupy the same close advisory relation to the president that the Council of Economic Advisers does in fiscal monetary matters." In his environment message he had stated that the Council on Environmental Quality "will be the keeper of our environmental conscience and a goad to our ingenuity; . . . it will have responsibility for ensuring that all our programs and actions are undertaken with a careful respect for the needs of environmental quality . . . and I shall look to it increasingly for new initiatives."

We took seriously our role as "environmental conscience" and hoped to be able to argue face-to-face with the president for positions favorable to the environment. But that was wishful thinking. We had to go through several intermediaries to get our views to the Oval Office. Our main channel was John Whitaker, who was responsible for environment, agriculture, and energy matters on the White House Domestic Council. Whitaker was a straight shooter and represented our interests fairly within the framework of the president's political priorities. But try as we would, we could not get to the president. The Nixon operating style did not allow discussions of proposals with advocates or opponents. Every proposal or suggestion had to be represented on paper, first to the Domestic Council or designated presidential assistant—Whitaker in our case. The proposal then usually went to the budget officials. Finally it would go to John Ehrlichman, who, if he saw fit, would reduce the proposal to a short position paper for the president, stating the pros and cons.

In our naive expectation of personally advising the president we also had not reckoned with the power of the Bureau of the Budget (reorganized in 1970 as the Office of Management and Budget). OMB sets priorities for how the budget pie is to be divided and establishes absolute money and personnel ceilings for each department and agency. Legislative proposals from all federal agencies have to be cleared through OMB before going to Congress, as do reports and policy studies. Ostensibly these powers are to be exercised in accord with presidential desires. But the budget officials have wide latitude in interpreting those desires. And they successfully layer themselves between the president and other branches of the Executive Office of the President as well as the line departments and agencies.

One of the Council on Environmental Quality's first responsibilities was to direct and coordinate a major intergovernmental program to develop the presidential environmental message for 1971. We eagerly started work and asked for a meeting with the president to explain why we thought strong legislation was needed in areas such as land use and toxic substances controls. We wanted to get Nixon's backing before the opposition of his industry-minded friends and advisers got to him. Five months later we were still trying to meet with him.

Finally, in July, we were invited to the Oval Office, but not in response to our requests. The president had just sent to Congress a reorganization plan establishing the Environmental Protection Agency (EPA) as an independent agency and the National Oceanic and Atmospheric Administration (NOAA) as part of the Department of Commerce. We had helped in the planning for EPA but strongly objected to placing NOAA in Commerce where it could be under extreme pressure from industrial interests and under the thumb of Secretary Maurice Stans, no friend of the environment. Evidently the president had been advised that it would be a good idea to "stroke us" a bit. And it wouldn't hurt his environmental image to have his published daily schedule show a meeting with his environmental advisers.

President Nixon greeted us at the door of the Oval Office somewhat as he might welcome visiting firemen, rather than as members of his executive family. He showed us to chairs circling his desk as Ehrlichman came in and took a seat next to him. Whitaker was also with us.

After some pleasantries, Russell Train spoke of our travels around the country and the environmental spirit we found everywhere. The young people were out in front in perceiving environmental needs, he said, and were willing to work on the issues, even trying to do their own monitoring of industrial polluters.

I added that a highly vocal group of young people felt that too much emphasis was being placed on an ever-increasing gross national product and that this excessive emphasis on growth and production of consumer goods was wasteful.

"If they don't like it they can go to some other country," the president responded. "The environment is no better in Russia or the other East European countries where the government controls everything." And he spoke disparagingly of what he called the "back to nature people" who oppose growth.

I tried to explain that many of these proponents of "slow growth," both young and adult, only wanted a change to an economy based more on service jobs and crafts instead of having all the priority placed on more and bigger products using scarce resources.

When Train mentioned that many people saw population control as one of the major environmental issues, the president went into a long monologue. He saw population as a foreign-aid problem and was bothered by the amounts of money we were spending in countries like India and Peru where it was doing little good because the population kept growing so fast.

Train coaxed the conversation back to environment by pointing out that the developing nations also have many of the same pollution and land-use problems as the United States, and that it was important to work with the United Nations on international aspects of these issues.

President Mobutu of the Congo (later Zaire) was coming to Washington soon, the president replied, and it would be a good thing if Mobutu brought along his top environmental adviser so he could meet with our council while other Congolese advisers were meeting with their U.S. counterparts. He turned to Ehrlichman and told him to arrange for all visiting heads of state to bring along their environmental chiefs. As it turned out, Mobutu did not bring an environmental adviser because he didn't have one. The president forgot the idea and Ehrlichman did not follow through.

Toward the end of our meeting I mentioned that in September 1972 the National Park Service would be celebrating the 100th anniversary of Yellowstone, the world's first national park, with a world conference on national parks at Yellowstone and Grand Teton parks. I suggested that the president might want to speak at the world conference.

The suggestion set off a discussion among the president,

Ehrlichman, and Whitaker of how much it would help the Republican ticket in Wyoming. Or should he visit a national park in a state where Republican candidates would be needing more help in the 1972 election? As we were to learn all too well, the Nixon White House was quick to turn any action or occasion to political advantage in the all-important goal of assuring an eight-year term of office.

We left the meeting vaguely frustrated, feeling like outside visitors as the president handed each of us souvenir paperweights, pens, cufflinks, and golf balls. The president had done most of the talking. He had not once sought our advice on anything. Nor had he given us any direction or indication of his feeling about environmental legislation we were working on. I think the meeting clinched for us the feeling that had been growing over the months that whatever we hoped to accomplish as a council, we would have to do without the president's personal support.

We focused on doing what we could to encourage the strengthening of present air and water pollution-control laws and expand legislation in new fields such as control of toxic substances and pesticides, added restrictions on ocean dumping, solid-waste management and recycling, general land-use legislation, and strip-mining controls.

Our excellent small staff, directed by Alvin Alm, operated as a coordinating unit, drawing on the expertise of all the government agencies connected in various ways with environment. This often took a lot of diplomacy. For instance, we had to blend the disparate views of the thirteen different agencies involved in activities affecting the oceans before we produced a report on protection of the oceans against the dumping of wastes and poisons. The study provided a basis for legislative proposals.

I was getting a crash course in political and bureaucratic maneuvering. When we were not arbitrating conflicts between two or three agencies whose priorities and pressures were at odds, we were fighting off intervention from yet another. The Department of Commerce was especially cool to ideas that would restrict or regulate business and industry, its constituency. And all along the way, the Office of Management and Budget tried to keep us from proposing initiatives that might be too bold or cost too much to carry out.

Our toughest battles involved land use and toxic substances. The

Office of Management and Budget vigorously opposed our land-use proposals, partly because of the $100 million we proposed giving states over a five-year period to inventory their natural resources and prepare statewide land-use controls. We appealed to Ehrlichman and our proposal stayed in the package. But in toxic-substances control, the Commerce Department succeeded in knocking out our requirement for manufacturers to conduct tests on products *before* marketing. (When a toxic-substances control act was passed in 1976, it still excluded pre-market testing.)

The Commerce Department and the Treasury Department ganged up on our most innovative proposal. We wanted to curb sulfur oxide pollution, which was costing billions of dollars each year in damage to health, crops, and property. Our idea was to tax industry for excessive sulfur oxide stack emissions. Funds generated by the tax would then be used for expanded environmental programs, including developing the technology to reduce sulfur oxide damage. The two old-line departments blocked us so completely that we couldn't get the tax provision into the package. All we managed was a mention of it in the message, with the president saying that the Council on Environmental Quality and the secretary of the treasury would develop a system to be submitted to Congress later. This never came to pass.

Yet despite the demise of some proposals and the watering down of others, the final product emerging in the February 10, 1971 environmental message to Congress presented some significant legislative concepts. And most remarkable—in an administration committed to reducing federal interference—was the proposed entry of the federal government for the first time into such matters as land-use planning, control of toxic substances, strip mining, ocean dumping, and power plant siting.

The Council on Environmental Quality's other major area of concern, the environmental impact statement process mandated by the National Environmental Policy Act, provided further education for me in the difficulties of nurturing an environmental ethic in a large bureaucracy. One of the possibilities that had excited me about the appointment to CEQ was that I would have a part in making the new impact statement process work. When the law passed, some conservationists hailed this requirement as revolutionary and predicted it would transform government by forcing officials to build environmental concerns into their decisions in the same way they automatically considered costs and technical feasibility. Critics, on the other hand, predicted it would cause extensive delays and even stop progress. Both predictions proved to be exaggerations.

As the council sought to implement the environmental impact statement requirement, I began to see that the new laws on the books and those we were hoping to add could not alone protect the environment and assure a better quality of life. There would have to be an understanding of the need for the laws and a willingness on the part of the agency decision-makers to accept the new value concepts that accompanied the legislative actions. Senator Jackson and Congressman Dingell and their staffs, who wrote the key policy and action-forcing provisions into the National Environmental Policy Act, were probably a few years ahead of the times. They accurately gauged the new-found political strength of the environmental movement and got their legislation enacted because the environment in 1969 was an issue with strong emotional appeal. No member of Congress could afford to be against a better environment. But neither those in Congress nor the public officials who would have to carry out provisions of the act really understood what the new policy might mean.

No wonder the federal bureaucracy found difficulty following the specific directions Congress spelled out in section 102 of the National Environmental Policy Act. That section required the agencies to "develop methods and procedures . . . which will insure that present unquantified environmental amenities and values may be given appropriate consideration in decision-making along with economic and technical consideration." Could we expect that the head of the Federal Highway Administration, whose mission has always been to lay down the concrete as far and as fast as he can—with individual members of Congress applying pressures for more roads in their districts—would suddenly seek "to quantify environmental amenities and values," even if he knew how to do it?

Although aware that these provisions put the federal agencies in a tough position, I felt disappointed that so many agency heads fought, ignored, or delayed compliance. Practically all of the impact statements we received clearly had been prepared *after* the decision was made. I could understand this in the first few months when the new act affected programs already under way or far down the planning road. But the "post-facto" approach became standard.

The environmental impact statement became a "paperwork" exercise to justify the decision already made and to ward off a legal challenge. Some agencies, including the Department of the Interior, established special staffs, far removed from decision-making, to prepare impact statements with no guidance from above. And there were no signs that the decision-makers at the top made use of the environmental data being prepared at lower echelons.

The environmental impact statement could not *force* the agency official to do the environmentally best thing. It only required taking the environmental factors *into consideration* in decision-making. If, after investigating and studying the environmental factors, and weighing them against technical or economic considerations, officials decided to pursue an anti-environmental course, they were free to do so if willing to bear the public criticism that might follow. CEQ was given no power under the act to regulate compliance with the law. The president's executive order establishing CEQ provided only that the council should issue guidelines to the agencies for preparation of the environmental statements.

It took months to get most of the agencies to prepare any impact statements at all. Some agencies demanded to know exactly which of their actions required statements. They wanted CEQ to declare a minimum dollar value that would determine which programs would be considered "major" and hence come under the section 102 umbrella requiring agency heads to prepare statements for "major federal actions significantly affecting the quality of the human environment." Some agencies quibbled about the word "significantly"; others asked us to define the difference between natural environment and human environment.

The official guidelines we published in the *Federal Register* helped to clarify the issues somewhat. The guidelines provided that agencies develop preliminary or "draft" environmental-impact statements and then allow at least 60 days for review and comment by other agencies and the public before publishing the "final" statement. And no action could be taken until 30 days after the final statement was submitted to CEQ and released to the public.

We suggested in the guidelines that, whenever appropriate,

public hearings should be held on the proposed actions, and that the draft environmental-impact statements should be made available to the public at least 15 days before a hearing. And in line with the act's provision requiring proposed actions to be reviewed by other federal agencies with jurisdiction or expertise regarding environmental impacts, the Environmental Protection Agency and the Department of the Interior's Fish and Wildlife Service became in-government monitors. After some initial hesitation, these two agencies, equipped with staff scientists and ecologists, frequently challenged the impact statements of other federal agencies.

It was environmentally concerned citizens, however, with assistance from some open-minded judges, who saved the environmental-impact statement process and made it a partial success. Being in the Executive Office of the President, the Council on Environmental Quality could take no public positions. If we felt an environmental statement was inadequate or if an agency failed to file one on an action, we could not complain publicly. The environmental organizations and legal groups, led by the Environmental Defense Fund, the Natural Resources Defense Council, and the Sierra Club, more than made up for our official silence by bird-dogging agency actions, ready to challenge officials who were not complying with the act. What CEQ was unable to do in bringing executive agencies into line—especially without support from the White House or the Office of Management and Budget—environmental groups accomplished through the courts.

In key cases, the courts forced agencies to prepare impact statements when an agency sought to evade the requirement by claiming the project had already been under way before the National Environmental Policy Act was passed. Judges forced agencies to consider economic costs of alternative solutions when the agency tended to dismiss the alternative out of hand as being economically unfeasible. Lawsuits forced several federal agencies to stop their practice of having a private contractor or a state agency prepare an environmental-impact statement, which was then almost automatically approved by the federal agency. Other lawsuits made the Federal Trade Commission and the Securities and Exchange Commission change their procedures to allow more environmental considerations

Despite the help from the courts and citizen organizations,

however, the process of giving adequate consideration to environmental concerns was steadfastly resisted by many federal decision-
makers. The controversy over the proposed Cross Florida Barge
Canal was typical of the bureaucratic resistance and political
maneuvers surrounding many projects.

I had covered President Johnson's ceremonial launching of the
canal project back in 1963, and had followed its hectic history ever
since. Barge interests and Florida chambers of commerce had been
working for years to have a 185-mile-long navigable ditch built
across the northern part of the peninsula, connecting the Atlantic
and the Gulf of Mexico. Congress had authorized the project
during World War II when proponents argued that the canal
would allow U.S. ships to avoid Nazi U-boats by cutting across
Florida rather than going around Key West. Congress never
funded it, however, until President Kennedy, making good on a
1960 Florida campaign pledge, put it in his budget and pushed it
through Congress. In addition to being a multi-million-dollar
boondoggle offering little real benefit, the canal would ruin the
scenically wild Oklawaha River which meanders 75 miles across
Florida. But when Kennedy made his go-ahead decision, the
environmental problems and alternative solutions received no
national attention.

The Council on Environmental Quality became involved in the
controversy by mistake, as it turned out. Not long after we set up
our offices, a letter protesting the canal was sent to the president by
fifty Florida environmental scientists. Joined by a hundred experts
from all parts of the nation, the scientists urged Nixon to declare a
moratorium on canal construction until appropriate environmental
studies could be carried out and evaluated.

The scientists pointed out that the canal was already obsolete
even though only one-third complete. It would drastically alter
ecosystems associated with two major river valleys, especially the
Oklawaha. And halting construction would fit the administration's
avowed anti-inflation policy. More than $50 million had been spent
on the project already, and costs had risen so much that another
$130 million would be needed for completion.

The letter was referred to a minor White House aide who should
have sent it on to the agency most concerned—in this case the Army
Corps of Engineers—for a reply. Instead, the White House aide
wrote an answer himself, expressing the president's thanks to the

scientists for their concern, and adding that "He [the president] has asked that your suggestion for declaring a moratorium on construction be forwarded to the Council on Environmental Quality."

As frequently happens when someone receives a letter from the White House on a controversial issue, one of the scientists immediately contacted the news media. And the next day an Associated Press story appeared in the *Washington Post* under the headline: NIXON ORDERS NEW STUDY OF FLORIDA CANAL.

Our council staff was not in shape to take on a study of that magnitude. And the White House really didn't want a study done, anyway, because of the canal's inflammatory political status in Florida. With the fat already in the fire, though, Whitaker told us to prepare a paper making recommendations for presidential action. This would also mesh with the effort to cut federal spending. The budget office had recently asked us to prepare a list of Corps of Engineers and Bureau of Reclamation high-cost projects that might be canceled "for environmental reasons."

So the Cross Florida Barge Canal headed our list of nine "expendable" projects totaling more than $1 billion in estimated costs to the federal government. Nothing came of our list. Stopping any one of those projects, of course, would have had severe local political and economic implications.

On April 14, 1970, we completed the Cross Florida Barge Canal paper Whitaker had suggested. In it we recommended that the president place a freeze on all canal construction funding during a study period and that $200,000 be made available for a study. Our reasons: The canal could degrade water quality in the area, affect the water supply of central Florida, alter a natural area, and endanger the habitat of wildlife including three endangered species—alligators, panthers, and wild turkeys. We even included a draft statement for the president to issue.

The Corps of Engineers, sensing the mounting pressure, decided to give a bit. It prepared its own draft presidential statement ordering suspension of construction on the portion of the Oklawaha River that could still be preserved in its natural condition, but allowing other construction to continue. It would then consider rerouting the Oklawaha portion of the canal.

The White House did nothing. From time to time we would raise the question with Whitaker. In January 1971 Sen. Henry Jackson, considered to be a potential threat to Nixon's re-election, began using the White House indecision on the canal as a political issue when he gave speeches in Florida. And a lawsuit to stop the canal was also nearing decision.

We tried again. Russell Train sent a letter to the White House urging the president to stop the project, and we enclosed another proposed presidential statement. Train's memo added: "I believe there are probably more political advantages than disadvantages in stopping the project."

This time, to our surprise, the White House responded. It set a date for announcing a halt to construction, but then delayed the announcement. During the delay a federal court judge hearing an Environmental Defense Fund lawsuit against the canal granted an injunction to stop certain parts of the construction.

But before the judge handed down his written opinion and the order could be implemented, the president ordered suspension of further canal construction. His statement on January 19, 1971, followed nearly word for word the letter we had sent to the White House, and read like the message of a president with a firm environmental concern. It said in part:

> The Council on Environmental Quality has recommended to me that the project be halted, and I have accepted its advice. The council has pointed out to me that the project could endanger the unique wildlife of the area and destroy this region of unusual and unique natural beauty.
>
> The total cost of the project if it were completed would be about $180 million. About $50 million has already been committed to construction. I am asking the secretary of the army to work with the Council on Environmental Quality in developing recommendations for the future of the area.
>
> The step I have taken today will prevent a past mistake from causing permanent damage. But more important, we must assure that in the future we take not only full but also timely account of the environmental impact of such projects—so that instead of merely halting the damage, we prevent it.

Long afterward, John Ehrlichman told me that he himself had made the Cross Florida Barge Canal decision without clearing beforehand with the president. And it was evident that the president's attitude toward Corps of Engineers projects had not really changed when, a few weeks later, he personally went to Tennessee to participate in ground-breaking ceremonies and to make a speech in favor of an even more environmentally harmful project then in its infancy, the Tennessee Tombigbee project.

After the president's next trip to Key Biscayne, and after hearing from some Florida interests, he told Ehrlichman that the decision to stop the Cross Florida Barge Canal had been a mistake.

"No, it was a good decision," Ehrlichman replied, and he told the president that thousands of favorable letters and telegrams had been sent to the White House congratulating the president for his bold action.

The Corps of Engineers and some members of Florida's congressional delegation did not readily give up. Florida interests took CEQ to court, and the council's senior scientist, Lee Talbot, worked for five years testifying at hearings or in lawsuits and attempting to work out ecologically sound solutions to the problems raised by the construction halt. Nevertheless, Nixon's cancellation of the canal served the environment well, even though the action resulted more from political circumstance than from environmental concern.*

At CEQ we found all too often that political considerations unnecessarily became the deciding factor in decisions affecting the environment. My experience as a reporter during the Kennedy and Johnson administrations had prepared me to expect that White House staffs would squeeze the utmost political advantage from presidential action. Nixon carried this proclivity to extremes.

The Council on Environmental Quality's efforts to influence presidential decision-making also were thwarted by the White House courting of industry executives whose objectives often ran counter to ours. Soon after CEQ was organized, Nixon created a National Industrial Pollution Control Council (NIPCC) with a membership list of 200 that read like a Who's Who of big polluters. The council had 30 vice-chairmen, each a top officer of his company and each heading a six- or seven-member subcouncil representing an industry with pollution problems. Though not

---

* It was not until late in 1976 that the Cross Florida Barge Canal was finally laid to rest, when Florida Governor Reuben Askew and his cabinet voted to have the canal program dropped and the Corps of Engineers requested permission from Congress to deactivate the project.

established by law, NIPCC was supported by a small, salaried staff and a budget of more than $1 million—almost half as much as CEQ's entire budget!

The group produced some useful reports on industry's pollution-control efforts. But it frequently used its muscle on the side of opposing those pollution-control standards it considered unfair. Several of its powerful members had easy access to the president and his close advisers, an access not available to CEQ.

Richard Nixon's grasp of the real significance of environmental matters was slight and his awareness of ecology or the value of nature almost nil. Apparently nothing in his background or training had given him a regard for the world of nature. Yet the reasoning that led him to support measures for more parks and cleaning up the air and water early in his administration seemed to be based on genuine concern for the well-being of the people. White House staff members have told me that on occasion in those early days the president complained privately about industry's cavalier pollution of the air and water.

His natural inclinations, however, favored the interests of the business sector, which he regarded as his major constituency, and were responsible for his support of the SST, the Alaska pipeline, and coal strip mining. His pro-business leanings were abetted by his close association with Secretary of Commerce Maurice Stans, presidential adviser Bryce Harlow, who was on leave from Proctor and Gamble, and close personal friends such as Pepsico board chairman Donald Kendall or multimillionaire industrial tycoon Robert Abplanalp. Nixon had no close friends among environmentalists, whom he seemed to link with anti-war liberals and the Eastern establishment.

Though Nixon's background and inclinations included nothing that could be classed as an environmental ethic, it must be admitted that his record is much better than some of us, who sought so much more, are usually willing to admit. He must be given credit especially for his three environment messages with their positive legislative proposals, support of land-use planning, creation of the Environmental Protection Agency, support for the expansion of wilderness and urban parks, cutting down on pesticide use, and eliminating the use of poisons in the control of predators on public lands.

4

FROM TEDDY
TO JIMMY

My observations in the Executive Office of the President, as well as earlier experiences while a White House reporter, led me to wonder whether it is possible for a president of the United States to have and practice an environmental ethic. Can a president really be expected to give as much weight to environment as to other concerns? Has any president ever had a real overriding sense of environmental values? If so, what happened when he faced the counterpressures and political exigencies that inevitably confront the occupant of the White House?

President Theodore Roosevelt, of course, was a great champion of conservation. He worked hard at both preaching and practicing respect for nature and preservation of natural resources.

A big-game hunter in Africa and America, and an outdoorsman, Roosevelt founded the Boone and Crockett Club in 1887. The club's mission was to end the ruthless slaughter of big game by commercial hunters and to preserve threatened species for future hunting or, if hunting would destroy the species, to establish reserves where the animals could be saved from extinction. He was also a bird watcher and helped bring attention to preservation problems by starting the annual Christmas bird count on the White House lawn—a practice that grew into a nationwide bird count by volunteers.

He was a wilderness devotee, and while vice-president, he was deep in the Adirondacks wilderness on a camping trip when word reached him in September 1901 that President McKinley had been shot. Roosevelt became president a week later and soon started a crusade to correct environmental wrongs of the previous century.

Exploitation of public lands and natural resources and taming of the wildlands had been accepted as a normal part of a nation's growth. Roosevelt considered this policy wasteful, and he resented the way a few people and companies profiteered off the public lands and built monopolies. He set out to reverse these practices. The first step was to popularize interest in nature and preservation of resources.

On his first presidential trip to the Far West, in 1903, Roosevelt took time out for a camping trip in California's High Sierra with John Muir, the great wilderness advocate. Today it is hard to imagine a president of the United States giving the press the slip and disappearing into the wilderness for a weekend. Yet Roosevelt hiked into a secluded part of Yosemite National Park, talked with John Muir over a campfire, and slept in a bed roll, despite a heavy snowfall. And coming down from the Sierra, Roosevelt made a speech that rang with an environmental ethic.

Roosevelt visited Yellowstone National Park, the North Dakota Badlands, and Grand Canyon National Park. On the Yellowstone and North Dakota trips, he took along the noted nature essayist John Burroughs, and the trips helped to publicize Burroughs' writings, which were leading many Americans to appreciate the outdoors.

Roosevelt used the rim of the Grand Canyon as a "bully pulpit." The canyon was at the time threatened by mining interests. He urged Americans to "leave it as it is. . . . You cannot improve on it. The ages have been at work on it, and man can only mar it. What you can do is to keep it for your children, your children's children, and for all who come after you as one of the great sights which every American . . . can see."

Five years later, the canyon rim was still threatened by mining and also by land speculators. Roosevelt realized it might be years before Congress could overcome the opposition of mining interests and create a national park around Grand Canyon. So he used the then new Antiquities Act of 1906 to withdraw the canyon and its rims from mining claims by declaring the area a national monument. The action went beyond that contemplated by Congress when it had passed the act, but the protection held until Congress created the Grand Canyon National Park in 1919.

At the same time Roosevelt was promoting preservation of nature he was also implementing his utilitarian land stewardship concepts. His good friend Gifford Pinchot, founder of the Progressive Conservation movement, first promoted widespread use of the word "conservation." Roosevelt agreed with Pinchot's definition of conservation as the use of natural resources for the greatest good to the greatest number for the longest time. Pinchot, the American leader in the technique of managing forests as a crop, had been chief of the federal Forestry Division since 1898. Roosevelt set out to extend his constitutional authority to its limits by taking control of millions of acres of western lands ostensibly for forest protection. By presidential proclamation Roosevelt enlarged the national forest lands from 42 million acres to 172 million acres. Included in the new federally protected areas were the best waterpower sites on 16 western rivers, 75 million acres of coal and phosphate lands, and 138 wildlife refuges. He used the Antiquities Act to proclaim as national monuments 18 areas of unique scenic value, four of which later became national parks (Olympic, Lassen, and Petrified Forest in addition to Grand Canyon).

Roosevelt's efforts on behalf of natural resource protection climaxed with a White House conference on conservation to which the governors of all the states were invited. The 1908 conference included among its thousand guests the cabinet and the Supreme Court. The president urged the governors to start conservation commissions and within a short time 41 states had done so. Most of those commissions have grown into the state conservation or resource agencies.

"In the past we have admitted the right of the individual to injure the future of the Republic for his own present profit," Roosevelt said in his conference keynote speech. "The time has come for a change. As a people we have the right and the duty ... to protect ourselves and our children against the wasteful development of our natural resources, whether that waste is caused by the actual destruction of such resources or by making them impossible of development thereafter."

Years later, when asked which of his achievements he considered most important to the national welfare, Roosevelt unhesitatingly named his conservation policies. His era marked the first phase of the environmental movement, the awakening to the fact that the nation's resources were being plundered and that something had to be done about it. It also established the federal government role in protecting migratory birds, creating large national forests, and aggressively seeking new national parks, monuments, and wildlife refuges. And though Roosevelt's efforts at popularizing his brand of conservation did not produce an immediate flowering of citizen activity, they did plant seeds that kept germinating for several generations.

President Herbert Hoover showed a degree of commitment to conservation and protection of natural resources. He encouraged scientific research in conservation agencies and promoted flood control and oil conservation.

Hoover enjoyed fishing and relaxing at a camp on Virginia's Rapidan River, which later became a part of Shenandoah National Park. At his camp one day he conceived the idea of the Skyline Drive along the crest of the Blue Ridge Mountains, and authorized use of some federal relief funds for starting construction of what developed into the federal parkways.

He tried to protect public lands in the West from overgrazing, and he set up a blue-ribbon commission to study the grazing issue. The commision's recommendation called for turning over to state control all public lands except those to be added to national parks, forests, wildlife refuges, reclamation projects, and areas needed for defense—with the federal government retaining the mineral rights. This approach appealed to Hoover's political philosophy of keeping the states powerful. But it ran counter to the needs of the times for strong federal controls over those who would plunder the natural resources. The states wanted no part of the arrangement, either. And the conservationists fought the proposal, struggling to hold on to the federal protection of public lands.

By bringing the grazing lands controversy into public discussion, Hoover helped his successor. It enabled Franklin D. Roosevelt to push passage of the 1934 Taylor Grazing Act, which brought better—though still inadequate—regulation to the western public lands.

FDR, both as New York governor and as president, left an active record as a utilitarian conservationist. He also gets good marks for protection of wildlands, parks, and historic areas. While not physically able to pursue outdoor recreation as did his cousin Theodore, FDR nevertheless appreciated nature and was a dedicated bird watcher.

By the time FDR took office, many of Teddy Roosevelt's conservation programs were still waiting to be solidly launched. In starting the Soil Conservation Service and Civilian Conservation Corps FDR was able to help prevent future dust bowls and improve conditions in the national parks and national forests. His choice of Harold Ickes as the vigorous secretary of the interior helped to form a good conservation record.

The Tennessee Valley Authority (TVA), another Roosevelt creation, is controversial today among environmentalists for its coal strip mining, advocacy of more dams, and resistance to putting air-pollution controls on its power plants. But TVA was hailed originally for its comprehensive national planning in water power, flood control, soil erosion control, and industrial development for a complete river watershed covering a vast region. It also showed how the federal government and private enterprise could cooperate.

FDR also had the political acumen to tie his concern for conservation to his social welfare goals. He successfully combined both interests in the Civilian Conservation Corps and other programs that gave jobs to the unemployed while furthering conservation and moving ahead with construction of public works.

Harry Truman did not give much priority to conservation. He was sympathetic and open-minded toward resource preservation and established the Paley Commission to survey the adequacy of natural resources to meet future needs. He carried on many of the New Deal conservation programs.

Dwight D. Eisenhower showed little understanding of environmental matters, and his first secretary of the interior, Douglas McKay, infuriated conservationists with his giveaway of timber on public lands. The Eisenhower administration is remembered among conservationists for such actions as turning over to the states the off-shore oil reserves, and the attempt to put dams on the Snake River and in Dinosaur National Monument.

But he did some good things such as defending certain wildlife refuges against unneeded military use and protecting Olympic and Glacier National parks from development proposals. His intentions were good when he launched the ten-year Mission 66 program for improving national parks. Although Eisenhower meant well, the Mission 66 effort was opposed by many conservationists, because it encouraged development of roads, concessions, and other commercial activities within the parks.

During the Kennedy and Johnson administrations, I was covering the White House as a reporter, and I got a fairly close look at their conservation and environmental actions.

Kennedy did not evidence much personal enthusiasm for conservation, but his secretary of the interior, Stewart Udall, pushed for water-pollution control, beautification of the countryside, improvement of urban environment, preservation and expansion of wilderness, state parks, wildlife refuges, and the national park system.

While not a great initiator of conservation activities, Kennedy was receptive to needs of the times. He called a White House conference on conservation in 1962. And when Rachel Carson's *Silent Spring* stirred controversy over banning the use of pesticides, Kennedy backed Miss Carson. He also ordered his Science Advisory Committee to make a study of pesticide use—a study that laid the groundwork for controlling pesticide abuses.

Kennedy took a swing around the country in the spring of 1963. It was labeled in advance as a "conservation" trip. I went along as a reporter. Kennedy started at the Pinchot Institute of Environmental Forestry in Pennsylvania with appropriate presidential remarks on conservation of forests. In upper Wisconsin he looked over a proposed new national lakeshore, and in Duluth, Minnesota, he addressed a farm convention.

Presidential aides were quick to note that the press was picking up Kennedy's off-the-cuff remarks on foreign affairs and anti-ballistic missiles and virtually ignoring the carefully prepared texts on conservation. From then on, at speeches in North Dakota, Wyoming, Montana, Utah, Washington, Oregon, California, and Nevada, President Kennedy discarded most of his prepared remarks on conservation and ad-libbed instead on foreign affairs.

During an overnight stop at Grand Teton National Park, Press Secretary Pierre Salinger announced at the evening press briefing that Kennedy would rise at 6:00 A.M. to lead a nature walk for all reporters who cared to join. At the appointed hour, I was bundled up, ready for the hike. But the president was still asleep, and his place at the head of the hike was taken by Udall. When we returned to the lodge we discovered that the president's own "nature tour" had consisted of feeding an apple to a deer from the balcony of his suite at the lodge, with photographers dutifully recording the episode.

Lyndon Johnson fancied himself cut from the FDR mold of utilitarian conservationist. But his interests were mostly on the side of rural electrification, soil conservation, stream channelization, flood control, and big projects such as the Tennessee Valley Authority. And they resulted in more talk than action.

He might have shown more interest in the environment had he not known that Lady Bird Johnson was taking care of beautification and parks from the east wing of the White House. His political feelers told him that the environment was a popular issue on the hustings. He retained Udall as interior secretary. Johnson pushed through Congress the Land and Water Conservation Fund, which Kennedy had proposed in 1963, and proposed boosting to $200 million a year the funds from offshore oil royalties to be used by the Interior Department for acquisition of new state and national parkland. Although LBJ did not personally visit any national parks, important new areas were added to the park system during his presidency. They included Redwood, North Cascades, and Guadalupe Mountains national parks; Assateague Island, Cape

Lookout, and Fire Island national seashores; and eight national recreation areas.

The First Lady's activities, meantime, had Lyndon Johnson's hearty blessing. He called a 1965 White House conference on natural beauty at her behest and expected Lady Bird to supervise the planning and guide the conference, which considered such topics as land use, water quality, air pollution, transportation, and solid-waste disposal. Mrs. Johnson also instigated cleanup campaigns and started flower gardens in Washington, D.C.'s public open spaces as a model to the rest of the nation. She helped to build public support for the Highway Beautification Act of 1965, which set up processes to screen junkyards and eliminate billboards from major highways.

Even Lady Bird Johnson's urgings were not enough to overcome the president's political loyalties. In the summer of 1968, for instance, Congress passed and sent to the White House a law intended to weaken the billboard elimination program and to mandate construction of a new bridge across the Potomac River into downtown Washington, with freeway segments passing beneath the Lincoln Memorial and close to the Jefferson Memorial. Mrs. Johnson and all major environmental groups pleaded with the president to veto the bill. But after he talked with some of his old congressional colleagues, he signed the bill. (The bridge was later blocked by lawsuits brought by environmental and citizen organizations.)

Johnson and Udall are also remembered by environmentalists for opening Santa Barbara Channel to oil drilling and for permitting an oil refinery to be built in the Virgin Islands.

Johnson had one last opportunity to make a truly significant contribution to the environment. After announcing his decision not to run for reelection, he sought ideas from his cabinet for lasting executive actions he might take without going through Congress. And in early December 1968, he agreed to deliver, as a farewell surprise to the nation, a mammoth conservation package proposed by Secretary Udall. He would use the 1906 Antiquities Act to protect certain lands by declaring them national monuments, a status guaranteeing protection almost equal to that afforded national parks. In one stroke of the pen he would sign executive orders adding to the national park system one-fourth as much land as had been protected in parklands over the past century: more than 4 million acres of wilderness in Alaska's Gates of the Arctic area, 2 million acres of the Sonora Desert and Marble Canyon in the Southwest, plus enlargement of several other national monuments. But the powerful House Interior Committee Chairman Wayne Aspinal found out about the proposal at the last minute and complained vigorously to Johnson that he was bypassing Congress. The president relented, and the day before leaving office, he signed executive orders for a conservation package that had by then been reduced from 7.5 million acres to 300,000 acres. When environmental values ran up against practical politics, the environment lost out.

After the Nixon years, some environmentalists had hopes that Gerald Ford, once he became president, would give high priority to the environment. In his earlier days, after all, Ford had worked as a seasonal ranger at Yellowstone National Park. And two of his sons had worked in the national parks and national forests. Instead, though, the Ford record turned out to be almost totally lacking in environmental concern.

Ford gave the Council on Environmental Quality short shrift, and never called on them for advice, although he did meet with the council twice. The post of White House environmental coordinator, left vacant when Whitaker's former deputy, Richard Fairbanks, departed during the summer of 1974, was not even filled for six months. The post finally went to someone with no access to the president.

Ford evidently turned a deaf ear to his son Jack, who urged his father to give more attention to the environment. Instead, Ford followed his own instincts, and they led him to believe that environmental improvements were gained only at the expense of business and the economy.

Among environmentalists he will be remembered most for twice vetoing the strip-mine protection bill. The League of Conservation Voters gave him very low ratings and labeled him "hopeless" on environmental concerns.

The record book on Jimmy Carter's presidency still contains many unwritten pages. But his background and first two years as president indicate that he has an environmental ethic that could lead him to elevate the priority of environment more effectively than any national leader since Theodore Roosevelt. And the time is right. Roosevelt had to educate the public to the need for conservation and had to apply the big stick of federal intervention against those who were despoiling the land and depleting the nonrenewable resources. But with the nation already alerted to pollution, energy shortages, and deterioration of environmental quality, Carter's task is to convince the people that not only must governmental and corporate decision-makers consider the long-range impacts of their activities, but also that every person's living practices need changing if the country is to solve the environmental problems of the latter 20th century.

Carter learned respect for the land from his early days on the family farm. And his devotion to a conservation ethic grew as he fished wild rivers and ran rivers in rafts, canoes, and kayaks. As governor of Georgia, he supported the addition of several areas to the national wilderness system, strengthened the state's protection of coastal zones and wetlands, and pushed through a strong park acquisition program, including a heritage trust program for protecting ecologically important lands. And he stopped the long-planned Corps of Engineers' Spewrell Bluff Dam on the Flint, Georgia's last free-flowing river.

Carter learned about the need for a holistic approach to environmental problems from Eugene P. Odum of the Institute of Ecology at the University of Georgia, author of the standard textbook on ecology. When Carter would go throughout the state to hold town meetings, he frequently took Odum along to speak to the people about environmental issues.

Although Carter did not make environmental matters a major part of his presidential campaign, his publicly circulated position papers sounded so good that environmentalists hardly dared believe them. During the campaign he stated that clear-cutting in national forests could be practiced only on small slopes where soil and esthetics permit, and he pledged himself "to end the unnecessary construction of dams by the Corps of Engineers." When economic and environmental objectives were in conflict, he declared, he would side with the environment.

Carter had been in the White House only a month when he surprised Congress, and even the environmentalists, by notifying

Congress that he was studying 19 Corps of Engineers and Bureau of Reclamation water projects with the intention of cutting off their funds, and would not back any new projects. The ongoing projects on the so-called hit list, announced Carter, "are of doubtful necessity now, in the light of new economic conditions and environmental policies."

Congressmen, angered that their pet "pork" projects were being eliminated, threatened to reinstate all the projects and to retaliate by holding up other legislation. The president finally yielded enough to accept a compromise that allowed half of the list to be funded.

At one point during White House staff deliberations on stopping the dam projects, Budget Director Bert Lance commented that the planning for one of the dams, the Dickey Lincoln, had been delayed by environmentalists because it would harm a "little old snapdragon." Commented the president: "I can't think of a better reason to stop the dam."

Carter irritated the business community by putting conservation and consumer advocates in a large number of subcabinet posts and key agency positions, especially in the Interior, Agriculture, and Justice departments.

In 1977 Carter sent a special presidential environmental message and package of proposals to Congress, something that had not been done for four years. The Council on Environmental Quality prepared a 25-page option paper for the president, proposing 35 actions. Carter backed all but one of the council's proposals (an idea for categorical grants to states for wildlife management, which OMB Director Lance opposed).

His environmental message proposed a $759-million program for developing new and existing parks. It requested four new wilderness areas, eight new wild and scenic rivers, three new national scenic trails, a $295-million program to rehabilitate and improve the wildlife refuge system, and $50 million for purchase of wetlands to protect waterfowl habitats. With the message, Carter also issued several executive orders, including one to ban off-road vehicles from certain portions of public lands where they might cause environmental damage, and another directing federal agencies to discontinue their support for development of floodplains and wetlands.

When Congress enacted the strip-mining bill in mid-1977 after strong administration lobbying, Carter held a signing ceremony to which he invited two hundred citizen activitists from all parts of the nation, who had worked for passage of the bill. And in contrast to President Ford, who twice vetoed similar legislation, Carter complained that the law did not control strip mining strongly enough.

The government reorganization task force put together by the president to cut the staff of the Executive Office of the President by 30% recommended that the Council on Environmental Quality be abolished and its duties spread among other agencies. This gutting of CEQ was supported by the vice-president, the OMB director, and all other key advisers. Carter considered the dissenting comments of environmental organizations and reversed the task force recommendation, keeping CEQ intact.

There seems little doubt that Jimmy Carter's sense of the environmental ethic is the most advanced of any president's yet. He has backed away from some of his pro-environment positions in the heat of strong opposition from Congress and from some governors and important industry voices, and his nuclear development position remains clouded. At a candid give-and-take cabinet-room session with a dozen environmental leaders in May 1978, Carter received some frank criticism, especially over policies of his Department of Energy. But by mid-term, he still had the support of most of the environmental movement. Whether the environmental ethic in President Carter can continue to hold its priority against competing pressures and priorities remains unknown.

5

THE REAL
BOTTOM LINE

Business and industry leaders whose activities were being regulated by government came in contact with the Council on Environmental Quality from time to time, and I took advantage of any such occasion to look for evidence of how deeply the environmental ethic had penetrated the corporate world. While most public attention centered on actions of government officials, I had come to realize that the decisions of business and financial leaders could have even more far-reaching environmental consequences.

One occasion presented itself when I represented CEQ at a meeting of the National Industrial Pollution Control Council in Washington. I had been asked to brief the thirty industrialists present about CEQ's current activities, a task that usually fell to CEQ Chairman Train, who was out of town at the time. The meeting took place in a conference room at the Department of

58 FOOTPRINTS ON THE PLANET

Commerce, an area that earlier had been picketed by Ralph Nader
and some of his associates, protesting the fact that the National
Industrial Pollution Control Council operated in secret, which
Nader claimed constituted a violation of antitrust law.

The public was still barred at the time I met with the council.
The NIPCC members, most of them chief executive officers of the
nation's major corporations, showed little interest in my briefing on
CEQ activities, and posed no questions when I concluded. Before
sitting down, I decided to ask them a question.

"I've been wondering," I said. "whether it would be possible for
each of your companies, on a voluntary basis, to prepare environmental assessments for your major actions that would affect the
environment." I quickly went on to explain that such an assessment
would not necessarily lead to their adopting the most environmentally acceptable method. "But at least it would give you a process
for bringing the environment into your considerations and enable
you to look at alternatives as government agencies are now
required to do. Is this a possibility?"

No one answered. I asked if they had any comments about the
idea. But I met a wall of silence. It must have sounded ridiculously
impractical to them.

On another occasion, while representing the council at a
conference, I ran into an old friend who was public relations
director of a large corporation with extensive interests in food
products and chemicals. I told him about my corporate voluntary
environmental impact statement idea. He was enthusiastic and said
he thought his boss, who was both board chairman and chief
executive officer, would be very much interested in having the
company be the first to institute such a system. The executive was
to arrive at the conference the next day to give a speech, and my
friend said he would get us together.

I could tell as I sat at lunch and talked with the company chief
that he had a good sense of corporate social responsibility. And he
liked my idea. He said it was the right way to approach
environmental matters. It would be difficult to implement such a
system, he said, but he wanted to give it a try. He promised to let
me know how it came out.

That was the last I ever heard from him. I found out later that
the board chairman had taken my idea seriously enough to have
the public relations director make a presentation at the company's

next executive meeting. It got shot down immediately by the head of the chemical division, who said the company was already doing more than enough just trying to follow federal pollution control regulations. The board chairman could not afford to buck the chemical division, which brought the company $80 million a year.

After I left government and returned to journalism, I continued pursuing this idea of an environmental ethic in business and industry. One of the major obstacles to more environmentally concerned corporate policies is the belief—right or wrong—that such policies may reduce the company's earnings and thus should automatically be resisted. I even found some corporate officials who claimed that taking actions which might result in lower company profits was illegal and could result in stockholders' suits.

A vice-president of a large multinational copper mining company told me: "The cost of environmental regulations is putting undue burdens on our company and hurting the economy as well."

Yet another business leader, Louis B. Lundborg, a member of the board of the world's largest bank, the Bank of America, insists that environmental and other social problems should get at least as much corporate attention as production, sales, and finance. "The quality of life in its total meaning is, in the final reckoning, the only justification for any corporate activity," he says.

These two statements represent viewpoints along a wide spectrum of attitudes among business and industry decision-makers regarding environmental concerns. The issue involves the amount of corporate social responsibility a company can legitimately be expected to sustain, and how to weigh this responsibility against corporate self-interest and immediate profits.

I found no uniform set of standards for measuring how well or how poorly business is doing in accepting responsibility for its environmental impact. Companies' organizational structures for dealing with environment vary widely, thus thwarting comparison. An observer cannot fairly judge an industry's real ability to afford all of the actions necessary to combat pollution or enhance the environment. And only those who sit at the board room conference table or have access to management decision-making sessions can answer questions like how adequate is the environmental information available and to what extent do competing factors and trade-offs affect a decision?

Nearly all decision-makers in business, industry, and agriculture are now required by local, state, or federal laws to apply environmental concern to their processes or products that affect the air or water or noise levels. Laws regulate use and production of pesticides and toxic substances. Many areas have laws controlling the way land can be used. There are laws to protect and preserve wildlife and endangered species, parks and national forests, wetlands and deserts, and historic and cultural areas. These many laws and regulations have been written in reaction to perceived problems affecting the quality of life, and were enacted because the great majority of those misusing the environment were unwilling to change their mode of operation voluntarily.

The laws, of course, apply only to direct, demonstrable instances of environmental impact. Many businesses, professional firms, and individuals take actions that contribute to environmental problems. For instance, banks and insurance companies may use their funds to finance projects that are environmentally harmful. Others may contribute to environmental degradation through legal, scientific, or technical consultation they give clients. Yet because their impact is indirect, they are not subject to the laws.

Many people in business, industry, and agriculture find the complex array of environmental laws and regulations extremely vexing. Sorting them out and bringing practices into compliance costs time and money. They charge with some justification that early environmental laws and standards were enacted in the heat of concern and were based on insufficient scientific data. And they bitterly complain of unclear, complicated, sometimes conflicting regulations.

Many companies have chosen to delay compliance, and a few have openly opposed the laws, forcing the regulatory agencies to take them to court, or in some cases initiating court actions against the regulators. Those who resist more vehemently do so in the belief that fulfilling environmental requirements would damage or destroy their business or industry. Most companies, however, have accepted compliance as a necessary cost of doing business. A few have even worked with legislators to help write the laws. And other companies have found ways to turn environmental improvements into financial gains, especially when costs for materials are reduced by recycling, or energy costs are lowered through more efficient processes or practices. And of course the manufacturers of pollution-abatement equipment are flourishing.

As I delved into the business area I did not expect to find the environmental ethic in full flower. I did hope to find corporate decision-makers who were demonstrating a concern for the public's environmental well-being by doing more than merely complying with laws. Under the profit-making pressures of the competitive free enterprise system, I did not anticipate finding much altruism. But I hoped to find managers who understood that environment, in addition to being a social responsibility, is a legitimate component of the pool of information on which to base decisions—as important a factor in its way as market research, current technology, and the cost of materials and labor. I realized this kind of outlook would be rare, and that circumstances made environmental responsibility more difficult for one company than for another. Some types of companies could pass on environmental expenses to the consumer, while others would be in competitive situations making this impossible. Business leaders complain that a company that takes costly or time-consuming actions not specifically required by law can meet resistance from stockholders, be put at a price disadvantage by competitors who declined to do the same, and face resentment from other companies in a given industry because of the precedent being set by the environmentally concerned company.

The attitude I hoped to find was one that would run counter to the prevalent approach of economists of the Milton Friedman school who believe that maximizing profits is the highest economic and social responsibility of business. States Nobel Prize winner Friedman: " ... there is one and only one social responsibility of business—to use its resources and engage in activities designed to increase its profits so long as it stays within the rules of the game, which is to say, engages in open and free competition without deception or fraud."

When I first started looking into how business and industry were institutionalizing their environmental responsibilities, I heard about a survey conducted by The Conference Board, an independent, nonprofit organization doing research in business economics and management. Study director Leonard Lund had mailed questionnaires on "corporate organization for environmental policymaking" to one thousand of the board's four thousand member organizations, and received replies from just over half.

The good news of the study was that 88% of the responding

companies said environmental policy decisions were made at a vice-president level or higher, and 85% indicated that environmental matters were viewed as actions reflecting social responsibility. The bad news was that over 60% of the companies answering the questionnaire had no kind of formal environmental policy.

Some of the statements of environmental policy Lund received were brief enunciations of the company's responsibility to be a good neighbor or a good citizen, and a pledge to comply with the law. A few published pamphlets in which a speech by a top officer stood as environmental policy for the company. And a number of firms said they had no formal policy but could point nevertheless to ongoing pollution control programs.

Lund's report noted that the director of environmental protection for a major corporation said that after reading several companies' policy statements, his firm concluded that there was no particular purpose in having a formal document "since they all seem to say that the company is in favor of protecting the environment and will do its share toward this end." The executive added that these policy statements sometimes "espouse corrective attitudes beyond what the company is really ready to support" and that these may "create adverse reaction if they give the impression of being too idealistic."

Lund commented that this frank expression on the question of policy statements seems to imply that there is as yet little purposeful connection between the company statement of intent and the actual record of accomplishment.

One promising survey statistic revealed that most of the companies having an environmental affairs officer had expanded the officer's role beyond pollution control to include a full range of company activities which may impact upon the environment. Although no details were given, over 60% of the reporting companies said that the environmental affairs officer participated in decisions on production procedures and plant siting. The officer participated in the planning of advertising campaigns in 43% of the companies and in product design in 25%. High-level environmental affairs committees were not widely used except in a relatively few large companies where they function primarily as a policy development mechanism.

"Increasing numbers of large companies have had to rely heavily upon ad hoc management networks to deal with effects upon company policy which have as their motivation newly accepted awareness of environmental influences," Lund reported.

More than half of the companies reported that their environmental policy officer's occupational background included engineering; the largest single broad grouping of those not from the engineering field were those with administrative or management backgrounds. Companies increasingly use their public affairs departments to direct environmental affairs. "Some companies, such as producers of packaging," the report stated, "have utilized the public affairs 'cover' for environmental affairs programs to reduce the high visibility of this issue as it related to the company's products."

The background of the chief executive officer of a corporation is far more significant than that of the environmental officer. In most big companies the chief executive officer (or board chairman or president) exercises enormous power to set policy. Although most major companies have management committees, the chief executive officer ordinarily can set the tone for such matters as social responsibility or how seriously to take environmental obligations.

A 1974 *Forbes* magazine study showed that 80% of the chief executive officers in the fifty largest U.S. industrial corporations had risen from career backgrounds in manufacturing and production, marketing and sales, operations and finance. A perceptive observer of this trend, Robert L. Stern, formerly with the Xerox Corporation and now with The Conference Board, noted in a speech that performance in this type of career "tends to be measured in the short term: meeting an annual sales quota, reducing a unit manufacturing cost, increasing sales or manufacturing productivity."

Stern said that a study of junior executives of the nation's largest corporations—men and women between 35 and 45 years of age— showed that over half hold technical degrees. This he considered encouraging because, "even if only to a small extent ... it will enlarge the prospects for a longer-range view of those corporate goals and social responsibilities that are affected by technology."

Since the average age at which the chief executive officers of the fifty largest firms assumed their posts was 53, and most have a retirement age of 65, they have only 12 years at the top. "The time-horizon in which to incorporate perceptiveness of values that have long-term merit is, then, not very forgiving within the age group of the managers currently leading the fifty largest firms," Stern said. "A younger CEO should be more able to set longer-term goals for his institution, in consonance with the needs of the future world in which he and it will live."

The environmental awakening of the late 1960s and early 1970s affected the attitude of many business leaders in ways that went virtually unnoticed. Some may have sensed that environment was going to become a major factor in doing business. Some were influenced by their own environmentally tuned-in children, and some simply believed protecting the environment was the right thing to do. Whatever the motivation, a scattering of corporate executives began to plan environmental measures beyond what the law required.

A combination of these forces converged several years ago when the New York State Electric and Gas Company planned to build a nuclear power plant on the shore of Cayuga Lake. A group of university biologists opposing the plant asked a brilliant young philosopher, David Comey, to help them. Comey was at the time a research associate at Cornell. He is now president of the Chicago-based Citizens for a Better Environment.

Comey organized statements by Cornell scientists concerning radiation problems and the thermal pollution impact of the proposed plant on Cayuga Lake. He drafted three pieces of legislation to stop the plant and helped lobby them to passage in the New York State Legislature. But Governor Nelson Rockefeller vetoed all three bills.

His conventional tactics having fallen flat, Comey turned to an unorthodox approach, working on the utility's board members indirectly—subversively, one might say. He got hold of the addresses of the directors' sons and daughters who were away at college and wrote to these students. He sent them materials he had written or collected on the proposed Lake Cayuga nuclear power plant, and suggested that when they were home over Christmas they ask their fathers about it.

Just before New Year's Day Comey got a phone call from one of the board members. "Enough, Comey, you bastard! I want to talk to you," the director said. He invited Comey to his club in another city, along with two other members of the board, who also had heard from their offspring.

Comey gave the three board members information the utility had not disclosed to them. He suggested that the three constitute themselves an ad hoc committee on behalf of the utility's board of directors and talk to the scientists who had been advising Comey, and to those advising the utility. The three met first with the pro-utility scientists, then with the opponents. They went back to a board meeting and recommended that the project be canceled. The full board sided with them, and the nuclear plant on Lake Cayuga was killed.

"When people ask me what's the most effective device you've ever discovered, I say: 'kid power,'" Comey told me. "Most of the times I have managed to get a corporate executive talking about environmental concerns it is usually because his children had been raising questions. This really makes them focus on it. An executive's wife can also be effective in getting him to discuss social and environmental values.

"I try to create a situation in which I force a confrontation between a man's corporate responsibilities and his own personal conscience," Comey continued. "Every corporate executive I have ever met has good intentions. But he gets inside of his office and he immediately sheds those personal values and begins to look at the bottom line. I want to create mechanisms that will make him reconcile the two values. He has got to bring his own personal values into the corporate boardroom. And the best way I know of doing that, frankly, is through his family. If, when he comes home at night, he can be motivated to focus on the social and environmental implications of what he did that day, I think we will see a lot more enlightened actions in the board room."

Another victim of "kid power" was Louis Lundborg when he was chairman of the board of the Bank of America. During a trip to California I learned from Lundborg, and from one of the exponents of kid power, how young people had helped in the transformation of a corporate chief executive officer into a maverick visionary.

By 1970, Lundborg was at the pinnacle of the bank's hierarchy, enjoying all the perquisites of the board chairman's position. Then, at the height of student unrest and violence, a mob of young people protesting the Vietnam war in particular and "the establishment" in general, set fire to the bank's Isla Vista Branch at the edge of the Santa Barbara campus of the University of California. The branch was destroyed.

Lundborg was furious at such violence against property and rights. His bank reacted with full-page advertisements in newspapers. The advertisements featured an open letter to California Governor Ronald Reagan, signed by Lundborg, in which he stated that the "wanton act of arson perpetrated on our Isla Vista Branch was a criminal act of violent proportions and in a very real sense an insurrection against the democratic process." The letter called for Reagan and local mayors "to take such steps as may be necessary to bring this wanton lawlessness swiftly and completely to an end," and to make certain "with all the means at your disposal, that citizens and their property are protected against senseless destruction."

This open letter angered many students, among them James Young, an environmental design student and president of the student body of California State Polytechnic College at Pomona. Young started organizing a boycott of the bank by his and other state colleges. His college senate suggested he first phone the bank, before withdrawing the student body funds. He did so. Young bullied his way through the secretary, demanding to speak to Board Chairman Lundborg.

"Who the hell are you to write a letter like that?" Young challenged. "You're our banker." (CalPoly Pomona had $129,000 deposited with the Bank of America.) "The last person we need to kick us is you. Who are you to give Governor Reagan a hunting license to shoot students?"

Lundborg sputtered: "Wait a minute, that's not what we meant to do."

"Well, that's what you did," replied Young.

The decibel level receded as the board chairman and the student talked. Lundborg felt he wanted to hear more, so he suggested Young come to Los Angeles, where Lundborg was then based, and have lunch with him.

Lundborg had a qualm or two when the young man with hair down to his shoulders appeared at his office to accept the invitation to luncheon at the very sedate Stock Exchange Club. At dusk the two were still talking.

Young arranged for Lundborg to meet with a group of student leaders from several campuses. As he listened to Young and some of the more radical students, Lundborg got an introduction to "the new world of youth culture that I had scarcely known existed."

One of the young radicals grinned at Lundborg and said, "You're a nice guy, but you're part of a dead system. Your days are numbered." Lundborg's defense of the American capitalistic system met vigorous questioning. Why did he support the Vietnam war? Why did the bank make loans to South Africa or to war contractors? Why didn't it hire more blacks? The discussion veered into smog and pollution, restrictive zoning, industry's rape of natural resources, people's wasteful lifestyles and emphasis on material values and excessive consumption.

Instead of arguing back or trying to preach to the students, Lundborg found his mind opening to many of the points they were making. He asked the students what he could do to help. For one thing, he could speak out against the Vietnam war, they replied. Five weeks later Lundborg was in Washington, testifying against the Vietnam war before the Senate Foreign Relations Committee.

When I met with Lundborg in his Bank of America office with its commanding view of San Francisco Bay, he had retired as chief executive officer but was still on the board of directors. He told me he had discovered back in 1970, at his conversion, that the activist environmentalists whom he and others had considered "do-gooders" were, in fact, dealing with the important issue—quality of life for all the people. "Some of us had been saying, 'You can't stand in the way of progress,'" Lundborg told me. "But I found the new generation saying, 'The hell you can't. Prove to us that it really is progress.'"

He spoke frankly about his colleagues in the business world. "Those in corporate life are going to be expected to do things for the good of society just to earn their franchise, their corporate right to exist. A bank is able to project into the future indefinitely because it has continuity. So it should be the one kind of institution that should have the long-range view in environmental terms. Most other kinds of corporations are under pressure to produce profits right now. But banks take on trust obligations that continue to third and fourth generations. So why not translate that into a trust obligation for physical and esthetic resources?

"Government obviously should be the first point of resort for looking after the well-being of future generations; it should have the longest continuity. But after government, no other kind of institution can offer more continuity and perpetuity than a bank.

"Most banks give as much as 5% of their pretax income to charities or community programs. This is really a postponement of shareholder enjoyment of profits for the sake of plowing it into public enjoyment or benefit for the long-range ultimate good of shareholders and everyone else.

"Shareholders, bank directors, and management are going to have to be reconciled to the idea that there will have to be more and more deferment of immediate use of profit for the sake of the longer-range interest of not only the general public, but also of the institution or company itself," he said.

"At some point, of course, you have to make a subjective judgment as to how much profit you can defer in any one year without wrecking your corporation or losing your job—depending," he added with a smile, "on how good a statesman you are and how skillfully you convince shareholders that they should get along with a little bit less."

I asked Lundborg how he would answer the arguments I had been encountering from business executives and even from one of his own bank's top officers—that the economy is in such bad shape one can't institute any environmental policies, because the corporation is doing enough just to survive.

"There never is a good time to do it," Lundborg replied. "Yet you can't afford to postpone adopting policies you feel are necessary, because the damage done now environmentally may be here for generations. You can't use any one cycle or period in the economy as an excuse. Future generations, including this one, are simply going to have to take their share of the social cost of environmental correction that has to be done. However, you're always going to have to weigh economic considerations with environmental ones, you have to have trade-offs. But it should be the longer-range economic considerations weighed against all other long-range considerations."

I commented that it was one thing for the retired chief executive officer of the Bank of America to have such a philosophy, but quite another for environmental concern to be practiced down through the organization, such as in loan policy.

Lundborg agreed and pointed out that the bank has six thousand loan officers. "It would be extremely difficult to suddenly impose an environmental perspective on the policy-making of loan officers who were selected for other skills and priorities."

While in California I discovered an interesting twist to the Lundborg story. It pertained to James Young, the anti-establishment college student who played the feature role in Lundborg's conversion. Young, it turned out, was working at the Bank of America in its Berkeley branch office. So I went to see him.

After graduation he was unable to find a job in the environmental design field, so he applied to the Bank of America. In his interview he told a senior vice-president that he wanted to work at things that involved the bank's taking environmental and social responsibility. The vice-president replied: "You've got to go slow and first change the values of people."

"We don't have time for that," argued Young. But experience has modified his outlook. He has taken the slow route, gaining experience, but still keeping his goals in sight. He helped get the bank involved in its low-income area rehabilitation and maintenance loan program.

He can now appreciate the business position, he told me. "The more I work here the more I see the potential within the marketplace for controlling a whole series of problems," Young said. "The system may be the only thing that's complex enough to consider all the different ramifications. I don't like laws myself because they're a cumbersome and meaningless way to do things. If you've got to sit down and tell people the law, then it's somewhat meaningless. Laws ought to be so logical that people follow them naturally. I like the market system because it's so immutable. It's not written down anywhere. But it's a force that's more powerful than law."

Young admitted, however, that his theory falters when it comes to the business sector accepting responsibility for what happens in the future. "How people make these management decisions, especially in regard to the environment, is where the rubber meets the road," Young said. "Man's mind sort of breaks down because of the time factor."

Louis Lundborg continues to work on his colleagues, trying to get them to adopt more environmental concerns. He believes that progress is being made toward this goal. Yet when I asked if he could give me some examples of corporations where the beliefs of leaders had brought about structural changes so that environmental concerns are given major consideration in decision-making, Lundborg had to admit that he did not know firsthand of any specific case. But, he said that surely there must be some, somewhere.

6

ENVIRONMENTAL ADVENTURES AT AMAX

Looking for companies giving high priority to environment in their decision-making, I remembered an article I had once written about a multinational mining company that had decided to cooperate with environmentalists instead of feuding with them.

The company, AMAX, Inc., was planning a new molybdenum mine in Colorado's Rocky Mountains not far from Denver. At the time of my article, January 1970, company representatives had been meeting with a small group of environmentalists for three years, hammering out plans for the company's new Henderson mine, which was to be located in a national forest. These two ordinarily opposing groups were pooling their knowledge to come up with methods of mining and ore processing that would do minimal harm to the forests, streams, and wildlife of this scenic area straddling the Continental Divide 40 miles west of Denver.

This unique effort had grown out of a chance meeting one blustery winter evening in 1967. Stanley Dempsey and Roger Hansen arrived simultaneously outside a locked gate in Denver to attend a meeting both thought was scheduled for that night. They went to a nearby tavern to phone and found that their meeting was not until the following week. So they sat down for a beer.

They discovered immediately a shared interest in hiking and the outdoors, and both were lawyers. But Dempsey worked for AMAX, considered an enemy of the environment. Hansen was executive secretary of the Colorado Open Space Council and had helped to lead several successful fights to preserve Colorado's scenic areas from developers such as AMAX.

As they talked and sipped their beer, Dempsey decided to go out on a limb and broach to Hansen an idea that had been in the back of his mind for a long time.

"Roger, what if a major mining company came to you and said: 'We have found a big ore deposit in a scenic mountain area. If we were willing to do completely open planning with some responsible environmentalists, would the environmental community be willing to make constructive suggestions, or would they jump on it and try to kill it?' "

Dempsey was treading on very risky ground. Details of the company's plans were a closely held secret and he had not cleared his idea with the top brass. If Hansen reacted the wrong way, there could be serious consequences. He chose his words carefully.

"Could a team of company people and environmentalists possibly work together to develop a major mine on the soundest possible environmental basis?" Dempsey continued.

Roger Hansen was quiet for a moment, thinking about the hazards involved in cooperating with a mining company. He could expect accusations of "sellout" or worse from environmental colleagues. But the idea was intriguing.

"I don't know. Maybe," Hanson finally answered. "It might be possible. Tell me a little more."

Dempsey explained that AMAX had discovered a huge molybdenum deposit on the east side of the Rockies within the Arapaho National Forest. It might be even larger than the company's old Climax mine, a huge deep-pit scar on the western slope of the Rockies. The Climax operation was a constant reminder to the company of an era when mines were operated without concern for the pollution they caused or the lands they despoiled. Times had changed, though, and now Dempsey wanted to bring in environmental considerations at the concept stage, nine or ten years before mining operations would begin, and make the Henderson mine a model of environmentally sound planning.

Neither Dempsey nor Hansen really thought that their discussion that night in Denver would lead to fruition. Yet both men relished the chance to give it a try.

The next day Dempsey went to his boss, A. J. Laing, then chief lawyer for AMAX's western operations, and suggested that the company was sitting on a powder keg of public opinion. When word of the Henderson mine plans got out, Dempsey warned him, environmentalists would likely try to block them, even though AMAX had the legal right to develop the mine. It could be especially controversial, located in a national forest and only 40 miles from Denver. "This is one time when we really ought to step back and see if there isn't some better way to do it than slugging it out with the environmentalists," he told Laing.

Hansen meanwhile received encouragement for the idea from two colleagues, E. R. Weiner, associate professor of chemistry at the University of Denver, and Beatrice Willard, then head of the Thorne Ecological Institute (and later a member of the President's Council on Environmental Quality).

Dempsey's top management gave a cautious go-ahead and named four officials of the new Henderson mine to serve on an ad hoc task force along with Willard, Weiner, and two other environmentalists Hansen had persuaded to join the effort, Robert Venuti of the University of Denver and William Mounsey, a mountain guide and wilderness advocate. At the first meeting they chose the name "Experiment in Ecology" for the project.

To demonstrate the potentially large scale of the operation and some efforts at revegetating tailing ponds, Dempsey took the group to several mines in Arizona. The task force also visited the Henderson mine site and looked at possible locations for the processing. The mining was planned as an underground operation, and the mine shaft would not be too bad environmentally, although the necessary roads and building would certainly end the unspoiled character of the forested mountainside. But the processing of the ore and disposal of the tailings presented major environmental problems.

Only six *pounds* of molybdenum disulfide is garnered from each *ton* of ore. AMAX planned to process 300 million tons of rock during the lifetime of the mine. So a total of 299 million tons of useless material—tailings—would be left in giant, unsightly piles. Runoff from these heaps of waste could pollute streams in the area.

The group examined some thirty processing sites and concluded that an area in the pristine Williams Fork Valley on the west slope of the mountains was the place where the least environmental damage would result. But the site was 14 miles from the mine shaft on the east slope and separated from the mine by the 12,000-foot-high Continental Divide.

The AMAX engineers joined the experiment and accepted the challenge to find an economical solution to this environmental problem. They devised a plan to tunnel 9.5 miles under the Continental Divide, a difficult and costly feat, but a concept that would produce some long-term economic benefits, especially by reducing costs of pollution control in processing the ore.

The company financed a complete inventory of plant and animal life in both the mine and milling areas. They hired Richard Beidleman of Colorado College to do animal ecology studies and John Marr of the University of Colorado to do plant studies. This ecosystems inventory would provide baseline data which, if continuously monitored, could show any harm being done to nearby plants or wildlife. Dr. Marr's biology classes assisted as part of their field work. Dr. Beidleman walked the entire railroad grade and made almost pace-by-pace notations of what he saw, including bird counts. He set up his data so that a decade later researchers could estimate the effects of railway construction and operation of the ore trains on the bird populations.

Electricity was to be supplied by the Public Service Company of Colorado on a route across the Arapaho National Forest. The task force suggested that the power company and the forest superintendent cooperate in the environmental planning. The ecologists advised how to avoid damage to the tundra above timberline, tundra being Dr. Willard's specialty. They suggested ways to clear trees for the powerlines with minimal harm to the environment. Instead of bulldozing wide corridors through forests, the power company cut trees selectively and had them dragged out by horses. Rather than burning the slash, the Public Service Company cut it into firewood and offered it free to the public.

Dr. Marr told the power company that its proposed power line route would disturb a stand of Douglas fir several hundred years old, trees not only scenically valuable, but important to scientific study in an area of mostly younger trees. So they set the power poles by helicopter, avoiding bulldozers; and they used wood poles, painted in three colors to blend with the landscape. The Public Service Company started a competition among crews to see which could do the best job, producing the phenomenon of rugged linemen carefully raking the tundra back into place after installing anchors for the poles.

The Experiment in Ecology reached into nearly every phase of construction as the mine and processing sites were developed. AMAX cleared only as much land as absolutely necessary for the mine, and revegetated where possible. At one time during early construction a foreman suggested moving the road 10 feet in order to save six pine trees. The road was moved. The company opened large areas near the mine and mill sites to public recreation. And when hunters began disturbing the area with their recreation vehicles, AMAX barred all motor vehicles. To protect Clear Creek, a stream near the mine, from pollution, AMAX installed a complex pipe system to route the creek underneath the buildings and roads. The warm water pumped from the mine is treated, cooled, and run through settling ponds before being released back into Clear Creek at near its normal temperature. A system of ponds at the milling and tailing site was constructed in such a manner that rain and snow run-off would be diverted or caught and recycled, thus preventing polluted water run-off from reaching the Williams Fork of the Colorado River.

All of these efforts of the Experiment in Ecology added considerably to the costs of the mine. But the company felt the added expense was justified because it prevented the delays that have plagued other mining developments in their efforts to comply with new state water pollution laws. AMAX avoided environmental lawsuits, received its polution control permits without undue delay, and opened the mine and processing plant on schedule in July 1976. And the environmental planning made it easier for the

mine to come into compliance with the strict demands of the new
Colorado Mine Land Reclamation Law.

This experiment also influenced the company's decision-making
process. AMAX Board Chairman Ian MacGregor * called a
company-wide conference on the environment in 1970. Fifty
representatives from the company's operating divisions met in
Denver. Dempsey talked about the Henderson mine development,
and other divisions reported on what they were doing about
environmental problems. At the close of the two-and-one-half day
session MacGregor announced that the time had come for a formal
environmental group to be established at AMAX and that he was
forming an Environmental Planning and Protection Committee, to
be headed by Dempsey. The committee would have 18 members
representing the various divisions—base metals, lead and zinc
mining and milling, molybdenum and special metals, fuels and
chemicals, and aluminum, plus financial and corporate officials
from New York headquarters.

They would not immediately hire a lot of people and just throw
money at the problem, MacGregor decided, but would communicate experience already gained by various divisions, and seek cost-
effective solutions.

"Management realized the environment was a serious issue,"
says Dempsey. "But it had to be viewed various ways—sometimes
as a public relations problem, sometimes technical, sometimes
political, sometimes economic—or a combination of these factors."
It was the first intercorporate activity the company had ever tried,
the first effort to cross division lines. Instead of meeting in country
clubs or at headquarters, they met at various plants to see firsthand some of the problems and solutions.

In November 1973, MacGregor called a second company-wide
environmental meeting at Tucson, with one hundred people
attending. At the close of that meeting MacGregor announced
formation of a full corporate department to be known as the
Environmental Services Group, headed by Dempsey, and reporting directly to the executive office of the company.

The Environmental Services Group has a staff of 16, including a
field ecologist, a wildlife biologist, two environmental control

* MacGregor retired as board chairman and chief executive officer in October
1977 but remains a member of the board of directors.

engineers, a mining engineer, a sanitation engineer, an attorney, two financial analysts, and a geographer.

Dempsey receives the long-range plans from all the divisions. Every Capital Project Appropriation Request (CPAR) goes to his group. Although the CPAR's principal purpose is to see if the company has or will have the financing available to make the proposed expenditure at the designated time, it also gives Dempsey the opportunity to check the proposal for its environmental acceptability. If he finds a potential environmental impact, he can ask senior management to turn down the request until the problem has been worked out.

Dempsey's method of operation is to get at problems early through a long-range plan for environmental control now required of every division. He has had several confrontations with divisions early in the process. But because appropriation requests for most major developments take a couple of years to put together, he has been able to resolve most conflicts without disruption of activities.

When AMAX considered possible locations for a new molybdenum roasting plant at Ft. Madison, Iowa, the Environmental Services Group hired Fred Glover, a biologist from the Thorne Ecological Institute, to make an ecological study of the two prime sites, both on the Mississippi River above St. Louis. Glover found that the location near Ft. Madison, favored by the engineers, might disturb a pool reputed to be the best canvasback duck habitat in North America. The alternative site also presented environmental problems. Glover and the engineers devised a way to make the Ft. Madison site acceptable to conservationists, who had raised objections. Company representatives discussed it with local rod and gun clubs, the game and fish commission, and other citizen groups.

As a result, the company allocated $9 million to develop technology adequate to meet the air and water pollution standards. On bordering land it owned, AMAX established a wildlife management area and donated it to the city for a park, with nature trails and wildlife observation areas, and with some sections closed to people so the wildlife would not be disturbed.

The Environmental Services Group does not solve all environmental problems. But Dempsey believes it has served to bring these concerns into front ranks of decision-making at all management levels up to the very top, and sometimes has bridged the basic conflict between developer and environmentalist.

"Working with ecologists and environmentalists has made our engineers and our management more sensitive to their interests," says Dempsey. "And I think that the environmentalists, by working with our people, have found that some of their own ideas were not practical."

Dempsey feels the Experiment in Ecology at the Henderson mine cannot necessarily be repeated in all situations. But he believes a number of general lessons learned from it can be applied in other cases.

"The first thing is that people in the mining business have to admit that any sizeable operation is going to cause change in the area—it can't be the same as it was before," he says. "Next, any industry should try to identify citizen groups that can assist in the design of the property to minimize this environmental impact. Third is the need for an inventory of the natural resources to use as a measure of potential environmental impact. The inventory should be started at the earliest possible moment. Fourth, the company should build contingencies into its planning—how will we respond if things don't work out as scheduled? And finally, there is a need for continuously generating and sharing information."

When working with AMAX managers and engineers, Dempsey does not talk about saving the environment just for the environment's sake. He seeks rather to frame the problems and solutions in terms of cost effectiveness. He tries to show the manager how the environmentally correct way will pay off in the long run even if it costs more in the immediate time frame. Dempsey's chief argument is that doing the right kind of environmental homework can prevent years of costly delay.

AMAX's MacGregor was a key to the company's willingness to institutionalize environmental planning. I went to see him, hoping to get answers to some of my questions. How did he balance the $50 million in environmental costs for the Henderson mine with the goal of maximum profits for which company executives usually strive? And why did AMAX—with its new process for building environmental concerns into decision-making—still stir so much opposition from environmental groups around the country?

We met in a small conference room at the company's New York

offices. He quickly showed himself to be a socially enlightened but pragmatic businessman.

"Carrying out a project in an environmentally correct way is a cost of doing business today," he said. "It's just good business to solve the environmental problems to the best of your ability before you start. Business is supposed to look at the quality of life for the people. My point of view is that we should look at the *real* bottom line—that is, we need that molybdenum in the 1980s and if we don't produce molybdenum in a way that is consistent with the environment, then we're not in business. And I mean the total environment, including the economic, the social, and the public understanding of what's good and what's bad. A lot of people will take the view that the way to solve the problem of opposition from environmentalists is to do it your own way and take a baseball bat in the other hand and beat away the people who want to stop you. That belongs to another age.

"I belive that in our particular business we've got to establish our own reputation by doing the things that we see should be done. And even if we can't convince all the population, we can convince people in our own immediate surroundings that we're doing things reasonably right, and that includes building in responsibility for the environment."

Why did he establish the Environmental Services Group, I asked.

"I have to give credit for that to my perceptive colleagues who kept bringing to me the message that our interface with the environment was going to be a major factor in the future progress of our business. If the concern for the environment was real—and I saw that it probably was because I happened to be a sort of broken-down scientist—I found no great difficulty in grasping that it was an absolutely basic assumption that the industrial process would have to be fitted into the envelope in an infinitely more compatible fashion than we'd ever thought of before.

"Just recently I heard one of my business colleagues say at a meeting that the social responsibility of business is to make a profit, that's what we're in business for. Unfortunately, he missed really what it's all about. Our industrial or business community exists to serve human needs. There is no other need. And the job is to bring together technology, money, people, and capital to get things done to improve the human lot. The first difference is between subsistence and something better than subsistence, and this is really the fundamental of the industrial revolution which produced our new concepts of business."

As an advocate of the free market system, MacGregor spent much of our interview complaining about the overzealousness of Congress and the Environmental Protection Agency in writing and enforcing pollution control laws.

"The idea of having instant correction for things that have been going on for a long time is a problem that we would like the environmentalists to understand more clearly. The world isn't made that way. The industrial process and the economic process are ill-equipped to cope with such demands. The environmental lobby will have to become more practical in terms of its demands and agree to have its long-term goals achieved in time spans that are practical within our technological competence and economic capability. We are undermining the validity of our legislative process by putting on the books insupportable legislation."

MacGregor especially singled out the sulfur oxide emission standards set by the Environmental Protection Agency—what he termed the "instant no-emissions"—as the wrong attack. And he objected to the strip mining bill then being debated in Congress. The people writing the surface mining bill were all residents of urban areas and hadn't a clue to what really goes on, he said. (Environmentalists claim this is completely untrue.) MacGregor, as president of the American Mining Congress, an association of mining companies, lobbied in Washington against the bill. "Those who wrote the bill were doing it not so much to solve the environmental problems as to serve their constituencies who had a whole flock of preconceived notions about things."

AMAX keeps close watch not only over strip mining bills but any proposed laws that might affect its mining activities. For instance, a company official testified in 1977 at a hearing on legislation affecting public lands in Alaska. The bill she opposed would place a large amount of Alaska public land in national parks and national wildlife refuges or in other designated wilderness areas where mining would not be allowed. "Locking up these lands from mineral development and exploration is short-sighted, we believe," stated Diane D. Rees, the company's legislative research director.

Most of the environmentalists I talked with in the Denver area, except those associated with the Experiment in Ecology, were either skeptical or critical of AMAX. They did not believe that AMAX was really an environmentally concerned company.

David McCargo, Jr., a member of the mining workshop of the Colorado Open Space Council, made it clear that Roger Hansen's praise of AMAX generally, and of the Experiment in Ecology particularly, did not represent the council or the views of its members, and at no time did the council back the project. McCargo admits that the development of the mine itself is a nice set-up in terms of a mining operation. But he feels the decision to do the milling on the west side of the Continental Divide amounted to a net environmental loss.

"What has been overlooked," McCargo says, "is that AMAX bought up forested lands in the state and was allowed to trade them to the U.S. Forest Service in return for 9,000 acres of national forest. The public thus lost all control of the 9,000 acres of public land they once owned, and on which they could have imposed mining regulations. And we don't know what it is going to look like forty years from now. The AMAX people say they will reclaim the land when the operation is finished. But now that they own the land, what would force them to do a reclamation job forty years down the line?"

McCargo also claims that AMAX in effect removed 7,000 acres of roadless land from wilderness potential in the St. Louis Peak area by running a power line from one end of the mill site to the other, when the company could have generated its own power at both ends. (Dempsey says the company did consider this, but abandoned it because the generating plants would have caused air pollution in otherwise unpolluted areas.)

Estella Leopold, a daughter of Aldo Leopold, and one of Colorado's environmental leaders at the time the Henderson mine was started, says that the public also lost control of an important piece of land in the Arapaho National Forest. "The land exchange between AMAX and the U.S. Forest Service required that the Arapaho National Forest be divided into two parts to give AMAX the strip of land for its tunnel under the Continental Divide," she says. "This required an act of Congress just for the benefit of AMAX."

AMAX is under fire from environmentalists at a number of

other operations around the country, including battles over a proposed open-pit copper mine at Kirwin, Wyoming, and plans for strip mining coal in several places in Wyoming, Illinois, and Tennessee.

At Catlin, Illinois, a farming community 120 miles south of Chicago, citizens found out about the planned strip mining and raised a ruckus before the AMAX Coal Company had worked out environmental plans. AMAX Coal is a division of AMAX, Inc. Dempsey's group sent an environmental team to Catlin and suggested to AMAX Coal better methods for reclamation of the land after mining. But Catlin citizens consider AMAX's efforts inadequate, and many are angered at what they consider a ruthless attempt to ruin the land and their way of life.

Terry Dolan, the mayor of Catlin (population 2,400), told me that the land AMAX Coal plans to strip mine is 6,000 acres of the most highly productive farmland in the state. And the strip mining site borders residential areas on both sides of the town.

"Nowhere has it ever been proved to us or anyone else that you can restore farmland like this to its original productivity," said Dolan. He added that strip mining right next to homes would render them unlivable.

"We're not environmental radicals here," the mayor said. "But AMAX has taken the basic attitude that they will do what the state law requires, and nothing more. And that is not satisfactory. An objective poll of this area taken by a University of Illinois team showed that 96% of the people oppose the AMAX project," said Dolan. "But they have gone right on. We're now in court trying to stop them."

AMAX Coal has also been in a running battle with Tennessee citizens and that state's Water Quality Control Board. The board denied AMAX a permit to strip mine one acre of coal per day for twenty years at a site in the Cumberland Mountains, and AMAX is fighting the board's ruling. The board claims the mining would destroy streams. But at a hearing, AMAX Coal argued that "some pollution has to be allowed for all human activity." And it complained that the state board's position places a burden on the coal industry "that they don't place on the chemical and paper industries that dump into streams."

As for the Kirwin copper mining operation, the people of the small town of Meeteetse, Wyoming, are divided, some favoring the mine, some opposing. AMAX supported an environmental study by the Rocky Mountain Center for Environment and the Thorne Ecological Institute, and has modified its plans to meet the study's recommendations. No solution is in sight, however.

Another unresolved battle with environmentalists involves a proposal by Alumax, Inc., an independent aluminum company owned half by AMAX and half by Japan's Mitsui Company. Alumax proposed placing an aluminum smelter near the mouth of the Columbia River at Warrenton, Oregon. Alumax had acquired rights for electric power from the Bonneville Power Administration, but needed air and water discharge permits from the state. Some Warrenton area citizens launched a campaign to stop the development. The AMAX Environmental Services Group arranged for an estuary study to assess the potential water pollution impact of the plant, and the Alumax management made changes in its plans so that the estuary would be protected. Opponents got the state of Oregon to set a pollution limit more than twice as stringent as the federal air pollution limitation on fluoride emissions. The federal limit was 2.2 pounds of fluorides emitted per ton of aluminum produced. The new standard set by Oregon was 1 pound per ton, which opponents of the plant assumed AMAX could not meet.

Dempsey, however, studied production processes in other countries, and AMAX sponsored a field test (costing $150,000) of a dry-scrubbing process it planned to use.

Engineers ran the field test at a plant in New Zealand owned by an Australian company. The test showed that the process gave out emissions of only 0.3 pound per ton! Alumax then agreed to meet the new Oregon standards. But the environmentalists persuaded the state Environmental Quality Council to establish a "critical environmental area" around Warrenton, which set a "zero" discharge standard for the area. Alumax, of course, could not meet this standard and gave up plans for the plant at Warrenton. It moved upriver to Umatilla, Oregon, where it received its discharge permits. Environmentalists then filed a lawsuit that held up allocation of electric power contracts to Alumax from the Bonneville Power Administration.

Some environmentalists feel that the credibility attained by

AMAX's Environmental Services Group is more than offset by the company's lobbying efforts and its actions in strip mining coal and in aluminum and copper development. The company's extensive program at the Henderson molybdenum mine and the planning efforts with local environmentalists have not been repeated. However, the measure of enlightened environmental awareness AMAX has demonstrated in its effort to institutionalize its environmental planning is far better than the old days at Climax and a vast improvement over some mining companies that have continued to pollute while doggedly fighting state and federal antipollution regulations.

7

WITH DRAGGING FEET

Driving along Interstate 90 as it traversed the valleys and low mountain slopes of eastern Idaho, I wondered what I'd find at Kellogg, site of the Bunker Hill Company's lead and zinc mining and smelter operations. The company's pollution problems had been in and out of the headlines for several years as Bunker Hill, a subsidiary of Gulf Resources & Chemical Corporation, battled federal and state efforts to enforce pollution laws. A brush with health authorities over lead poisoning cases among many of the town children had led to the company's purchasing in 1974 more than fifty homes nearest the smelter and helping to relocate the families. It also had caused the company to make some improvements in the smelting operation.

At the Environmental Protection Agency's regional office in Seattle, EPA officials had told me that although the lead dust threat to children was now under control, the company was in flagrant violation of both state and federal air pollution regulations, pouring tons of sulfur oxide into the air each day. EPA had also cited Bunker Hill for illegal discharges of zinc and lead into the South Fork of the Coeur d'Alene River.

One EPA economist explained that the smelter, about fifty years old, used technology that was long outmoded. It also had the problem of being situated in the worst possible location—Kellogg has temperature inversions more than two hundred days a year, causing the pollution to hang over the town and the neighboring communities of Deadwood Gulch, Silver King, and Smelterville. Of course, the smelter had been built in that location because it is close to the Bunker Hill mine and other mines are nearby. The company would not be able to meet EPA standards without almost completely rebuilding the smelter, the EPA economist said. And although Bunker Hill had made large profits in recent years when lead and zinc markets were high, the parent company had absorbed most of the profits that could have gone into improving the smelter. Gulf and Bunker Hill instead fought the federal regulations. At Gulf's 1975 annual meeting its board chairman Robert H. Allen commented: "The EPA is totalitarian in nature and pursues its course uncontrollably, regardless of fact or reason."

Idaho environmental activists had told me that Bunker Hill used every method possible to delay and fight for variances from state and federal pollution control laws while threatening to close down the plant if the variances were not granted. The environmentalists claimed that Bunker Hill officials were not the least interested in the welfare of the community, charging that when pollution control equipment had breakdowns the company kept operating regardless of the pollutants poured into the air and water.

After going through the mine and smelter on the regular morning tour, I met with Gene Baker, a vice president of Bunker Hill who had been promoted from his former job of chief engineer and, among other duties, headed a small Environmental Affairs Department. Baker explained that most of his "environmental" work consisted of commenting on EPA and Idaho State regulations and preparing testimony for hearings.

Baker complained that EPA had a very shallow knowledge of the Bunker Hill plant and its processing activities. "We get to the posture where we say this is all we can do technically, and they say, 'We don't believe you.' Right now we are out for bids on tall stacks and we're prepared to issue contracts. But if EPA insists we reduce our sulfur oxide emissions in other ways, we will just have to go to court and fight. We could try SO_2 scrubbers, but we don't think the technology is available now."

Bunker Hill President James H. Halley underscored the company's animosity toward federal antipollution regulators.

"EPA officials are going far beyond what the law allows them to do," Halley said as he sat behind his desk in the two-story company headquarters building in Kellogg. "They are trying to pressure us to do what is socially acceptable. We are perfectly capable of meeting our own social obligations."

Talking with me in his small, plain office, Bunker Hill's president wore his shirt sleeves rolled up, exposing a tattoo from his Navy days. He had finished high school after serving in the Navy in World War II, labored in the Bunker Hill zinc smelter summers while going to New Mexico School of Mines, graduated with honors, and worked his way up in the mining industry until chosen as president of Bunker Hill in 1971.* Outspoken, gregarious, a chain-smoker, reputed to be hot-tempered, Halley calmly continued his attack on the Environmental Protection Agency.

"If this plant were located anyplace else but in this valley, we would be able to meet EPA's standards. But they have to consider this valley. If we did everything that was possible, we still couldn't meet their standards because of the location. If EPA were to force us to do everything they have tried to force us to do, the plant would have to close.

"You have to remember that there are two types of industry," Halley continued, "those that can pass costs directly to a consumer, like the auto makers, and an industry like ours, that is in both national and international competition. There's no difference between our zinc and Canadian zinc. It's all the same quality and shape. So we can't pass on costs.

"Then you have to divide into 'before EPA and after EPA,' " he said. "This lead smelter was built in 1917, and the zinc smelter in 1927. Under old standards your conscience was your guide.

* Halley is now vice-president for special projects and assistant to the president of Bunker Hill's parent company, Gulf Resources & Chemical Corporation.

Whatever harm you did, you drew the line someplace. Over the years standards tightened. Acid treatment, for instance, was added here in 1968 and 1970. We recognized then that we could no longer discomfort our neighbors. But under EPA today, the standards already set or proposed are too far out. To meet all the standards we now know about, or that will be set later, would effectively take all of our cash flow for a five-year period. Should we do that, or shut down today? And who knows what EPA will be calling for in five years?"

I asked about the charges that Gulf Resources & Chemical Corporation was milking the company.

"That's not true," Halley replied. "This is a cyclical industry. We have gone on for years with little profit. EPA wants us to use this money now, when the prices are high. But the government doesn't offer a subsidy for when they go down. When EPA says it will only cost from four to nine million dollars to meet their standards, they don't have the slightest idea of the actual cost."

What about the lead pollution poisoning scare with the children, I asked. Why hadn't Bunker Hill cleaned up its operation after children near a similar smelter in El Paso had received dangerous doses of lead in 1973? Bunker Hill had sent observers to El Paso.

"At that time we made tests of school age children here, and didn't find any problems," Halley said. "Our mistake was that we should have tested preschoolers. But we have a study now going on and if the continuing examination of children should show that they are getting a dangerous amount of lead, even after the changes we have made in the smelter, we would have to shut down or completely change our system."

Halley insisted that Bunker Hill had been caught in the middle of changing attitudes of the American people. For years the people wanted cheap goods and didn't care about the planet or the environment—unless the polluting industry was operating next door to them. Now, he said, the public was crying that the planet was being ruined, and wanted industry to clean up the air and water regardless of what it cost. But the public has to understand that it has to be done in such a way that a company like Bunker Hill doesn't destroy itself in the process.

"If we had unlimited funds and complete disregard for whether or not we operated at a profit, it is possible that we could meet the

EPA standards," Halley said. "But many of the things we would have to use to meet the standards are highly experimental. And we do not feel it is right that we should be a privately financed experiment just for the EPA or for any other branch of government."

With the interview ended, Halley somewhat mischievously commented on some of the items decorating his office. On one table sat a ceramic black-robed judge with heavy spectacles—sort of an Ed Wynn type. The figure was labeled: "Sue the Bastards." And on top of a cabinet was a modernistic wrought iron sculpture depicting a wild, demonic character which had been given to Halley by a well-known Idaho sculptor. Halley said with a grin that he had named it "The Conservationist."

From Halley's office, I drove past the smelter, noting the leveled-off area where the lead-tainted houses had been removed. I looked up at the barren, scarred hills and down at the long mounds of black slag piled high alongside Interstate 90 running along the floor of the valley. I thought about my conversation with Halley. He obviously did not admit to doing anything illegal. He had his obligations to the parent company to run the mine and smelter efficiently and make a profit.

I recalled the comment of a workman I had spoken with as I toured the smelter that morning. He had pointed with some pride at the whitish plume curling out of the smelter's main stack, and said he had been with the company all his working life.

"When did it start getting clean like that?" I asked the worker. "When EPA started getting after us," he replied. "I hate to have to say that, but it's true. You don't do anything until the law requires it."

Subsequent to my visit to Bunker Hill, the company's plan to reduce sulfur-oxide pollution by building two tall stacks was rejected by EPA as being an unacceptable solution. Bunker Hill went ahead anyway and built a 715-foot-high stack for the lead smelter and a 610-foot-high stack for the zinc plant, at a cost of $11 million. The company says it has spent more than $23 million in programs to control pollution and is committing an additional $2 million for additional smelter controls. The health monitoring of children has shown no new evidences of excessive lead levels. An extensive program is underway to revegetate 18,000 acres of land disturbed by mining and smelting activities, and plans call for planting 350,000 trees a year.

EPA officials admit that most of the water-pollution problems have now been taken care of by Bunker Hill and that the tall stacks have improved air quality near the smelters in Kellogg but have degraded the air quality over nearby areas. And while EPA charges that the sulfur-oxide emissions are still violating the regulations, the Clean Air Act Amendments of 1977 allow the company a five-year period for compliance. So the battle between the company and its regulators continues.

Half a continent away another mining company has been waging a more highly publicized battle against antipollution laws and regulations. On the shore of Lake Superior at Silver Bay, Minnesota, 60 miles north of Duluth, Reserve Mining Company, co-owned by two of the nation's largest steel companies, Republic and Armco, for more than a decade has fought state and federal regulators and citizen environmentalists all across the nation.

I had been aware of the Reserve controversy and while at *The Christian Science Monitor* I had received materials about the company's polluting activities from an aroused citizen, Verna Mize, a government secretary. She was running a one-woman campaign trying to force federal officials to stop Reserve's dumping of 52,000 tons a day of finely ground iron ore tailings into the largest freshwater lake in the world.

At the Council on Environmental Quality the staff kept me informed on the developing controversy as Reserve continued to resist state and federal air and water quality regulations. Inasmuch as the situation came under the jurisdiction of the Environmental Protection Agency, CEQ never entered into the case officially. We were aware, however, that the White House considered the situation a potential source of embarrassment, since the president of Armco had been a major money-raiser for the Nixon 1968 election campaign, and the president of Republic in 1971 was vice-chairman of the Ohio Republican finance committee.

Despite interventions at the White House by Armco and Republic, EPA Administrator William Ruckelshaus refused to be pressured, and he formally requested the Justice Department to bring suit against Reserve, which it did in 1972. EPA charged that drinking water in Duluth contained large quantities of potentially cancer-causing asbestoslike fibers believed to originate from Reserve's discharge.

Reserve's activities became a national issue in mid-1974 when a federal district court judge closed down Reserve's Silver Bay operations because of potential harm to health, and two days later an appellate court panel ordered the plant reopened.

That fall I had to go to Madison, Wisconsin, for a meeting of the President's Citizens Advisory Committee on Environmental Quality, so I arranged to visit Silver Bay afterward and see for myself the pros and cons of the argument. When I mentioned my plans to fellow committee member Arthur Godfrey, he said he would like to go, too—he could fly us up to Silver Bay in his twin-engine plane before he flew on back to New York. Reserve officials enthusiastically agreed to add Godfrey to the tour, hoping (I assumed) that they could persuade him to quit condemning them, as he had done in speeches and during television talk shows.

On the way from Madison to Silver Bay we stopped overnight at Duluth, where I had arranged to meet two of the leading opponents of Reserve, Grant Merritt and Charles Stoddard, for a briefing on their side of the controversy. Merritt was at the time the aggressive director of Minnesota's Pollution Control Agency, while Stoddard had been Great Lakes regional coordinator for the U.S. Department of the Interior when the federal government first challenged Reserve in 1968.

They reviewed for Godfrey and me the history of the controversy, especially the events since Verna Mize and another citizen activist, Duluth resident Arlene Lehto, who organized the Save Lake Superior Association, had begun making a public fuss about Reserve, both in Minnesota and in Washington, D.C.

Stoddard explained that Reserve had been the first company to mine taconite (a low-grade iron ore) from the Mesabi Range of northwestern Minnesota. In 1947 Reserve proposed shipping the ore by rail from the mine at Babbitt to the shores of Lake Superior, 47 miles away, for processing. At the public hearings on Reserve's request to dump the iron-ore residue into Lake Superior, the company assured state officials that the tailings were nothing but "inert sand" that would sink immediately to the deep bottom within a 9-square-mile area, and would do no harm to fish or man.

Minnesota, eager for a new payroll, granted the permit, the Army Corps of Engineers approved dredging for a harbor adjacent to the plant, and processing began in 1956. For their ore sources six other companies followed Reserve to the Mesabi Range, but all built their processing facilities at their mine sites.

Under pressure from citizen activists, the federal government formed a federal interagency group in 1969, with Stoddard as chairman, to look into the charges being raised against Reserve. The committee found that the tailings were *not* all dropping to the bottom near Silver Bay, but were spreading. The official 1969 Interior Department report (never published; Stoddard claims it was suppressed after intervention by Minnesota Congressman John A. Blatnik) recommended that Reserve be ordered to stop dumping in the lake but that it be given three years to build on-land dumping facilities.

When the Environmental Protection Agency took over enforcement of water pollution laws late in 1970, Ruckelshaus ordered Reserve to develop a plan to correct the pollution. The company's answer was to propose piping the taconite tailings into deep water. EPA rejected the proposal. EPA also discovered at that time that the particulate matter from Reserve's stacks was exceeding federal air pollution standards.

Merritt recounted for us Minnesota's unsuccessful attempts to bring Reserve into compliance with state laws and regulations, and said that the air pollutants were even more hazardous to health than the water dumping that had received so much publicity. When the Justice Department filed suit, Minnesota, Michigan, and Wisconsin joined, as did the cities of Duluth and Superior, and several environmental groups.

The trial before Federal District Judge Miles J. Lord lasted nine months and revolved around whose experts to believe. Reserve's experts claimed the fibers found in the water were not asbestos, but were different from asbestos fibers, which in other cases had been related to cancers. Besides, they argued, in the other cases asbestos fibers had been ingested through the air. These minute particles were being swallowed, not breathed. Reserve's major defense was the absence of concrete evidence that the particles cause cancer.

Testifying for the government, a leading medical expert charged that Reserve's air and water discharges carried 35 toxic chemical materials, including arsenic, beryllium, selenium, and thallium. Another expert testified that a distinct public health hazard was present because of the fibers in the air and water. Epidemiological studies of 14,000 factory workers exposed to asbestos revealed excessive rates of cancer. But deaths did not occur until twenty years or more after the first exposure. Experts also testified that the level of pollution in the ambient air at Silver Bay was ten times greater than that measured in New York City near insulation spraying sites, which had led to a New York ban on asbestos spraying.

The trial set off a conflict about what actions Reserve could take or not take to mitigate the pollution, and how much such actions would cost. Although other companies mining in the Mesabi used on-land systems for disposing of tailings, Reserve insisted that it was not economically feasible to move to a land-based disposal system. It would take three to five years to convert to on-land disposal, would cost up to $500 million and cause the layoff of 3,000 workers while the change-over was underway. The Justice Department disputed these cost estimates as being greatly exaggerated. The company said its ore was of a lower grade than competitors' and it could not afford to make the change. The government introduced evidence that the firm had been making more than $50,000-a-day profit for many years, profit which went to Republic and Armco shareholders, not back into the Reserve plant.

The trial came to a heated climax, Merritt said, when company documents subpoenaed by the government showed that mining company officials had misled the court. A Reserve vice-president had denied under oath that the company had a plan for on-land disposal. But the subpoenaed company documents revealed that an Armco study group had concluded in 1972 that a deep-pipe system was not technologically feasible and that the company had investigated an on-land disposal system that appeared to be a feasible way to satisfy the regulatory agencies.

This discovery led Judge Lord to accuse the company of acting in bad faith in the lawsuit. On April 20, 1974, he ruled that Reserve's discharges of both air and water endangered the health of the people nearby. And he issued an injunction closing the plant.

Thirty-two hours later an emergency three-member panel of the

Eighth District Circuit Court of Appeals stayed Judge Lord's injunction until the case could be heard by the full appellate court, and Reserve went back to work on full schedule. The circuit court emergency panel ruled that the government had not sustained the burden of proof of a demonstrable health hazard, and that Judge Lord's resolution of a reasonable doubt in favor of public health might better have been left to a legislative body. In its ruling, however, the appellate panel admitted that the state's original permit allowing Reserve to dump into the lake was a "monumental environmental mistake," and the judges ordered Reserve to take prompt steps to stop polluting and move its disposal of tailings to an acceptable on-land site.

The federal government applied to the U.S. Supreme Court to overrule the stay granted Reserve. When the high court denied the government's application without hearing the case, Justice William O. Douglas issued a strong dissent. The three-member Court of Appeals decision seemed to hold, said Douglas, that "maximizing profits" was the measure of the public good. "If ... there is doubt, it should be resolved in favor of humanity, lest in the end our judicial system be part and parcel of a regime that makes people ... the victims of the great god progress. ... Our guiding principle should be Mr. Justice Holmes' dictum that our waterways, great and small, are treasures, not garbage dumps or cesspools."

Godfrey and I arrived at Silver Bay during arguments about location of the land disposal site. As we circled over the small one-industry town the unique characteristics of Reserve Mining became evident: the greenish discoloration in the water; gray smoke billowing out of the stacks; a mile-wide delta of tailings protruding into the lake; and two large outfalls dumping tons of material into the water.

A company official met us as we let down at the small airstrip and took us a few miles to the processing plant. He showed us how the low-grade taconite was pulverized in huge revolving drums into smaller and smaller pieces, then had the vital "magnetite" extracted magnetically from the crushed rock and milled into dark gray pellets about one-half inch in diameter. Each day Reserve produces 30,000 tons of these pellets, about 15% of the domestic ore used by American steel makers.

The company representative, Assistant to the President Edward

Schmid, explained to us that although the process and the plant were old, Reserve had spent millions on improving it and cleaning up its operation. Outside, as we saw the wind spreading dust from huge piles of pellets, and smoke coming out of the stacks, I asked about the charges of air pollution. Schmid denied that the company was violating any laws, but said it was planning to clean up the stack emissions anyway.

Then we drove to the waterfront and boarded a launch. It moved through the turgid waters of the bay and we got a closer look at the two outfalls that spilled their slurry into the lake 24 hours a day.

I asked about the results of this 52,000 tons of ground rock slurry discharged daily into the lake. And I received the stock answer: It all went harmlessly into the 900-foot-deep trough just offshore. The "green water" we had seen from the air only in the vicinity of the plant was not caused by Reserve Mining, but was simply a natural phenomenon that occurs in many large lakes. And no proof had been established that the particles, even if they did get into drinking water, were harmful to health.

On leaving the plant, our company host drove us through the town of Silver Bay, population about 4,500. As we passed the housing tract with its neat lawns, the official said that unless the state agreed to let them dump at the newly selected Lax Lake site 7 miles away, the company would have to go out of business, throwing 3,200 employees out of work at Silver Bay and at Babbitt, where the ore is mined.

The federal government had appealed the Eighth Circuit Court's three-man decision overruling Judge Lord's closing of Reserve. The government asked for a hearing before the full nine-judge appellate court. In June 1975, the court en banc overruled the earlier three-man decision that had allowed Reserve to continue dumping. The full appellate court ordered Reserve to change to a land-based dumping system within one year, and to take steps immediately to reduce air emissions.

The argument dragged on in the courts for another three years, the main controversy being over protecting nearby residents from air contamination resulting from the dumping of tailings. Finally, in April 1978, the Minnesota Supreme Court ruled that Reserve Mining must comply with the state's air pollution standards for the Milepost 7 dumping area. Armco and Republic company officials, after initially indicating that Reserve might have to shut down because of the costs required to meet the standards, agreed to comply and complete the Milepost 7 site as ordered by the courts. Reserve Mining is now being forced to spend an estimated $370 million (including $72 million to prevent air pollution at the plant) to meet the court-imposed requirements.

Out of the delays and costly litigation a milestone legal precedent may have been set in forcing Reserve Mining Company to obey the law. In doing so, the full Eighth Circuit Court of Appeals expanded the law regarding burden of proof. The court could not find under ordinary standards of proof that the government had proved by a preponderance of the evidence that people would get cancer from drinking the water or breathing the air polluted by taconite disposal or processing. But it applied another standard, that of the Court of Appeals for the District of Columbia in the *Ethyl Corporation* v. *EPA* case. The District of Columbia appellate court had held that the nature of the risk and the probability that harm would occur could be judged even when the government had not proved that actual harm would occur.

But has the result of this long litigation changed the policies of Reserve Mining Company? Its president, Merlyn Woodle, was asked recently if, in hindsight, Reserve would have done anything differently knowing what it does now.

Woodle replied, as recorded in a 1978 magazine article: "No, I don't think so."

8

"BEST OF
THE S.O.B.s"

What about a company whose business is completely intertwined with the nation's renewable natural resources, one that owns 5.5 million acres of timberland—an area the size of the entire state of Massachusetts? Does this company use its vast natural resources in an environmentally ethical way?

I went back to my native Pacific Northwest to look for an answer at the Weyerhaeuser Company. I had seen the huge timber company's advertisements in magazines and on televison touting its conservation practices. It had been given good marks by the Council on Economic Priorities which made a 1970 study of forest products companies and their pollution control efforts. While critical of most companies, the report pointed to Weyerhaeuser as one of two exceptions in the industry. It found the company willing to give technical personnel the freedom and funds to minimize environmental damage. The report noted that Weyerhaeuser had developed pollution control systems beyond the requirements of existing pollution laws. And it commended Weyerhaeuser for innovating techniques of pollution control and acting to anticipate controls "simply because it recognized problems and wanted to solve them."

A study made by the same council two years later, however, showed Weyerhaeuser only ninth among 21 major pulp and paper companies in its pollution control efforts.

The company came in for praise—though faint—from *Audubon* magazine (September–October 1974), which titled an article about Weyerhaeuser "The Best of the S.O.B.'s." But the magazine of Friends of the Earth (*Not Man Apart,* December 1974) carried an article strongly critical of the company's timber cutting operations. Brock Evans, the Sierra Club's Washington, D.C., bureau manager and former Northwest representative, who during 1970 Earth Day activities rated Weyerhaeuser as one of the "good guys," told me he has changed his mind. He now considers Weyerhaeuser "the worst of the worst."

Someplace between these opposing viewpoints I expected to find the extent to which the company practiced real responsibility for the environment. I knew that as the nation's leading producer of wood products Weyerhaeuser had pioneered in tree farming and conducted extensive research on how to maintain a sustained yield. That is, if it takes sixty years for a Douglas fir to mature, Weyerhaeuser programs the production schedule over a sixty-year period so that only as many trees are cut each year as will grow back within the cycle. With large holdings in Oregon and Washington and significant stands in the South, the company does not depend very heavily on national forests for its timber as do most of the other major companies. Its Pacific Northwest forests have extensive virgin growth, and these big trees constitute a major part of the current timber cutting. The company harvests the old growth in its prime, then moves on to second growth. It plans to do even more of the same. Weyerhaeuser has based its future on being—as the company motto emphasizes—"The Tree Growing Company," and has pioneered in tree farming and in methods of making trees grow faster and improving them genetically. It plants more than 185 million new trees each year, about 90% of them bare-root, foot-high seedlings nurtured for two or three years in outdoor beds. By 1980 the company will have planted about 1.8 billion trees, or 8 trees for every person in the United States.

By the end of the century, the 250-year-old Douglas fir and old hemlock growth will be a thing of the past on Weyerhaeuser lands—except for a few economically inaccessible stands. The company is hoping to reduce the growth cycle to 45 years through replanting programs and tree genetic improvement. The result will not be stately, magnificent trees living out their life cycle in "cathedral" forests, but an efficient crop of timber grown to produce more saw logs and more pulp.

To carry out these plans, Weyerhaeuser foresters clear-cut large areas, and although they replant quickly, the clear-cut area can look like a devastated battlefield for the five years it takes for seedlings to make significant growth. They treat the soil around young trees with nitrogen pellets to induce growth. And they use the herbicide 2,4,5-T to reduce or eliminate alders and other competing growth while the trees are young.

All of this, while good economics for the company, does not set well with environmentalists. They fought the use of the 2,4,5-T defoliant in Vietnam, and they fight it at home. They have doubts about the impacts of genetic tree engineering on future forests and soils. They question the Weyerhaeuser policy of considering trees only as crops to be manipulated as a farmer does his corn or wheat. And they are especially troubled with Weyerhaeuser's stated mission of removing the majestic cathedral trees at high elevations, wiping out virgin forests that include some of the Pacific Northwest's scenic heritage.

Comments Doug Scott, Northwest field representative of The Sierra Club and a forestry graduate of the University of Michigan: "Weyerhaeuser's motto should be changed to 'The LITTLE Tree Growing Company.' We need to get our timber production on a stable volume not by chopping down every old tree in private and national forests, but by balancing out the growth on all the ownerships so it is even."

Weyerhaeuser officials explain that mature trees over 125 years old decay more than they grow, that the old, giant Douglas firs are inefficient. Trees are, after all, a renewable resource, they argue. If the company is to meet society's need for wood products it must use the most cost-effective management techniques possible.

Environmental critics also object to Weyerhaeuser's exporting

25% of its production overseas, mostly to Japan. Even though the trees are felled on Weyerhaeuser's private landholdings, the exports diminish U.S. supplies and thus increase the number of trees that must be cut from the U.S. national forests to supply American demands.

On my visit to Washington I found that although the company was indeed controversial, there was general agreement among state and federal officials that, as the Council on Economic Priorities study had reported, Weyerhaeuser tried to anticipate pollution problems and solve them. For example, in 1970 the company's large but outmoded sulfite pulp mill at Everett, Washington, faced tough environmental regulations. The mill, built in 1936, poured thousands of gallons of wood sugars into Port Gardner Bay each day. Though the pollutant posed no known health hazard, it caused unsightly discoloration of the water.

Weyerhaeuser had to decide among several alternatives: build a new plant elsewhere; spend $10 million on pollution controls at the Everett site; or simply shut down and throw 330 employees out of work. The company was required to notify the state of its decision by March 31, 1972.

The Everett facility was Weyerhaeuser's most profitable pulp mill, yet the company saw no economical way to install controls that would meet the environmental standards, or to build a comparable mill nearby. Company officials announced that they would shut down the plant on May 31, 1973, the date when the permit would expire. This decision, announced 14 months before the permit ran out, brought instant outcries from labor and from environmentalists who would have preferred that the plant clean up. Weyerhaeuser searched for a better solution, but meantime, the Everett mill continued to operate—and pollute—while the permit remained in effect.

At about the same time the company wanted to rebuild and upgrade its mammoth wood products processing facility at Longview, on the southern border of the state. The improvements would cost $200 million to $300 million over a ten-year period, and before committing that kind of money, Weyerhaeuser was looking for some long-range guidance. It asked the state for a permit covering all phases of the Longview operations and setting forth in advance the state and federal pollution standards the facility would be required to meet over the entire ten-year period.

The state had no way to foresee exactly what the laws and regulations would require over the next decade. The Department of Ecology agreed, however, to coordinate the planning of some 27 agencies, both state and federal, to see if they could come up with immediate, midterm, and long-range environmental goals for Weyerhaeuser to meet.

Weyerhaeuser included in its application a provision for a new plant at Longview to replace the Everett sulfite mill, and the company asked to be allowed to operate the Everett mill until the new plant could be built. This aroused suspicions among environmentalists that the arrangement was no more than a ploy to give the Everett plant more time to pollute without paying the cleanup costs. And some saw the single-permit idea as merely a way of making it more difficult for the State of Washington to regulate the company.

The state finally turned down the application on the basis that a single all-encompassing permit was not legally possible. It gave Weyerhaeuser a year's extension on operating the Everett plant and agreed to coordinate a proposed master environmental program for the Longview facility. This fell far short of Weyerhaeuser's hopes, yet the coordination activities resulted in a number of benefits for Weyerhaeuser as well as for the state and county agencies.

The first segment of the ten-year building program ready to go forward was a satellite small-log sawmill near the Longview complex. A number of environmental factors were involved, including solid waste disposal, water discharge, air pollution, shoreline management on the Columbia River, and health effects. Teams from Cowlitz County, the state Department of Ecology, and the U.S. Environmental Protection Agency examined the problems together with Weyerhaeuser representatives.

The state's coordinator of the planning project, Donald Provost, said team members went through an extensive and unprecedented "what-if" exercise. What if Weyerhaeuser puts the plant on the river, or the hill, or in between? What if they haul by rail, by truck, by river? What if they burn waste on the site? What if the effluents are treated? Or diffused? Or hauled away?

Often an idea for decreasing water pollution would be found to increase air pollution or solid waste, or vice versa. By going through this kind of planning, problems could be anticipated and alternatives considered as required by the state and federal environmental impact statement process.

Weyerhaeuser obtained a permit and in December 1974, the new $10-million small-log sawmill opened, employing one hundred people and producing green lumber and chips for the Longview lumber mill and pulp mill.

Meantime, Weyerhaeuser's continued search for a solution to the Everett mill's problems uncovered a thermomechanical process being used in Europe. This process could produce a larger amount of usable paper fiber out of wood than the old sulfite process, and could do it with far less pollution. The state agreed to give the company a permit for the new process, providing that water pollution would be reduced 90%. Weyerhaeuser spent $20 million on the new Everett mill and completed it about the same time the old sulfite mill closed (60% of the sulfite mill jobs were saved, and most of the other workers were absorbed in other parts of the company). The process, however, presents an unfortunate negative tradeoff, requiring considerably more electric power than the old method. Thus pollution was cleaned up at the expense of energy.

Energy conservation has now become a major activity at Weyerhaeuser and plans are underway to make more use of wood wastes as an energy supply.

A written environmental policy distributed throughout the company calls for employees to identify and minimize the adverse environmental impacts of all production facilities and operating activities, the impacts of the uses of its products or services, and the impacts of the disposal of its products.

All employees are expected to assume personal responsibility for awareness and control of environmental problems both on and off the job. The policy delegates to individual managers the responsibility for performance in environmental efforts and measurement of results. In some companies this could indicate a cop-out, a failure to give responsibility to any one individual for overseeing environmental responsibility.

Weyerhaeuser officials claim that this system of leaving responsibility with the department head or even with the forest engineer keeps any single operating or corporate unit from having veto power over any other. Conflicts have to be recognized and agreement reached, or else the problem is forwarded to senior management for resolution. For instance, a mill manager cannot demand that the loggers in the nearby Weyerhaeuser forest "high-grade," that is, select only the best trees for lumber. He has to get his logs from a separately controlled Raw Materials unit, which in turn has to get permission from a Land and Timber unit to cut timber. And Land and Timber is charged with maximizing the timber resource on a long-term time frame, not maximizing production.

In the field, the responsibility for building roads, for instance, goes to the individual forest engineer. But his decisions are audited regularly. He must prepare continuous environmental impact assessments noting soil damage, harm to fishing areas, and safety factors. Logging plans must be prepared by the forest engineer three years before cutting starts, and be thoroughly reviewed. In the State of Washington, Weyerhaeuser's logging and road construction plans are submitted in advance to the State Fish and Game Department for agreement.

Company officials are mindful that environmental policy statements have not altered the views of some critics who object to certain corporate decisions and practices, and have developed an internal organization to identify responsibilities at several corporate levels. All environmental activities are coordinated under Jack Larsen, the director of environmental affairs, who returned to the company in 1976 after serving in the governor's cabinet as director of the State Department of Commerce. Larsen came to Weyerhaeuser from the U.S. Forest Service, and holds an undergraduate degree in biology, wildlife management, and forestry, and a master's degree in public administration.

The company has 145 people working full time on environmental problems, most of them involved in research, new technology application, and monitoring impacts of activities on air and water. Several hundred others spend part of their time on environmental matters. Day-to-day issues at the facilities are supervised by regional environmental managers who report to Larsen. Issues needing policy decisions at higher levels are taken care of by three corporate managers of environmental affairs—for facilities and manufacturing, land and timber, and environmental planning.

In addition to supervising these activities Larsen chairs an environmental steering committee of five vice-presidents—energy, land and timber, pulp and paper, research and technology, and facilities planning. The steering committee reviews all company activities and plans that might have significant environmental ramifications.

If an issue needs attention at the highest corporate level, Larsen prepares an issues assessment paper that includes background on the issue and possible alternative actions, an estimate of capital and operating costs, and an assessment of possible risks to the company. He personally discusses the issue at a meeting of the Senior Management Committee chaired by George Weyerhaeuser, the company president. On this committee are seven senior vice-presidents including William Ruckelshaus, former head of the U.S. Environmental Protection Agency and now Weyerhaeuser's vice-president for law and corporate affairs.

At the time I visited Weyerhaeuser, Larsen had just submitted the company position on changing the federal water pollution control law with specific recommendations for modifying the 1983 standards, but not requesting delays in applying the regulations. He was preparing a company position on the federal regulation of privately owned wetlands, backing the proposal to have the Army Corps of Engineers administer development around the headwaters of river basins but urging that normal silviculture practices that do not involve dredging be allowed without special permits. He was working on a plan for use of 2,4,5-T and other chemicals in forest management, coordinating with state and federal pollution control authorities to track potential harmful impacts. And he was working up an authorization (later approved by Weyerhaeuser top executives) to spend $1.25 million for environmental baseline research on natural resources around the site of a projected new port facility near critical marshland habitat at the southern end of Puget Sound. The port proposal has aroused vigorous objections from environmentalists and the U.S. Fish and Wildlife Service, which administers the nearby 1,700-acre Nisqually National Wildlife Refuge. The port would accommodate cargo vessels over 900 feet long.

Larsen has direct access to the company's president and chief executive officer, George Weyerhaeuser, who takes a keen personal interest in environmental problems. The great-grandson of the founder, Weyerhaeuser took the reins in 1966 at the age of 39. He has led the 75-year-old company to its most profitable years ever, with programs he says are aimed at markets of the year 2000 and beyond, and which include responsibility for the environment.

"We are a long-range company, a long-range land manager," George Weyerhaeuser told me at the corporate headquarters near Tacoma as we sat in his open office, separated from the large executive area only by screens and planters. "We don't allow ourselves the pleasure of short-term expediency. Sure, we have company officials under the pressure of performance standards and production targets. But they have to work within the frame of long-term standards.

"We don't have to spend a lot of time convincing ourselves the environment is important. What we do in the management of land and timber, game, water, fish, and soil is the heart of our business. If we were making toys it might be different."

He feels that the environmental evaluation of a proposed action is vital before the decision, not only because it can prevent public criticism and lawsuits, but because managing the forests and the soils is a matter of stewardship for an important natural resource. And he has publicly taken the position in meetings of his own industry that the burden of proof that an action may or may not be harmful should be on the company, not on the environmental activist. "If only 2% of the people are environmental activists, we must look seriously at the concerns they express," he said. "For they may be expressing concerns common to the other 98%.

"It is not a question of whether they can prove that a practice is harmful. It is a question of whether we can prove conclusively that it is not. We cannot handle this resource with only the harvest in mind, and neglect the long-term effects and esthetics. Short-term economic gains should not be taken at the expense of the long-term health of the prime assets, the soils and the trees."

Weyerhaeuser also expresses views on wilderness preservation that are considered unusual for a lumber baron. "We must address the question of how much wilderness we need to preserve, and address it positively, providing constructive inputs into the process. We cannot afford to be merely defensive; until and unless the lands best suited for wilderness are firmly and finally identified and pinned down, *all* lands will be up for grabs."

At times the company lobbyists have followed an industry-wide position and worked for smaller wilderness areas than those advocated by environmentalists. However, in a recent dispute over legislation for an Alpine Lakes Wilderness Area in the North Cascades, a Weyerhaeuser lobbyist took the lead in working out a compromise that expanded the area by 13,000 acres over the size advocated by the industry. And George Weyerhaeuser became personally involved in having the company donate to The Nature Conservancy 13,000 acres valued at $6 million for an addition to the Great Dismal Swamp National Wildlife Refuge in Virginia.

Although the chief executive officer of a company has the ultimate responsibility, Weyerhaeuser believes that it is the strength of each individual employee's own ethical system that will determine the good or bad practices of a company.

As an example, George Weyerhaeuser pointed out to me the ethical problem a forest manager faces in deciding on a program of fertilization. It may increase growth and productivity, which is good in economic terms. But what impact may it have on water quality or game animals or use of the forest for recreation? Those noneconomic issues are important factors in the decision the manager makes because of their impact on society.

"In such a situation the manager has an obvious ethical obligation. No formula can be written to give absolute guidance. In the end, the person responsible for the decision is responsible not only for its economic but also for its ethical quality. Business corporations as they impact society are really collections of individuals working toward certain shared goals. And there is no reason for people to change their ethical standards between the hours of 8:00 A.M. and 5:00 P.M., checking their off-hours ethics at the door as they enter the office and retrieving them in the evening."

Environmental critics respect George Weyerhaeuser for his philosophy, for the high quality of professional foresters he employs, and for most of the field operations of the company. But they feel that the company's stated environmental policy does not square with some of its basic management directions, especially its merchandising of almost all of the old virgin growth at high elevations.

"They may call it tree farming, but I call it tree mining," says outdoor writer Harvey Manning, a critic of Weyerhaeuser and all the major timber companies. Manning backpacks more than one thousand miles a year through the Northwest's forests. He believes that at high elevations high-yield forestry can be extremely harmful. "At elevations above 4,000 or 5,000 feet where timber is interfingered with alpine meadows, you can't simply plant a seedling in the ground and get a new forest forty or fifty years later," Manning says. "Generally a seedling has to grow upward from the shelter of older trees. Take the forest cover off and you may be talking of a replacement in terms of three hundred to five hundred years. And in the process of taking off the old trees Weyerhaeuser, even with the best practices, will lose much of the soil, soil that has been accumulating for thousands of years. And for what purpose? The character of the land is being changed completely for a one-time crop which probably will be shipped to Japan.

"These high-elevation forests even when in private ownership ought to be withdrawn from production," Manning argues. "They should be left intact for their watershed values, for wildlife, for a gene pool, for clean air production, for esthetics—all the other things a tree is good for besides providing cellulose."

Director of Environmental Affairs Larsen denies that Weyerhaeuser now cuts in any areas where it cannot regenerate and have a harvestable crop within the forty-five- to sixty-year time frame. Nor does it cut at sites that do not meet the company's standard of being able to plant a tree and get acceptable stocking within one year of harvesting the old trees.

To the criticism that Weyerhaeuser is cutting the "cathedral" trees and thus limiting the esthetic opportunities of this and future generations, Larsen answers: "We concur that there is a public interest in the preservation of some of the areas with those kinds of trees. Our view, however, is that it is not the responsibility of a private land owner. Preserving the cathedral trees is a function of government."

9

THE VIEW FROM DETROIT'S BIGGEST

A conversation with a friend piqued my interest in taking a look at America's biggest automobile manufacturer, General Motors. The friend, a scientist who happened to own a few shares of GM stock, had been troubled by company actions that he felt demonstrated a basic lack of concern for the environment. He was disappointed that neither GM nor any of the other U.S. manufacturers had been able to design a high-quality, small, fuel-efficient, nonpolluting car. And at the time we talked, he was particularly irked by a letter he and the 1.3 million other GM stockholders had received from the chairman of the General Motors board asking him to write to his congressman urging a delay in imposing automobile emission standards.

Research scientists had discovered in 1953 that the automobile was the chief cause of smog. Yet not one major U.S. automobile company developed devices or methods for controlling pollution until more than a decade later when federal regulations forced them to do so. Even when the federal Clean Air Act Amendments went into effect in 1968, improvements the industry devised to meet the air-quality standards were hardly worthy of American ingenuity, and failed to control auto pollution adequately.

While I was a member of the Council on Environmental Quality the council exercised general supervision over a federal assistance program aimed at "producing an unconventionally powered virtually pollution-free automobile within five years," as President Nixon described the program in his 1970 environmental message to Congress. Reviewing data collected by the CEQ staff and sitting in on sessions of the Advisory Committee on Advanced Automotive Power Systems, I got the impression that while auto makers publicly espoused the goal of a new cleaner and more energy-efficient automobile, it was not a very high priority with them. The eight-member committee had been appointed to advise the Council on Environmental Quality and the Environmental Protection Agency on use of program funds for development of low emission power systems to replace the internal combustion engine. Chaired by Ernest Starkman, dean of the mechanical engineering school at the University of California at Berkeley, the committee included representatives from Ford, Chrysler, and General Motors.

As the advisory committee discussed the matter, it became evident that the automobile company experts did not believe that their own experiments with steam-type engines, electric-powered cars, gas turbines, or stratified charge combustion systems were anywhere near the point of being adopted, and their companies had no plans to shift away from the polluting internal combustion engine. It was known that one Japanese company was ready to market a "clean" stratified charge engine, but the American manufacturers all took the position that any change away from the internal combustion engine was a decision to be made at some time in the distant future. Current technology, they believed, was not adequate to allow production of a satisfactory new clean and energy-efficient engine.

Detroit's answer to the federal auto emission control standards applicable to 1975 model cars was the catalytic converter. For all of its problems such as overheating and unpleasant odor and the

strict requirement for using unleaded gasoline, it did satisfy the
federal standards temporarily and helped achieve better fuel
efficiency.

When I visited the General Motors headquarters in Detroit, I
found a much more active environmental program than my earlier
contacts had led me to anticipate. In 1971 the company had
combined various sections into a four-hundred person Environmental Activities Staff headed by Professor Starkman, whom it had
hired away from the University of California and made a GM vice-
president. Although the majority of the environmental staff's
efforts involved automobile and truck emission controls, its responsibilities included supervision of plant environment, vehicle fuel
economy, resource recovery, vehicular noise control, automotive
safety engineering, and product quality assurance.

David Potter, who currently heads the environmental activities
staff,* is a physicist who served during the Ford administration as
under secretary of the navy. Much of his staff's supervisory and
research work focuses on the plants of General Motors and its
subsidiaries. One staff group prepares environmental assessments
for all manufacturing facilities, evaluating the impact that new
facilities or major modifications of existing plants may have on the
environment. A resource recovery unit is in charge of a recycling
effort that reuses almost all of the company's scrap metal,
cardboard, wood pallets, and oil. A task force is looking for ways to
improve the recyclability of automobiles by changing the materials
used. At more than one hundred of its facilities GM installed water
pollution control systems, many of them in operation before
federal law made them mandatory. The Chevrolet plant at Parma,
Ohio, has built an experimental sulfur oxide stack scrubber system
that makes it possible to use high-sulfur coal to generate electricity
and still meet Ohio air pollution regulations.

GM employs as a consultant one of the nation's leading
ecologists, David Gates, who advises on the problems involving
siting of new plants and on manufacturing processes that present
threats to health and the environment at existing plants. Gates
operates as an adviser to the environmental activities staff as well
as to GM's corporate Public Policy Committee.

In 1975, when Environmental Protection Agency researchers
* Ernest Starkman died in 1976.

suspected that catalytic converters being used in all 1976 model cars were causing potentially harmful concentrations of sulfuric acid, GM's environmental activities staff proposed a test to assist in determining the actual extent of the problem. In cooperation with the Environmental Protection Agency, GM's environmental group and research laboratories ran a test involving 352 cars from four U.S. manufacturers. For a month the cars were operated on a straightaway track while air quality measurements were made at sites on both sides of the track. General Motors ran the risk that if the results showed a health problem, EPA would enforce more stringent standards, or else require that the converter be modified or possibly abandoned. But the tests—along with other experiments—demonstrated that the converters did not pose a health risk.

GM's pollution control efforts, while important and commendable, did not, however, touch upon some of the fundamental environmental problems presented by the design and manufacture of automobiles. I was still unconvinced that top managers were adequately considering the environmental effects of such policies as continued reliance on planned obsolescence rather than durability. They were responding more quickly than other American manufacturers in curtailing fuel consumption by developing lighter engines and designing smaller overall dimensions for their standard size cars. Yet I had questions about the extent to which environmental concerns were figuring in major decisions at the highest corporate level where the long-term direction of the company is decided. I also wondered why the vice-president in charge of the environmental activities staff did not serve on any of the company's major policy-setting committees as did some other vice-presidents, or why GM's Public Policy Committee, made up of corporate board members from outside the company, had no environmentalist on it. There was not even a member who could claim to represent consumers until the Reverend Leon H. Sullivan, the black leader from Philadelphia who had been a GM board member since 1971, was added to the Public Policy Committee in 1975.

In separate interviews with General Motors Board Chairman Thomas A. Murphy and President E. M. (Pete) Estes, I had an opportunity to explore the company's attitude toward environmental concerns. I asked Murphy if he felt the present organization of his company allowed environmental issues to get an adequate hearing.

"I would say that the developments of the last five years have brought all of us to the point where we are more aware of the environment," Murphy told me. "Initially, it took a lot of things to get our attention—you know, you had to wield the old two-by-four. But environment has our attention now. And I think we are structured so we can get all the proper inputs and the proper environmental evaluations. That doesn't mean we can't continue to improve. That's why we have a Public Policy Committee—outsiders looking in at us. And we have a Science Advisory Committee—whose members make recommendations to the Public Policy Committee—who are monitoring both our research and engineering, and who work with our environmental staff."

At the time of the 1976 interview with Murphy, Congress was considering more stringent auto emission standards. I asked why GM was opposing the tougher standards, and why he had written to GM stockholders the previous year asking them to pressure their congressmen to delay imposing new standards for five years.

"We've come a long way in a relatively short time, and the environment has been improved," Murphy replied. "If we stay with present standards the environment will improve every day from now on. We feel we can continue to make progress with the present standards while we sort out and see where we should be going and what gives us the best cost benefit. When the decisions on standards were made, they were based more on emotion than on studies. And at that time energy was available and cheap and not of much concern. Today we have another dimension, the cost and availability of energy. We would like to see a careful examination of what we have accomplished, where we can go, the cost of getting there, and a determination of the health and environmental needs of the country. We think we can stand very well on the five-year pause before putting stronger emission standards into effect."

When I met with Estes a short time later I asked how the decision to produce the Chevette had evolved. I knew he had participated at the beginning of the planning for a small car back in 1970 when he was vice-president for overseas operations. What part had energy conservation or the environment played in the final decision to go ahead with the Chevette? I asked.

"I'd be less than honest if I told you the decision was made strictly for environmental reasons," Estes said. "If we are going to accomplish anything in the area of what we call social concerns, we have to sell vehicles. So I would have to say that the decision in late 1973 to go ahead on the small car was really made because there was a market that we were not meeting for about 700,000 vehicles that were smaller and more fuel-efficient than the Vega, our smallest vehicle at that time. And the inroads from imported cars had become large enough that we thought we ought to have a car on the market quickly."

Estes explained that what eventually became the Chevette started in 1970 when GM engineers in West Germany were ordered to come up with a suitable successor to the Opel Kadett.

"Less than a month after President Nixon made his speech asking for energy conservation, on November 25, 1973, we made a commitment to bring out the Chevette within eighteen months. At the time we had five other designs for completely new small cars but we couldn't wait the three years it would have taken to get those into production. The overseas version of the Chevette was already underway in Brazil, England, Germany, Japan, and Australia. The whole thrust of our decision was on the basis of the nation's energy situation, and that we had to level off gasoline usage in the United States. We also decided to reduce the size and improve the fuel economy of all our big cars."

I put to Estes the same question I had raised with Chairman Murphy: Why was General Motors fighting the Environmental Protection Agency's standards on automobile emissions and trying to delay them?

"Whatever the legislation calls for, it should be health effective, cost effective, and energy effective," he replied. "If in our opinion it isn't, we're going to continue to fight it. If we don't meet those three criteria it's bad for every one in the United States, including environmentalists.

"We don't think there's enough experimental data on health standards, on where we have to be in order to make sure we're not damaging the health of our people. We believe that by 1985 only the Los Angeles Valley won't be clean from an automotive point of view by adhering to current standards.* Anything tighter than that is just unnecessary waste of both money and energy. And until we get another breakthrough like the catalytic converter, we're going to lose fuel economy. It's going to cost energy if we tighten the emission standards further.

"We're not trying to push a policy or a principle that's wrong. The only thing is, we want to be sure whether it is necessary. And if it is, we'll go all-out to meet the requirements. But if it's not a problem, then we shouldn't even be working on it. Everyone thinks we're strictly self-serving in everything we say and do. Maybe we are, in the short term, in order to get the end that really counts for the country and for the customer."

Before we ended our conversation I asked Estes, who has been with General Motors for more than forty years, if he had seen a change in attitude to the point where the company accepts an environmental responsibility.

"Sure, I think we're much more conscious of the environment," he said. "There isn't any question that the work of the environmentalists, our critics, has improved us and our method of operation."

---

* When Congress finally got around to passing new air pollution regulations in 1977, the GM request for continuing the 1975 auto emission control requirements until the 1980 model year was not accepted. In a compromise move Congress voted to keep the standards the same for 1978 and 1979 model years, with slightly higher standards for 1980, before requiring the strictest standards beginning with the 1981 model year. GM management accepted this compromise and no longer opposes federal standards. With these standards Estes believes that even the Los Angeles area will be rid of major automotive air contaminants by 1985.

10

ENVIRONMENT'S STAKE AT CUMMINS

In 1970, when automobile and truck engines were being regarded as a major cause of air pollution, the Cummins Engine Company of Columbus, Indiana, the world's largest independent producer of diesel engines, announced a startling environmental policy:

> Concern over pollution is proper and overdue. Cummins's commitment is to manufacture products which will not contribute to the degradation of the environment. ... Federal agencies must decide which elements are harmful, at what levels, and in what operating environments. This applies equally to emissions and to vehicle noise. ... Once standards necessary to protect our health are determined, it is up to the manufacturer to achieve them. ... Some feel that industry is being asked to do too much, too quickly. Although standard-setting must recog-

nize the realities of development time, society's needs transcend the individual needs of any one firm, including ourselves.

The automotive and truck industry was at the time battling federal and state pollution-control regulations, and Cummins's statement was equivalent to heresy. Nor did the company, producer of more than half the nation's heavy-duty diesel truck engines, as well as engines for tractors, boats, oil rigs, and mining equipment, endear itself to its competitors when in 1971 then Board Chairman J. Irwin Miller testified at an Environmental Protection Agency hearing on motor vehicle pollution control.

"Manufacturers, ourselves included, sometimes tend to sell themselves a bit short," Miller told the hearing. "The answer is for the government to set tight standards to cause everyone to run hard at them, ease up only if *nobody* makes them, but always remember why the standards were set." Miller also testified that Cummins felt it appropriate that all products bear their full cost. "The by-products of certain products such as emissions represent a real cost to society either in deteriorating quality of life or in the cost to clean the environment. We feel that it is far better to put the cost of cleaning the environment on the particular product that causes the pollution rather than to use public funds to clean the resources later. . . . It is up to the manufacturer to find the appropriate product solution to the market demand that does meet the needs on a full cost basis. No particular product, our own included, has any inherent right in the marketplace."

In carrying out its environmental policy as well as the company's entire corporate responsibility philosophy, Cummins applies what it calls a "stakeholders" model. To find out what that means I talked with the company's young board chairman, Henry B. Schacht, who came to Cummins as vice-president in 1964 when he was only 29. He rose to the presidency five years later, became chief executive officer at 39, and was named chairman of the board in 1977 when Miller stepped down. Schacht told me: "In dealing with the variety of responsibilities that a corporation has, we asked ourselves—to whom are we responsible? When we started to examine the process it became clear that our responsibility was not merely to the company's shareholders, because they were by no means the only people who have a stake in the business. A great many people are what we call stakeholders in our business: our 22,000 employees, our customers, our suppliers, cities in which we operate, regulatory agencies which have jurisdiction over our products, stockholders and bondholders, and, in our case, the various general publics, since our products move throughout populated areas and our engines put out exhaust gases. So there are a legion of claims on the corporate responsibility. And it is management's job to balance the claims."

To help management adjudicate among the competing claims, Cummins established, under the leadership of James A. Joseph (who was appointed undersecretary of the U.S. Department of the Interior in early 1977), a 22-person corporate action division to participate at all levels of corporate decision-making and ensure that all claims are heard and that company policies protect these various interests. Joseph was succeeded by Charles W. Powers, a former Yale University ethics professor and co-author of *The Ethical Investor,* a book which includes an assessment of corporate social responsibility. The corporate action staff participates in the long-range planning process so that top management will not be faced constantly with intolerable choices. Corporate action also encourages policies in the public interest, policies which Schacht says will stretch the corporation toward what society identifies as its needs.

The stakeholder concept is applied to every major action or new investment decision by the company. Internal environmental impact assessments as well as social and political assessments are made and executives weigh the effects on the various stakeholders to whom the company is accountable. Although Cummins does not have environmental problems as severe as companies in the natural resources area, its policy is reflected in such things as unusual attention to environmental factors when siting a new production plant, as well as in dealing with diesel engine pollutants.

Cummins obviously is no ordinary company. Operating out of a town of 30,000 population, it grossed more than $1 billion in 1977, had after-tax profits of $67 million, has several overseas plants and sells its products worldwide. The company has 1,200 of its 22,000 employees working in technical and engineering research and, in 1977, spent $40 million on research. Company officials say they have not been able to develop an alternative type of engine that

drastically reduces pollutants. But the company devotes a significant portion of its research resources to reducing emissions in its
present designs and continues to explore alternative possibilities.

Cummins does not have a corporate public policy committee,
but 10 of the 17 members of the board of directors are from outside
the company and represent wide areas of the public sector. The
board includes William Scranton, former Pennsylvania governor
and U.S. ambassador to the United Nations; William Ruckelshaus,
former head of the Environmental Protection Agency and now a
senior vice-president of the Weyerhaeuser Company; Hannah
Gray, president of the University of Chicago; Franklin Thomas, a
New York lawyer who started the Bedford-Stuyvesant community
program in Brooklyn; and Sir William Hawthorne, an engineering
authority from the University of Cambridge in England.

About one-third of the Cummins stock is held by the family that
founded the company. It was started in 1919 when J. Irwin Miller's
great uncle, William G. Irwin, decided to finance the diesel engine
experiments of his chauffeur, Clessie L. Cummins. For years the
Irwin-Miller family provided funds for the company while Clessie
Cummins improved his engines. He developed the first diesel-
powered vehicle to finish in the Indianapolis 500 race, produced a
diesel truck and drove it in 1931 from New York to Los Angeles in
97 hours and 52 minutes using only $7.63 worth of fuel, and wrote
a book, *My Days with the Diesel.*

Each year the company, through the Cummins Engine Foundation, donates the maximum 5% of its domestic pretax profits to
charity. Miller himself has been nationally prominent. He was the
first lay president of the National Council of the Churches of Christ
in the U.S.A. and led that organization's work in the civil rights
movement in the early 1960s, helped Columbus, Indiana, pass an
open housing ordinance, and recruited black executives for Cummins. A liberal Republican, Miller was suggested by a national
magazine in 1968 as a presidential candidate.

With Cummins Foundation help, Columbus has become an
architectural showcase and a mecca for architects and students of
architecture and design. Miller was a Yale University classmate of
Eero Saarinen, and in the 1930s the Miller family was instrumental
in persuading the First Christian Church 'in Columbus to hire
Saarinen's father, Eliel, to design one of the first "modern"

churches in the nation. And Miller had enlisted Eero Saarinen to design the Irwin Union Bank building in downtown Columbus, and, later, the new North Christian Church. Disturbed by the uninspired design of the city's school buildings, Miller in 1954 offered to have the foundation underwrite the architectural fees of all new school buildings in Columbus on one condition: The school board must select an architect among six recommended by an impartial panel of experts. The Cummins Foundation would have no connection with selecting the architect but would pay the architectural fees.

Under the program, 11 schools have been built in Columbus, in addition to 11 other public buildings as Cummins extended the offer to them. Not to be outdone, businesses, churches, and other organizations have on their own hired nationally prominent architects to design 20 more buildings. Thus it is that little Columbus attracts 40,000 visitors a year, most of them to take public tours of the buildings. In addition to schools designed by Harry Weese of Chicago, Caudill, Rowlett and Scott of Los Angeles and Houston, and Gunnar Birkerts of Birmingham, Michigan, Columbus now has a downtown library, designed by I. M. Pei of New York, with a massive Henry Moore sculpture in the library plaza, an enclosed civic square and shopping mall designed by Gruen Associates of Los Angeles, and a modern glass-fronted newspaper plant designed by the Chicago office of Skidmore, Owings & Merrill, and several modern church buildings. Many downtown buildings have torn away artificial plastic and glass façades to highlight the original architecture, following a master plan by Alexander Girard of Santa Fe, New Mexico, for restoring old storefronts.

Aside from Cummins's contributions to Columbus's esthetic environment, how do the company's impressively stated policies and internal structure work out in practice, especially as they relate to the natural environment? They were put to a major test when Congress in 1975 started to rewrite and strengthen the 1970 Clean Air Act. In that legislation, heavy-duty vehicles had been lumped with motorcycles in an "other vehicles" category, and the Environmental Protection Agency had been given authority to require the "best available emissions control technology" for this miscellaneous category.

But trouble for the heavy-duty engine industry appeared imminent when the Subcommittee on Health and the Environment of the House Interstate and Foreign Commerce Committee adopted an amendment which set target goals or standards for emissions reduction so high they would have been impossible to meet. Largely at the insistence of one subcommittee member, with no supporting health data and no information as to whether industry could devise technology to meet them, the subcommittee adopted standards that would require by 1983 a 90% reduction of the three traditional gaseous emissions—hydrocarbons, carbon monoxide, and nitrogen.

This action brought immediate protests from the heavy-duty engine and vehicle industry, and lobbyists started working on members of the full House Commerce Committee urging them to strike the provision entirely. Even members of the committee staff felt the subcommittee's amendment was not workable. If it were adopted into law the Environmental Protection Agency would be forced to admit that the standards could not be met nor the law enforced. EPA would then have to administratively adopt regulations based on the lowest common denominator of technology available in the industry.

Cummins's management was as concerned as the rest of the industry. But instead of joining with the lobbying efforts, Schacht brought together senior executives to seek a solution.

"We didn't think the manufacturers of the products should have the responsibility of setting standards," Schacht told me. "But the government has a responsibility to set *reasonable* standards that take into account what they are trying to do. For government to say lower emissions are better without knowing why is as irresponsible as for industry to try to set self-serving standards on nothing but empty phrases.

"We felt that the government in setting standards should have input from the scientific community, the manufacturing community, the academic community, and from other interested parties. Then it ought to decide as the elected representative of the people what is in the best public interest, considering tradeoffs of health, cost effectiveness of various methods of meeting standards, energy efficiency, and availability of the technology. Of course, if the health hazard is severe enough, you don't worry about the availability of the technology. The companies either find it or they go out of business, because the needs of society transcend the needs of any individual firm.

"Our premises were that public health should not be impaired by emissions from our products, and that it was government's job to keep figuring out which emissions those are and at what levels they are harmful. We also had to figure out just where and how market forces could be brought to bear to create incentives to find the technological alternatives to reduce the specific emissions.

"But because emissions reduction ordinarily affects fuel economy and inflation, we had to find an incentive system which encouraged us to find the breakthroughs which either got beyond the social tradeoffs or which best took them into account. So we decided to identify criteria which a new regulatory approach would meet, a decision in effect to figure out how the law *could* work, not why it couldn't."

After analyzing the situation Cummins decided in 1975 to see if company representatives could work with the committees of Congress to find a reasonable *process* for setting the standards. The project was assigned to the corporate action division. The staff, working with the company's technical people, made a study of the known data on health effects, the history of previous standards-setting procedures, and the existing technological capabilities of its own company to reduce polluting emissions, its future technological potential, and how long it would take to get from the research drawing boards to finished products.

Cummins's corporate representatives presented to members of Congress and their committee staffs an integrated four-part process for standards-setting and obtaining compliance with the regulations that would be set:

(1) A revised set of standards starting off slightly less stringently and with a later compliance timetable than the one proposed by the subcommittee but capable of being raised or lowered before being imposed. The standards would be based on a study to be made by the Environmental Protection Agency of the effects of air pollution from heavy-duty engines on the public health and welfare. Although Cummins felt that ideally standards should be

set administratively by EPA, Cummins recognized as a political fact of life that Congress itself wanted to set target goals for emission controls.

(2) A periodic review and revision of the standards to take into account health needs, technological feasibility, and economic factors.

(3) A system for monitoring actual compliance with the standards by checking engines coming off the assembly line.

(4) Financial penalties to be assessed for noncompliance with the standards, the penalties increasing in scale to provide an incentive for compliance and to eliminate any competitive advantage to the manufacturer of a nonconforming engine.

The Cummins people worked with the staff of the House committee and with staff assistants to a number of Congressmen on the committee, with the Environmental Protection Agency, and with other engine manufacturers. The four points were incorporated into a broadly supported amendment, and the new proposal became a part of the bill first passed by the House in 1976. The whole bill failed to come up for a Senate vote in 1976, however. In 1977 both houses passed the bill with the Cummins proposal intact. And after considerable work by a conference committee to resolve differences in the House and Senate versions, the Clean Air Act Amendments of 1977 were enacted and the Cummins proposal became part of the new law.

Although the legislation set up the process, the specific emissions regulations have yet to be established. Schacht believes that if the law is carried out as written, the regulations adopted as a result of the new process should help produce the improvement in air quality necessary to protect health. Schacht admits, however, that the resulting standards may turn out to be such that Cummins might find it hard to meet them.

"If the public interest provides a standard that meets the tests of health effects, cost effectiveness, energy consciousness, and technological availability, then the mechanism will force the technology," says Schacht. "Without a law required by health effects, it does no good for one company to be more concerned about the environment or health than another company. If we produced a nonpolluting engine that cost $1,000 more than a polluting engine and there were no laws to be met and no ready evidence of the effects of the pollution, people would buy the cheaper engine. We would go out of business and we wouldn't be helping to solve the health problem. Therefore, we need a rational regulatory process that we all can live with and that meets society's needs. Once we have that, then the rest of us will compete like crazy for the most cost-effective solution."

11

A SWAMP AS
COLLATERAL

A senior vice-president of one of the nation's leading insurance companies expressed something akin to shock when I asked him whether his company applied environmental standards in its lending. His company, of course, acknowledged the need for social responsibility. It was an equal opportunity employer. But to pass judgment on the purpose of a loan just on the basis of environmental considerations or to inquire about the environmental record of an organization in which he would invest was unthinkable.

"My sole responsibility is to the interests of the policyholders, investors in my company, and our employees," he said. "That responsibility is to make as high a return as possible on the investment."

The financial institution—bank, insurance company, or mortgage trust—plays a significant role in determining what development takes place. If an oil pipeline is planned, or a shopping center, or a second-home development, someone has to put up the money for it. Rarely does it come from the developer. I wondered, therefore, whether any banks or insurance companies saw themselves as a first line of defense in protecting the quality of life for citizens in their own community or farther afield. So I looked around for examples in the world of lenders and investors.

The premise that lending institutions might be able to build environmental considerations into their banking policies was, I discovered, part of a study, Environment and Banking, made by the Center for New Corporate Priorities, a public interest group in Los Angeles. The center looked at the significant environmental impact of lending and trust policies at thirty major commercial banks around the nation whose loans to business and industry amount to $177 billion. Only six of the banks said they had policies to protect and improve the environment, and none of these was very specific, nor did the banks have any process by which to follow up with their policies.

Said the Bank of America: "The Bank must be sure that environmental protection standards are met by projects for which it lends funds." But the bank had no process for deciding that standards were being met other than checking the formal environmental impact reports required by the State of California for all major development projects.

Said the Chase Manhattan Bank: "Those at Chase involved in lending, investment, and other banking activities, as well as in external relations, will take environmental factors into account in making their judgments. The bank will also cooperate in environmental efforts undertaken by industry and government and will share its own expertise with other banks, businesses, and the public at large." But in practice, Chase has no process through which to take environmental factors into account in lending and investment activities.

A New York State bank official said: "We are bankers, not engineers, not ecologists, and certainly not policemen." That expressed the prevalent attitude I also found among bankers—that protecting or enhancing the environment should be the concern of government, not of financial institutions. They believed that they have neither the right nor the expertise to try to inject any persona' environmental commitments into their corporate banking activities.

I thought I might have found an exception when I heard about a "polluter's code" that had been proposed for some banks in Maine. I was referred to Halsey Smith who, my source said, was with the Casco Bank and Trust Company of Portland, Maine.

When I tracked him down, Smith had left the banking business and was head of the University of Maine's Center for Research and Advancement. Yes, he told me, there had been a proposal for a polluter's code when he was board chairman of the Casco Bank in 1970.

At that time the Maine Legislature had passed a Site Location Law requiring environmental permits for large developments, but the state had no laws to regulate the environmental effects of smaller developments. These individually and cumulatively could pollute, create esthetic damage, or lead to destruction of wetlands and other ecologically important areas.

Smith believed that the state's banks might be able to play a helpful role in protecting Maine's unique natural heritage. Why couldn't banks adopt a code for judging potential construction loans where the Site Location Law did not apply?

He convinced his own bank's board of the merits of the polluter's code idea. He also persuaded the Maine Bankers' Association, of which he was then president, to write and approve a code. In addition to protecting Maine's environment, it could protect banks, Smith suggested. It would limit the possibility that borrowers might default if they ran afoul of environmental regulations and were prevented from finishing their work due to local restrictions or to public pressure.

The code the Bankers Association adopted appeared to be an environmental landmark. It stated:

"The bankers of Maine individually and collectively agree, as a matter of basic philosophy, that pollution control and abatement must be an integral consideration in credit decisions attendant to the financing of new industries, expansion of existing industries and new and existent commercial ventures to insure that such financing shall not encourage or abet pollution of the air, land or water of the State of Maine."

One of the code's six provisions required banking institutions to satisfy themselves that, in granting credit, no significant pollution of air, land, or water would result. In instances wherein licensing was not required, banks were to accept informal expert opinion from the State Environmental Improvement Commission as to whether or not significant pollution of air, land, or water could result from approval of a credit request. The code would also have the banks seek to persuade customers presently polluting to stop doing so. When possible, the banks would offer additional credit to encourage pollution abatement.

After adopting the polluter's code, the Maine Bankers Association sent it to member banks for ratification. The association, says Smith, felt it had no right to dictate policies to member banks. Half of the 44 banks claimed they were already meeting most of the standards, and refused to sign the code. This caused the 22 banks that had already approved the code to back down. They feared that unless their competitors went along, they would lose business.

"I argued that for many other reasons they turned down loans their competitors accepted, so what was wrong with doing it for environmental reasons?" Smith recalled.

Maine Bankers Association Director Roger Ayers told me that no check was ever made to see which, if any, of the banks followed the polluter's code. And the association has done nothing about it since 1970.

Smith believes that even without formal acceptance, the standards served a purpose by creating an awareness of environmental considerations. Some of the state's banks have encouraged their loan officers to become more conscious of environmental concerns. And they may have had some influence on other state banking associations that requested copies of the Maine code. Smith is disappointed that it did not catch on. He saw the code as leading to more environmental responsibility in the banks, which could then have been picked up by the communities to help preserve the environment of the state. "But you don't sell moral responsibility very easily in this age," he now admits.

I found that in recent years some major banks have taken environmentally progressive steps, even though I discovered none in which loan officers applied environmental criteria in determining the acceptability of a loan request. A number of banks exercised their social responsibility by engaging in inner city redevelopment programs, the most outstanding of which is that of the South Shore National Bank of Chicago. New owners in 1973 set out to prove that a commercial bank in a declining neighborhood could both succeed in the marketplace and help rebuild its neighborhood. Its program in "greenlining" has produced mortgage and rehabilitation loans on housing in run-down areas where other lending agencies had "redlined." The bank's extra efforts in community development are guided by a 19-member Resident Advisory Board nominated by South Shore organizations. And the bank has increased its profits.

The Bank of America in California, in addition to participating in several urban rehabilitation loan programs, has made some efforts to further its environmental concerns. It has hired as environmental consultant Dr. Marjorie W. Evans, formerly with Stanford Research Institute. When called upon, she reviews the state-required environmental impact reports to determine the suitability of projects submitted for loan consideration. She is involved in the urban rehabilitation programs. And she has been working on a program to give banking customers advice on using solar energy. The bank in 1972 published an environmental handbook *Getting Down to Earth* which attempted to define for the layman the causes of pollution and the effects on the environment, with suggested solutions to the problems of solid waste disposal and air and water pollution. Evans is chairman of an ad hoc environmental policy committee of the bank, which as yet has not come up with any major new policies. She does not believe that banks should consider environmental factors in making loans.

"I refuse to acknowledge that banks have some quasi-governmental obligation," says Evans. "Some people talk about banks as if they were some governmental institution which had this special obligation. If you ask a bank to make a distinction among lenders on environmental grounds, you are asking it to assume a governmental role, which it should not do."

New York's Chase Manhattan Bank in 1970 created a post of technical director, environmental systems, a position now held by Sheldon Sixfin, who has been an industry consultant on environmental engineering. Sixfin is available to advise bank officers on implications of any of their actions with regard to the environment. He helps municipalities with their resource recovery and energy conservation, attends environmental conferences and seminars, and was an adviser to the U.S. Department of State for a 1977 international conference on environmental education.

An unusual environmental effort was started in 1976 by the Seattle Trust and Savings Bank when it initiated an Energy Conservation Loan program devised by energy expert Wilson Clark. Under the program, reductions of 0.5% to 1% below standard interest rates are given to loan applicants who can furnish evidence that their planned new homes or rehabilitation work meet certain energy conservation and efficiency requirements in line with standards advocated by federal, state, and local agencies as well as some utilities and professional associations. The standards involve insulation, efficiency of the heating plant, and energy consumption of appliances. Home owners are allowed flexibility in choosing the methods used to meet a minimum overall acceptability required by the bank. Reduced loan rates are also given on purchase of new cars and diesel trucks that get 25 miles or more per gallon of fuel.

Seattle Trust's president, Joseph C. Baillargeon, testified before a congressional committee developing the Energy Conservation Act that the bank recognized energy conservation "as the common denominator by which we felt we can profitably market our services to the consumer everywhere and attract customers who had opted for thrift in their own affairs, thus creating an environment of better risk. . . . We are actually demonstrating that it is possible to market conservation very much the way we have marketed consumption."

Small investors who might desire to put money into corporations with good environmental practices find it difficult to get reliable information on the companies. To help the environmentally minded investor the Natural Resources Defense Council went to court in June 1971 requesting that the Securities and Exchange Commission require more environmental disclosure by corporations filing reports with the commission. The NRDC claimed that "investors now have no available and reliable means of assessing the environmental impact of the particular corporation. . . . It is difficult and perhaps impossible for investors to make either socially responsible or financially sound investment decisions."

In a court ruling more significant for its findings than for its results, U.S. District Court Judge Charles R. Richey wrote: "NRDC and some of its members have funds which they want to invest prudently and with a minimum adverse impact upon the environment; some members own common stock which they want to vote prudently and with a minimum adverse impact on the environment. The Court agrees with NRDC and its members that their interest in protecting the environment, in investing their funds, and in voting their shares in a socially responsible manner, have been and continue to be adversely affected and aggrieved by the SEC's failure to adopt corporate disclosure regulations which will require disclosure of a corporation's impact on the environment.... There are many so-called 'ethical investors' in this country who want to invest their assets in firms which are concerned about and acting on environmental problems of the nation. This attitude may be based purely upon a concern for the environment; but it may also proceed from the recognition that awareness of and sensitivity to environmental problems is the mark of intelligent management. Whatever their motive, this Court is not prepared to say that they are not rational investors and that the information they seek is not material information within the meaning of the securities laws."

Despite the strong language, however, Judge Richey's decision required only that the SEC hold hearings to determine what environmental information was required to be made public and how.

In testimony before the hearing examiner, the Sierra Club's Executive Director Michael McCloskey said that the club's investment committee had been looking for information about the environmental performance of companies to help guide their investment policies, but had been unable to develop reliable criteria to help them. (The Sierra Club had been embarrassed by news stories that its own investment portfolio included a number of oil companies and other firms which it had been attacking for degrading the environment—investments which the club has now dropped.) McCloskey suggested the kind of information that the Sierra Club felt the SEC should require of corporations:

(1) What share of the firm's fixed assets is invested in pollution control equipment (should be presented as a percentage, as well as in actual dollar terms)?

(2) What is the actual total tonnage of effluents and emissions released by the firm into the environment each year (portion which is not in fact controlled), and what ratio does this bear to the production cost of sales?

(3) What is the actual amount of money spent each year by the firm to conduct research on solving environmental problems, and what ratio does this bear to the production cost of sales?

(4) How much energy does the firm consume annually in BTU's and what is the ratio of this consumption to the production cost of sales?

(5) For firms or portions of firms that use or sell natural resources (other than agriculture but including forestry, fisheries, and mineral development of all sorts), what percentage of their resource inventory is used or sold each year?

(6) For firms developing natural resources (as defined in (5) above), what amounts are invested annually in rehabilitating development sites and what ratio does this bear to the production cost of sales?

(7) Finally, all firms should be asked to provide concise information in a narrative form on toxic substances which are included in its products, hazardous wastes which result from its production processes and any irreversible environmental impacts of its operations. Such substances, wastes, and impacts should be described, with appropriate statistical data, and it should be indicated whether corrective action is contemplated and possible.

After considering the testimony from 54 oral presentations and 353 written comments on both sides of the issue, the SEC rejected most of the Natural Resources Defense Fund demands.

The commission said, in effect, that the only instance in which corporations might need to disclose environmental information was when they had been cited for not complying with federal antipollution laws. It rejected the concept that the commission could protect the interests of environmental investors by requiring comprehensive disclosure of the environmental effects of corporate activities. The costs and administrative burdens to companies would be excessive, and no uniform method exists to comprehensively describe the environmental effects of corporate practices, the commission stated. SEC also rejected the suggestion that corporations be required to disclose pending environmental litigation, general corporate environmental policy, and all capital expenditures and expenses for environmental purposes.

Insurance companies—both in their stock purchases and in their investment loans to industries and developers—are among the country's most powerful investors. I found that several have shown some interest in bringing environmental considerations into investment decisions and other aspects of their business.

The John Hancock Life Insurance Company produced an environmental policy report in 1971 that is the most comprehensive *written* policy I have ever seen. It was prepared by a staff committee composed of John Hancock management representatives and headed by Ralph L. Gustin, Jr., senior vice-president and general counsel.

This remarkable statement called for the company to "infuse environmental considerations into its decision-making processes." The recommendations applied to all areas of the company, with specific policy guidelines for investment operations, city mortgages, farm mortgages, and administrative operations. The report recommended that John Hancock investment department analysts be required to qualify themselves to consider environmental regulatory control factors just as they qualified themselves to consider other factors in business and financial analysis. The analyst responsible for electrical utilities should be familiar with storage of nuclear fuels, utility plant siting, pollution abatement technology, and other relevant environmental factors. Each presentation on investments made to the Finance or Real Estate committees should include an environmental assessment.

The City Mortgage and Real Estate Department, which deals in specific urban buildings and projects, should analyze prospective investments "from the point of view of the needs of the community in which the land is located and the appropriateness of the land and area for the project," the Gustin report recommended.

Site plans should be designed to minimize environmental damage. "The developer, loan correspondent, or broker should be required to describe in detail the method of provision for recycling, the adequacy of public facilities for handling waste generated by the proposed development, the compliance of public facilities with existing state and federal regulations, and the method of ultimate disposal of waste, treated and untreated, from the public system and the impact of that disposal on the environment. Loans should be avoided in communities with outdated treatment practices or in communities with an unsatisfactory record of compliance with state or federal regulations."

The Farm Mortgage Department's field organization should be trained to recognize and consider environmental protection measures when modifying existing investments or negotiating new ones. It should consider factors such as soil erosion control, water quality, waste disposal problems, and runoff control, especially in large feedlots. The report cautioned that "funding of the investment should not take place until all permits are obtained and the manure treatment or disposal system is complete and operative."

The committee even recommended carrying environmental considerations into voting of proxies. "In cases of abuse [of the environment] where the company holds a significant position in a company's stock or debt, company views should be made known where indicated. In some instances, it may be more effective to state shareholder views to management than to sell the stock of a corporation which is abusing the environment."

A recommendation was made that procedures be established to lend credibility to the company's environmental policy. "A record of investment refusals based on environmental considerations should be maintained," the committee said.

The report also recognized the need for following environmental standards in the company's administrative operations as manager, as purchaser of goods and services, as property owner and occupant, as contributor of funds, as employer, as participant in civic activities, and in legislative efforts.

A policy category called "employee participation" recommended that the company should advise employees of existing programs and opportunities for volunteer work in the environmental area. "Employees can be encouraged," the report said, "to use environmentally sound practices in their daily work habits by actively soliciting their ideas and giving them recognition in employee suggestion programs."

When I discovered this impressive report, I traveled to Boston to see Ralph Gustin, the head of John Hancock's environmental policy committee, and find out how his recommendations had fared.

The company's governing executive committee had accepted the report, Gustin told me. But he was not able to give me the results because once the report had been submitted, he no longer had any connection with environmental affairs. My expectations began to fade as he went on to explain that John Hancock's highest decision-making body, its executive committee, had referred the recommendations to the appropriate operating departments for implementation. And no one had been appointed to guide or direct environmental policy.

Gustin felt certain, though, that the recommendations had made a significant change in the way the company operated, and he said he would try to obtain the information for me. He warned that he probably would be able to find out about only a fraction of the effect, however, because any new procedure circulated throughout the company has results far beyond those known to top management. Also, he was aware that some of the recommendations were not being followed because many specific requirements thought necessary in 1971, such as checking on the environmentally harmful activities of loan applicants or companies to invest in, had been rendered unnecessary by strong federal and state pollution control laws. It was now sufficient, Gustin said, for the John Hancock analysts to make certain the company or project under consideration was in conformance with all the various laws, regulations, and standards set by government.

Later, when Gustin passed along to me the information he received from within the company on the results of the environmental policy's adoption, the reports gave a mixed picture. Loan agreements now include a covenant requiring that the borrower be, and remain, in material compliance with all federal and state environmental regulations. For a loan on one new steel mill, for instance, the covenant required the company to comply promptly with all laws, codes, or acts of all governments, including those laws related to pollution control, zoning, and land subdivision. When an electric power company applied for a loan but could not meet the sulfur oxide emission requirements of state and federal laws, John Hancock wrote into the loan agreement a covenant requiring the applicant to get certification from independent engineers that no technique or method exists for such control, or that control of emissions is not at the time commercially feasible.

One loan officer said that when a borrower is not presently in

compliance, but is on a step-by-step schedule to clean up its
pollution, the loan officer requires a certificate, signed by a public
official, assuring that the company is continuing to meet its
compliance schedule. The loan officer in each case is required to
establish the borrower's "environmental status" and make a
judgment on the applicant's ability to meet antipollution regulations. The environment, however, is only one of many factors to be
considered in judging each prospective loan.

Some loan applications have been rejected on wholly environmental considerations. In one case, John Hancock turned down a
loan on a new mine when the loan officer determined that the
applicant's strip mining operations did not include plans for
adequate reclamation of the land.

John Hancock's City Mortgage Department requires loan applicants to fill out an environmental certificate form. Applicants check
"yes" or "no" to questions such as: Is any portion of the land a
protected wetland? Will construction affect existing historical
property or landmarks? Would the improvements on the property
create significant air or noise pollution? Is there a waste disposal
problem? Is an environmental impact report required, and if so,
has it been approved? (If "no," it must be explained.) Mortgage
loan analysts or mortgage loan correspondents or brokers use these
certificates to help identify items of concern to John Hancock, and
sometimes they request additional information.

The company required a major shopping center loan applicant
to get an analysis of the development's environmental impact.
Would it increase air pollution in the area? Were storm and
sanitary sewer systems adequate to handle the center? And would
noise from automobile related traffic be excessive?

On a loan application for a large shopping center in New
England, John Hancock required an independent study. It revealed
that the center would destroy an inland wetland covering 35% of
the site. After extensive engineering studies and modifications by
the developer to mitigate drainage problems, the state granted a
construction permit subject to several conditions concerning potential flooding. John Hancock wrote covenants into the loan requiring that the borrower comply at all times with all applicable
federal, state, and local environmental laws and regulations, and
maintain all detention ponds, drainage and sewer lines and pipes in

good operating condition at all times. But John Hancock did not take into consideration the wetland's value to the community, and whether the applicant should have chosen a site that would not have destroyed a wetland.

The City Mortgage Department has not followed the Gustin committee's recommendation to train loan analysts to recognize environmental factors. Each analyst is expected to become self-educated on environment and to keep abreast of changes in federal and state regulations.

The Farm Mortgage Department does not use environmental certificates. But its analysts, brokers, and mortgage correspondents are expected to be familiar with the company's environmental standards. And a number of applications have been rejected, or the applicants required to make changes, before receiving loans.

When a cattle operator requested financing for a feedlot that would handle 15,000 cattle, the environmental investigation revealed that houses were being built within one-half mile of the proposed feedlot. John Hancock rejected the loan. The project was financed, however, by another corporate lender having less stringent environmental standards.

A pork producer wanted financing for a sow feeder-pig facility one mile from a western city. The review process disclosed that the city would be expanding in the direction of the facility, and John Hancock turned down the loan.

When a milling company sought financing for new construction, the John Hancock agricultural representative discovered that the planned waste treatment equipment would treat only 20,000 gallons of the plant's daily effluent. The loan acceptance was delayed until the borrower had agreed to equip the plant to treat 80,000 gallons per day, the full daily load of effluent.

In the investment of company funds, there was a disappointing lack of environmental standards. Gustin was unable to find any record of John Hancock withdrawing from any public investment because of environmental considerations. He explained this on the basis that the company had never found it necessary to do so because the large, well-known corporations in which it invests have corporate images that depend on their ability to react to such politically sensitive matters as environmental problems. That seemed to me a less than satisfactory explanation inasmuch as a number of well-known companies have openly defied state and federal regulations.

Gustin's committee had recommended that the various departments keep a record of investment refusals based on environmental considerations, in order to lend credibility to the company's environmental policy. Gustin told me that one department reported it had concluded this would not be practical because most investment refusals are based on a wide range of considerations, of which environmental factors would be only a part. Another department said that the public dissemination of investment refusals would, by implication, cast John Hancock in the role of a super environmental regulatory agency, and this could have adverse consequences on future company activities.

The Administrative Services Department has implemented several parts of the company environmental policy. In 1972, John Hancock advised all major suppliers that the company required them to furnish statements about what they were doing to comply with existing environmental regulations. The company stipulated as a part of all purchase orders that if a seller was not in compliance, John Hancock might terminate the order without liability.

John Hancock falls short of completely abiding by that far-reaching policy report the company leadership accepted in 1971. It has no continuing corporate structure for dealing with environmental concerns, not even a single individual responsible for environmental affairs. "We compete for loans," said one company official. "That we have money to lend does not mean that we have the right to dictate to others." Despite its inability to follow fully the guidelines in the environmental report, however, John Hancock does follow some excellent environmental practices in carrying out its function as a lender and insurer.

The Equitable Life Assurance Society, one of the nation's largest financial institutions, has been led into activities beneficial to the environment by its president and chief executive officer, Coy Eklund. The most unusual is an active corporate policy of considering social goals in voting of proxies on Equitable's extensive stockholdings in other companies.

According to Eklund, Equitable takes a stand on the affairs of those companies in which it invests when it thinks it is necessary, as in the case of a large company that planned recently to expand its activities in coal strip mining.

"When the issue came up at the company's annual meeting, we abstained from voting the large block owned by Equitable," Eklund said. "That got management's attention, and they changed their policy on strip mining."

When considering loan applications, Equitable uses a social evaluation checklist, and the company's high-level Investment Committee sometimes turns down an applicant because the project does not have adequate environmental protections. Equitable also was one of the first companies to aid The Nature Conservancy. Its loans helped the Conservancy acquire Little Egg Harbor in New Jersey and a sandhill crane sanctuary in Mississippi. And Equitable has made grants to the Conservancy, the American Land Trust, the Audubon Society, the Conservation Foundation, and the Natural Resources Defense Council.

Aetna Life and Casualty is another large insurance company with some good environmental practices. It does not have an extensive written policy but, due chiefly to the influence of its board chairman, John H. Filer, Aetna demonstrates a measure of environmental awareness. Aetna checks on companies applying for liability insurance protection and denies coverage to those it believes are knowingly and wantonly polluting the environment. The company also tests products in its own laboratory, and if potential danger to consumers is detected, Aetna denies the manufacturer liability protection.

Board Chairman Filer's personal interest in conservation is a strong factor in actions the company takes to protect the environment. In 1973, for instance, he received a call from Patrick Noonan, president of The Nature Conservancy, whom he had met at a Connecticut conservation meeting where they shared an interest in saving a natural area threatened by commercial development. Noonan wanted an appointment to discuss a possible loan to the Conservancy for the purchase of a property in the Great Dismal Swamp in Virginia. The Nature Conservancy, a nonprofit organization that has preserved thousands of acres of ecologically vital private land, sometimes takes options on development-

threatened land sought by government agencies, and acquires the
land temporarily, until the federal or state agency can obtain funds
for purchase.

Noonan told Filer that some 14,000 acres in the Great Dismal
Swamp had been optioned by the Conservancy in order to buy it
and hold it until Congress appropriated funds for its purchase by
the U.S. Fish and Wildlife Service as an addition to a national
wildlife refuge. Ordinarily the Conservancy would have drawn on
a line of credit it held at a bank. But when this particular
opportunity came up, the 12% interest rate was too high for the
Conservancy to absorb. (The organization tries to buy land below
the assessed valuation and recoup its operating costs and interest
when a government agency repurchases it later at the assessed
valuation.)

Noonan recalls that when he went to see Filer he pointed out
that Aetna lends a lot of money for construction and development,
so the company ought to make special efforts to lend money for
conservation as well.

Filer and Edwin B. Knauft, Aetna's vice-president for corporate
social responsibility, considered the request. "We wouldn't ordinarily make a loan on a swamp," Knauft told me. "And there
was some risk that Congress would not appropriate the money, and
we might end up holding a swamp that we would then have to sell
to a lumber company."

But on investigating, Aetna discovered that The Nature Conservancy had a record of no failures whatsoever in eighty lending
transactions. And the U.S. Department of the Interior verified that
the Great Dismal Swamp had a high priority for congressional
appropriations. Aetna agreed not only to give the loan, but did so
at about one percentage point below the going interest rate.

"Normally a situation like this would have required a higher rate
of interest than the market rate because of the risk involved,"
Knauft said. "But we feel that conservation is a part of our social
responsibility."

I asked John Filer how he justified charging the lower rate in
light of the reasoning I had heard expressed by most business
leaders. Didn't he feel, as they did, that the responsibility to
stockholders to make as much profit as possible prevented special
environmental considerations?

"I don't think you can say that your only responsibility is the short-term maximization of profits for your stockholders," Filer replied. "Granted we can't do so much that we become noncompetitive or that in fact we are frustrating the expectations of the stockholder. We are in the business of financing things but we also have a corporate responsibility. And it seemed to me that the preservation of the Dismal Swamp is in everybody's interest.

"I would defend this action as part of Aetna's social responsibility, but also as necessary for the long-term survival of business in this country. I happen to think that if the business community is perceived as having only one objective—that of making money for the stockholders—we won't be in business in twenty years. If we don't do business in the public interest as the public defines it, I think we are going to be so strangled that we won't be in business."

What about those who believe the business of business is profits, I asked.

"I disagree with them," Filer said. "We've got the constituencies of our shareholders, our employees, our customers, the community in which we do business, and the public at large. And people say, how come? And I say: because we have the capacity to affect all those people."

How does Aetna make certain it is not adversely affecting the public at large? I asked.

"What we try to do in the investment function is to have an assessment of whether we are contributing actively to something that retrospectively we might wish we hadn't," Filer said. "Both our real estate investment and bond investment departments look into these things. We say to our bond investment analysts, investment officers, and real estate investment officers, we want you to be very certain, as you process a loan, that you have looked at the environmental and other social issues in concert with the safety of the loan, the adequacy of the yield, and so forth."

Aetna, Equitable, and John Hancock may not find it comfortable to add environmental judgment to other factors normally considered in granting a loan. But they have found out that it does not cost them anything. On the contrary, it serves to protect them against losses or defaults on loans that can occur when a developer with unsound environmental plans runs into delays or is actually stopped by the inability to get necessary permits.

12

TO SAVE
A PIECE OF
THE PLANET

In the late 1960s, the few people in Jacksonville, Florida, who knew Willie Browne, or knew of him, considered him a kindly, eccentric, penniless old man. He never traveled, he had no telephone, no electricity. He lived alone on his 361 acres along the St. Johns River in his flimsy, tin-roofed, two-room shack and enjoyed walking about the woods watching the birds and the small animals.

People in Jacksonville thought him even more eccentric when they found out in 1968 that he wanted to give away all of his land, which was valued at $1 million. He wouldn't even talk to land developers or real estate people. He had no close relatives to look after the land. He wanted to find someone who would agree to keep the land just as it was.

In 1905, on Willie Browne's sixteenth birthday, he had made a pact with his father, William Henry Browne, a lawyer who had left

New York City in 1877 to settle in Jacksonville. "From now on, this land is yours," said the elder Browne. "Now you look after it. And don't let the hunters in."

Browne did not know anything about ecology—formally, that is—but he loved the way all of the wild living things related to one another. And he wanted the land preserved in its natural state so future generations would be able to see it too.

Approaching his eightieth birthday, he tried to give the land to the state or the city or even to a famous private agency. Several years earlier he had given a small part of it to the Campfire Girls for a camp. But now he couldn't find a taker who would accept his conditions. Finally, a friend told Browne about The Nature Conservancy.

Although Browne's land had been logged, it contained very old palmettos, excellent marshland, and abundant wildlife habitat. After a period of negotiations, the Conservancy agreed in 1969 to accept the land and keep it in its natural state in perpetuity. One other condition imposed by Browne was that the area not be named after him but that it be designated the Theodore Roosevelt Sanctuary.

The gift received a great deal of publicity throughout the nation and brought hundreds of letters to Willie Browne. In the remaining year before he died, Browne, with a friend's help, answered every one of the letters, including one from an 8-year-old boy in Racine, Wisconsin, who wrote: "If everyone donated their land like you did the world would be a very nice place to live in." The Conservancy has kept Browne's land in its natural state and in 1977 added an adjoining 176 acres donated by the Seaboard Coast Railroad.

Willie Browne exemplified an aspect of the environmental ethic that has shown a good deal of strength among Americans—the desire to save land or historic and cultural sites so that they will be preserved for future generations. Land saving has been most prevalent among private citizens and volunteer or nonprofit organizations. But their efforts have succeeded because individuals in government and business have been willing to put the ethic into action and set up systems to protect the land.

Preserving land and wildlife in the interests of all the people and for future generations has been an American tradition. It had early expression in the writings of Ralph Waldo Emerson, Henry David

Thoreau, and John Muir, and in the efforts of a few 19th-century explorers. Emerson and Thoreau emphasized immersing oneself in the world of nature, allowing unity with nature to lift one beyond ordinary materialistic values into spiritual awareness. Thoreau urged preservation of wilderness and areas of great natural beauty as national parks, and his phrase "In wildness is the preservation of the world," written in 1862, became one of the rallying cries of the 20th-century preservationists.

Even during the nation's expansionist period when the land was seen as a commodity to be exploited, there were individuals who were working to preserve natural America. When California's giant sequoia trees were threatened with destruction in 1864, some far-sighted citizens appealed to Congress. Acceding to their pleas, Congress turned over the federal lands in Yosemite Valley and the nearby Mariposa Grove of big trees to the state for protection. A quarter of a century later, through the influence of John Muir and others, the area was made a national park. When Yellowstone had been made the world's first national park in 1872 it was considered something of a miracle that 2 million acres of federal lands could be withdrawn from settlement or resource use to be preserved as a park. In the succeeding years millions of acres of public lands were set aside as national parks, forests, and wildlife refuges, historical and cultural areas, wilderness, wild rivers, scenic trails, and seashores. The National Park Service, established in 1916, was given the dual charge of conserving the scenery, wildlife, and natural and historic sites and providing for people's enjoyment of them in a manner that would leave them "unimpaired for the enjoyment of future generations."

Although all early national parks and forests were designated from public lands, a precedent was set in 1916 when some conservation-minded philanthropists assembled privately owned lands to form Acadia National Park in Maine. One of these wealthy men, John D. Rockefeller, Jr., was also involved in acquiring private lands in Wyoming which he and others donated to the federal government to form part of the Grand Teton National Park established in 1929. In 1956, his son Laurance S. Rockefeller donated the land that constitutes the Virgin Islands National Park.

In small and large ways other individual citizens and corporations have had a role in land saving. One unique effort took place in southern Arizona where Ariel and Frank Appleton owned a 3,200-acre cattle ranch and held grazing rights to another 4,600 acres of federal and state land. In 1968, the Appletons took a step that shocked their ranching neighbors in the scenic, mile-high country along the western piedmonts of Arizona's Huachuca Mountains about 70 miles southeast of Tucson.

They sold off their cattle and arranged for their land to be leased for $1 per year and donated over a period of time to a nonprofit foundation they set up called The Research Ranch. Their four grown children agreed with the plan and willingly gave up a potentially valuable inheritance.

The entire family has a keen environmental awareness and a special feeling that the land is really a trust to be cared for and to be left as a better place for future generations. To the Appletons, cattle grazing was not an appropriate use of the land, for the land's sake. They had often wondered what their land—comprised of short-grass prairie, oak savanna, oak woodland, and piñon juniper ecosystems—had been like originally. More than two centuries of grazing and other uses had ruined the natural balance the land had maintained in the days when native Indians roamed the country.

By 1968, the grasses on the Appletons' Elgin hereford ranch were just managing to survive. The ever-flowing streams of earlier years now ran only occasionally, remaining wildlife was dwindling, and each year more seedling cottonwoods along wet river washes failed to survive, until only a few remained.

The Appletons knew they could never completely restore the land to its original condition. But they could let it serve scientific purposes, not only as a preserved area, but as a test plot for research. They hoped to have the land serve as a gene bank for the diverse abundance of plant and animal life native to the area. They wanted to see the reintroduction of indigenous species that had been eliminated, such as the Mexican pronghorn antelope. They also thought it would be good to provide restricted areas for breeding certain select endangered species such as the Bolson tortoise, whose native Mexican habitats are similar. And finally, the Appletons hoped the ranch could serve as a catalyst, encouraging other private landowners to take similar steps to preserve areas that would be valuable for scientific study.

Now the ranch represents the only sizeable short-grass prairie in the Southwest from which domestic grazers have been removed so that plant and animal successions can occur in their natural settings. Human activity is kept to a minimum, and an assessment of long-range environmental consequences is made before any activity is conducted. The National Science Foundation has designated the ranch as one of 67 ecosystems throughout the nation officially selected as experimental ecological reserves.

The first scientist to use The Research Ranch was Charles D. Bonham. In 1969, while at the University of Arizona in Tucson, he took advantage of the opportunity to study the ecological changes resulting from the Appletons' letting the prairie return to its natural state. Later, while at Colorado State University, he used the ranch as a test area for a program sponsored by the U.S. Atomic Energy Commission. His project involved developing a new technique for reclassifying the 280 million acres of short-grass prairie east of the Rockies. The Research Ranch provided the large, ungrazed area needed for having periodic photographs made from planes and satellites with the information stored in computers. This data, added to ground samples made during the project, provides a soil inventory of plant species and establishes a basis for other ecological studies.

The husband and wife research team of Carl and Jane Bock are conducting studies on the role of wildfires in the grassland-savanna ecosystems in the Southwest. In most other places, human use and livestock grazing would prevent the Bocks from separating those impacts from the effects of fire.

Taking away the land's normal source of income has made the financial going rough for Ariel Appleton, who heads the foundation's board of trustees now that the Appletons are divorced. She spends much of her time raising funds and generating use of The Research Ranch. Despite the hardships and uncertainties, she remains committed to this land "laboratory," and is encouraged by growing recognition of the need for places like it.

"I had never realized how little is known about the interrelationships of all living things that make up a prairie community," she says. "How can we conserve or repair the land, plants, and wildlife systems unless we have a better understanding of their requirements and behavior—and how nature, on her own, stays healthier and more varied than when we step in with changes. It's like the field of medicine—how could a doctor treat a sick patient if he's never seen a well person?"

The land preservation ethic that motivates Ariel Appleton can also be seen in varying degrees in dozens of individual and corporate land owners who contribute in one way or another to preserving land. Many of them, motivated partly by a sense of altruism and partly by an enlightened self-interest, donate or sell below market value many ecologically important lands that would otherwise fall to development.

The ethic is most evident, however, in the dedicated professional land savers working in national nonprofit organizations such as The Nature Conservancy and the Trust for Public Land.

As a reporter I first started looking into The Nature Conservancy in 1969 and became fascinated by the highly motivated professional staff and the working membership of this innovative organization founded in 1951. Keeping alert for ecologically significant natural sites up for sale or areas needed by government agencies for parks, forests, or wildlife refuges, The Nature Conservancy staff obtains options on property, then seeks to raise money to purchase it. Sometimes the Conservancy acts as agent, showing a potential donor how the property can be used by a public agency and finding a public entity willing to accept the land and able to protect it. The Conservancy also shows the owner how a substantial tax deduction for the land can be obtained as the result of an outright gift or from selling below market value. Some of The Nature Conservancy members throughout the nation also help out by spotting lands to be saved, raising funds, conducting environmental education programs at the sites, or by helping to manage or protect the areas.

In 1969 I visited the Mianus River Gorge. A virtual wilderness where the Mianus River flows out of New York into Connecticut, less than an hour from Manhattan, it was the Conservancy's first land-saving success. It began in 1953, when a group of local citizens, who had formed a Mianus Gorge Group, joined forces with the then fledgling Nature Conservancy. The local citizens held benefits, borrowed money, sought contributions, and, with the help of The Nature Conservancy, purchased 60 acres in the gorge—an area also sought by a land developer. By 1969, subsequent land purchases had enlarged the reserve to over 300 acres. I watched a group of school children enjoying an environmental education outing at the site. Volunteers—mostly from local garden clubs—were serving as guides along the 5 miles of trails. They helped to identify some of the 800 species of plant and animal life in the habitat and explained the geologic history of the narrow gorge with its 150-foot cliffs, white water cataracts, and forested glens.

Today, Mianus Gorge is still protected and has more than 7,000 visitors a year. But that early success has been overshadowed by some of the more recent acquisitions and activities of The Nature Conservancy, which, in its first 27 years, saved more than a million acres in 1,985 projects scattered over 47 states, the Caribbean, Latin America, and Canada.

The Conservancy has helped create new areas or vital additions for 18 national parks and national recreation areas, 24 national wildlife refuges, and 40 national forests. The areas include the 4,300-acre Kipahula Valley, added to Haleakala National Park in Hawaii; 2,800 acres added to the Golden Gate National Recreation Area in California; creation of the Great Dismal Swamp National Wildlife Refuge in Virginia and North Carolina; and the Mason Neck Wildlife Refuge in Virginia.

A whole string of barrier islands off the coast of Virginia, ripe for second-home or resort development, has been purchased by the Conservancy. The 35,000 acres constitute the largest privately owned refuge in the world. In the Midwest, the Conservancy has preserved examples of diminishing grasslands and prairies in 20 sanctuaries in five states.

The Conservancy staff now numbers about two hundred, including several ecologists working on a natural heritage program that assists states in inventorying their natural features and developing plans for preserving a state's most critical areas. The Conservancy works with corporations to secure gifts of land or to buy land at far below its market value, and also receives cash contributions from corporations. In 1976, the Exxon Corporation, U.S.A. gave the Conservancy $60,000 to establish a data bank on U.S. natural areas and to help support the Conservancy's Natural Heritage Program. The following year, the Andrew M. Mellon Foundation granted the Conservancy $600,000 to consolidate and expand the Natural Heritage Program, already underway in nine states.

In North Carolina's state natural heritage program the Conservancy helped inventory natural areas that needed to be preserved. Noticing that the inventory showed that the Federal Paper Board Company, Inc., owned a unique geological formation called a pocosin, an upland swamp area that was home to five endangered plant species, Nature Conservancy president Patrick F. Noonan arranged to see the company's president, John R. Kennedy. When Noonan mentioned the specific area, Kennedy replied that the company did not consider it to be economically productive woodland unless it was drained. Noonan emphasized its value as a wildlife habitat, and the company wound up donating the land, valued at $4 million, to the Conservancy, receiving a tax credit for half that amount.

Noonan, who brings youth and dynamism to his leadership of the Conservancy, holds a master's degree in both business administration and regional planning. He has been a real estate broker, professional appraiser, and land planning consultant, and combines expertise in these areas with a single-minded determination to wrest important pieces of land from exploitation. He describes The Nature Conservancy as the "real estate arm" of the conservation movement. "We don't lobby, we don't know anything about toxic substances or clear-cutting," he says. "But we do know a lot about natural areas that need to be protected, and how to acquire them."

Noonan and his associates, realizing that neither they nor the government can purchase all the land that ought to be preserved, are also seeking to promote ways of protecting land short of outright acquisition, such as through conservation easements. Property owners can sell or donate an easement to the Conservancy or to a government agency, giving up their rights to develop the land. The advantage to owners in most of these cases is the promise or assurance of a lower tax rate on the land.

The Conservancy owns and manages 670 areas and most of them are open for public hiking or nature study, although some are reserved for scientific research. At a number of areas, student stewardship programs have been started in which nearby high school and college students and teachers participate in gathering information on the diverse natural elements that make up the preserves. The students also work with adults on local committees to preserve and protect the areas.

Almost every one of the Conservancy's land-saving transactions includes some element of the land ethic, manifested in the private owner's desire to see the land preserved for posterity or in the efforts of those contributing funds for preservation or working to raise these funds. Noonan acknowledges that some of the acquisitions are seen by the seller as a good business deal. But in most cases, while tax advantages are a consideration to the seller or donor—and in the case of corporations, the public relations value is important—the concept of saving the land for the future becomes a factor in every transaction. And each one, like Willie Browne and his Florida homestead, has its own little story.

One of these transactions involved a large area around the Santee River north of Charleston, South Carolina, a habitat for many birds and animals including two endangered species, the southern bald eagle and the American alligator. The area also sheltered the oldest known egret colony in the nation. Since 1896, some 25,000 acres around the Santee had been the private hunting preserve of the Santee Club, with an exclusive membership limited to 25 which for a time included President Grover Cleveland. By 1974, the club was being used sparsely by its 21 members. The club property, however, was the key to a vast wild area bounded on the south by the Cape Romain National Wildlife Refuge, on the west by the Francis Marion National Forest, and on the north by other private shooting preserves.

But the Santee Club's property also had become a potential resort development area, and the property was valued as high as $21 million—if the members wanted to sell. A nearby island had just been sold to the oil-rich government of Kuwait for resort development.

Two of the Santee Club members familiar with the work of The Nature Conservancy, Forrest Mars (of Mars Candy Company) and John T. Dorrance (of Campbell Soup Company), got in touch with Noonan. The club had long protected rookeries and conserved wildlife—hunting was minimal, they told Noonan. The members had not joined the club to make money, so they did not feel a need to sell the land for profit.

"They weren't acting as businessmen or even stewards of their own fortunes," says Noonan, "but mostly as stewards of the land." In deciding to give the Santee Club's land to the Conservancy, however, the members were not acting entirely out of altruism. Each member was able to take a sizeable tax credit on the gift. On the other hand, if monetary gain had been the motive, a sale to a developer could have brought a considerably higher net gain.

Noonan and his staff then worked with South Carolina Governor John C. West to reach agreement for the state to accept and maintain the club property. After receiving the gift of the 23,000 acres of Santee Club land, The Nature Conservancy deeded the land over to the State of South Carolina, which agreed to manage it as a state wildlife area, the first part of a planned larger coastal reserve. The state allows controlled surf fishing along the 14 miles of ocean beach, provides nature trails and a canoe "trail" through the marshes, and maintains two primitive camping areas. A reverter agreement assures that if the state should ever permit commercial development or exploitation, the property would go back to the Conservancy.

In many instances lands have been saved as a result of joint efforts of corporate interests, the federal government and The Nature Conservancy. The acquisition of a large block of land in the Great Dismal Swamp is one such instance. In 1970, the Union Camp Paper Company, in the process of reviewing its landholdings, pondered what to do with its 49,000 acres in the Great Dismal Swamp in southern Virginia bordering North Carolina, land that had not been logged since the 1940s. There was little chance that it could ever be logged economically, and the company was thinking of joining another corporation in farming a major section of it. Or the company could sell or give it to the government, but nobody at Union Camp knew how to value the land for such purposes. And how would the stockholders' interests be protected in a gift of land worth millions of dollars?

About this time The Nature Conservancy found out that a planned interstate highway with its resulting commercial development might endanger part of the land, an area of both ecological and historical value, which local citizens had been trying to save. Although logged at least once, the land supports loblolly pine barrens, mixed swamp forests of red maple, pond pine and cedar, cypress swamps and evergreen shrub bogs, and is a crossroads of northern and southern species of wildlife. George Washington once owned much of the area, and it is the setting of Henry Wadsworth Longfellow's poem "The Slave in the Dismal Swamp" and Harriet Beecher Stowe's novel *Dred: A Tale of the Great Dismal Swamp.*

The Conservancy made scientific studies to determine the preservation need and secured the support of conservationists in the two states. Then the Conservancy approached Union Camp executives, suggesting a donation of the land in the public interest or a bargain sale at half the fair market value.

Company officials acknowledged that preservation might be the highest and best use for the Dismal Swamp holdings, but had to recognize the interests of their stockholders with such a large capital asset involved. Negotiations continued for two years.

The Conservancy meantime approached the U.S. Fish and Wildlife Service to see whether the area could be made into a federal wildlife refuge, providing a gift could be arranged. Finally, the government agency, the corporation, and the Conservancy reached agreement. In a ceremony at the Department of the Interior on February 22, 1973, Union Camp Corporation donated its holdings, valued at $12.6 million, to the Conservancy, which in turn conveyed the land to the federal government for a wildlife refuge. Union Camp was able to deduct the appraised value from taxable earnings, thus adding about $6.3 million to corporate net income.

On a visit to Union Camp headquarters in Wayne, New Jersey, I asked board chairman and chief executive officer Alexander Calder, Jr. if there had been any adverse reaction from stockholders to giving away 49,000 acres of land, even if the company did get a tax advantage.

"I sent all stockholders a letter beforehand, telling them what we were doing. I wrote that although it was an economically sound thing to do, Union Camp was proud of having the opportunity to participate in the preservation of the country's heritage in this way," Calder said. "And you know, we got 500 letters back approving of it and not a single criticism. We put the tax savings into a fund for purchase of replacement land. And we started a land legacy program to identify and preserve other parts of our holdings that have special ecological or historical significance," he added.

Since 1970 the company has donated eight other pieces of land, including 16,000 acres in Okefenokee Swamp to be added to a national wildlife refuge.

As we sat at his long conference table, Calder explained how his own interest in conservation had expanded since the Dismal Swamp venture. "Until that time we had never had close dealings with any conservation group," he said. "We were guilty of the same feelings in reverse that some of the environmentally concerned groups have about business. We put them all in the same pocket and looked at them with considerable suspicion—just the way they looked at us.

"Several of the pieces of land we gave the Conservancy I had no idea were significant at all ecologically. But the Conservancy had identified them as vital to the nation's heritage, and we decided the gift process was the best use of the land. Then I decided to do my share (in 1977 Calder became a member of The Nature Conservancy's Board of Trustees) by going to a number of my friends in the corporate area who perhaps hadn't done an inventory of their lands. I explained the Conservancy's operations to them and asked if Pat Noonan or one of his people could talk with them. Every one of the ten corporate leaders I've approached so far has contributed either land or money."

Realizing that government policies can change, The Nature Conservancy made certain that the Dismal Swamp would be kept intact by placing restrictions in the deed before turning the property over to the secretary of the interior. For instance, vehicles are excluded from all except existing roads and no materials may be removed except to manage and improve the integrity and natural character of the refuge.

"The refuge must be used for environmental and ecological purposes consistent with the enhancement of the ecosystems of the swamp," says Noonan. "If these concepts are not followed, the swamp reverts back automatically with title vested in the Conservancy. The Conservancy can file suit to prove the misuse of the area, as can any citizen, since the Great Dismal Swamp is a gift to the people of the United States." Similar restrictions or "reverters" are placed in all the property deeds which the Conservancy turns over to public bodies.

During 1976 and 1977 The Nature Conservancy directed the two-year bicentennial conservation project of the American Land Trust, a national citizens' committee of business, conservation, and civic leaders formed "to save vital portions of the nation's diverse ecological heritage as a lasting contribution to the future." Citizens and corporations made outright donations of property or combinations of gifts and sales, or sales at far below market value. More than $320,000 for purchase of lands was raised in a special program of the four thousand local clubs affiliated with the National Council of State Garden Clubs. At the end of the two-year project the land trust program had succeeded in preserving 335,000 acres of land. The value of the land saved and cash gifts received exceeded $100 million.

The single most valuable corporate gift in the program was 26,000 acres valued at $13 million donated by International Paper Company. Known as the Savannahs at Genesis Point, the area includes marshes, wooded uplands, and live-oak hummocks along the Georgia coast bordering the Intracoastal Waterway. A week after the International Paper Company donation, a Georgia philanthropist, George W. Woodruff, put up $4 million toward acquisition of 25,000-acre Ossabaw Island, a barrier island just across the waterway from the Genesis Point property. Ossabaw Island's owners, Eleanore Torrey West and her niece and three nephews, agreed to sell the land, valued in excess of $15 million, to The Nature Conservancy for $8 million. The State of Georgia put up the other $4 million and Ossabaw is now a State Heritage Reserve to be protected in perpetuity by the State of Georgia.

In May 1978 the Conservancy's acquisition of 90% of Santa Cruz Island near Santa Barbara, California, resulted from actions that demonstrated elements of an environmental ethic in the owner, several corporations and foundations, and the public. The owner, Dr. Cary Stanton, had turned down fabulous offers from developers for the 55,000-acre ranch—most of a 21-mile-long island lying 25 miles off the California coast. The flora and fauna, including a number of endangered and threatened species, are much the same as when the Spanish explorer Cabrillo discovered the island in 1542. Stanton, who has lived on the island since 1950, wants it to be kept the way it is for future generations of Americans. The Nature Conservancy received a $75,000 grant from Atlantic Richfield Foundation to put an option on the purchase of

154 FOOTPRINTS ON THE PLANET

the Stanton land for $2.5 million, a mere fraction of what it might bring commercially. Atlantic Richfield also gave $1 million on a "matching" basis of $1 for every $3 raised by the Conservancy toward the $4 million needed for purchase of the property and future management of the island. Within 60 days of taking the option, $2.5 million had been raised. Funds came from another oil company and two foundations, plus $175,000 from 1,500 citizens participating in a nationwide "Save an Acre of Santa Cruz" campaign. The Conservancy will own 15,000 acres of Santa Cruz outright and have a 30-year "conservation easement" on the remaining land, which it will eventually acquire. The Conservancy plans to open the island to the public under conditions that will allow its natural values to be preserved, with environmental education becoming a major use of the land.

To help finance small local land saving projects The Nature Conservancy often advances money for acquisition from its revolving fund (which has grown from a few thousand dollars to $4 million). It loans the money at a low interest rate, and Conservancy members and other local people raise the money to pay back the revolving fund as quickly as they can. It is often a challenge to raise the funds, and some unique methods have been used.

To pay back an advance for purchase of the shores of Thompson Pond, one of the best locations for waterbirds in New York's entire Central Hudson Valley region, the local committee sold "shares" of beauty. Their slogan for the campaign was "Buy now, enjoy always." Among items which buyers could purchase but not own were:

1 black oak 19 feet in circumference.................	$500
1 acre of blue sky with silhouetted wood ducks	100
1 hollow tree with pileated woodpecker's nest..........	10
1 muskrat house (present occupant will remodel in fall) .	5

Willing purchasers of these invaluable bargains went a long way toward repaying the original $20,000 loan.

While The Nature Conservancy has given priority to ecologically significant remote areas that ought to be saved, some conservationists in recent years have recognized another need—to provide more open space and natural areas right where the majority of Americans live, in or near big cities. These areas would not rate as national parks—they might not even be very "natural"—they might be as small and seemingly insignificant as a vacant lot.

One who decided to do something about this urban need was Huey D. Johnson, former western regional director of The Nature Conservancy, who had been the organization's star land saver. In 1973, Johnson formed the Trust for Public Land, a nonprofit group that concentrates on providing urban open space while also saving wilderness and other large remote natural areas. In addition to vigorous nationwide land saving activities and pioneering new techniques of land preservation and funding, members of the Trust's small staff operate a training program.

When I visited the informal Trust for Public Land offices in a second-floor converted loft just across Market Street from San Francisco's financial district, I found negotiations underway for donation of land for a city park. The conference room was filled with black inner-city residents finding out how to acquire, without cost, a rubbish-filled vacant lot in their block that they could turn into a community garden. In a back office a retired business executive was taking a videotape recorded training course in how to outfox a land-hungry developer in the competition to acquire choice open space that suddenly comes on the real estate market.

In its first five years the Trust for Public Land acquired major new parks and open-space lands for the cities of San Francisco and Los Angeles, for Lincoln City, Oregon, and for Volusia County, Florida. It has saved shoreline and county parkland for Marin County, California, is working to provide an 1,100-acre addition to Point Reyes National Seashore in California, acquired a dozen ranches to add to the Golden Gate National Recreation Area in California and the Sawtooth National Recreation Area in Idaho, obtained a 2,400-acre regional park for the State of New Jersey, 20 miles from downtown Manhattan. And it is well into an innovative program making garden plots and small parks out of vacant city lots, beginning with Oakland, California, and Newark, New Jersey.

One urban project started with a phone call from a woman who said she and her brothers wanted to give a surprise eightieth birthday gift to their father, a San Francisco philanthropist and civic leader. She asked if some land could be obtained and given to

the city in the name of her father, Daniel E. Koshland. Huey
Johnson and his associate Gregory Archbald suggested the possibility of acquiring land for a small park in a poorer, inner-city
section where there was great need.

The family liked the idea, and the Trust for Public Land began
an extensive search. It discovered a site in the Fillmore district,
where a fire had just gutted a 30-unit tenement adjacent to two
vacant lots. The land was on a hill with an excellent view. It was
near two federal housing projects and was in a depressed neighborhood. About 8,000 residents, mostly black and Mexican-American,
many elderly people, and a host of young children live within a six-
block-square area which has no regular park.

For several months the Trust for Public Land worked on the
various owners trying to talk them into selling the three pieces of
property. When TPL staff members finally secured options on the
property, they had to talk the San Francisco Park commissioners
and the mayor into accepting the park. The Koshland family
agreed to supply the $300,000 purchase price and an additional
$300,000 for developing the lots into a park.

After the neighborhood residents raised objections to the landscape architect's original design, TPL arranged for the residents to
have a say in the planning. Delegates from the neighborhood met
once a week for twelve weeks, then went en masse to the architect's
office for a discussion. The final plan met their desires.

When I went to see it in the summer of 1977, the park was in
final stages of completion, and had something for everyone—except
supervision. The city had not yet put in professional staffing. Some
of the original palms and pine trees had been saved, in keeping
with the feeling of the original site. At the top of the rectangular,
hilly, acre-size park was a small circular cement area for skating or
a half-court game of basketball, and next to it a small amphithea-
ter. A sitting area with checker tables for the elderly had been built
behind a windscreen at the highest part of the park, with a view of
the San Francisco skyline and a glimpse of the Bay Bridge. On the
lower end were two structures for climbing, swings, and a
sculptured cement slide.

At the entrance, a plaque contributed by the neighborhood
reads: "This park is a gift from the Koshland children to their
father and the city he loves. The realization of this dream was

made possible with the help and support of this neighborhood."

The activity in inner-city areas has been the most difficult but the most satisfying for the Trust for Public Land staff. Their National Urban Land Program, with its experiments now underway in Oakland and Newark, seeks to develop a process whereby neighborhoods can acquire land without relying on the government. The TPL staff helps them acquire, design, and develop some of the rubbish-strewn vacant lots into community gardens or recreation areas.

On a huge tax parcel map of Oakland, TPL people plotted all of the vacant land. In one East Oakland area that had 950 vacant lots, they held meetings with thirty community organizations to see if the citizens had any interest in turning some of them into parks or other uses. Although the organizations agreed to cooperate, the local citizens shrank from the responsibility of owning the land individually.

In 1976, TPL staff member Steve Costa approached six savings and loan associations in the area, explained the program, and asked for donations of lots that had been returned to them through foreclosures. Costa sold the program on the basis of giving the savings institutions an opportunity to make a contribution to improving the community as well as showing citizens that the savings group had a sense of social responsibility. The institution would also have the financial advantage of not having to pay taxes on the land. All six of the savings and loan associations agreed to cooperate and, in the first six months of the program, donated 18 lots.

To bolster community participation, Johnson enlisted two black community leaders in the program. The Bank of America loaned one of its real estate appraisers, Arnold Bellow, to work with TPL for a year. And Bellow, who had become interested in the urban land program through the early community meetings, encouraged the minority groups to become involved in improving the land, setting up gardens, and developing small parks. TPL also hired Leonard Colar to develop a "Green Guerrilla" program for the summer in which high school students clear areas, plant trees, and do other conservation work in Oakland.

When I visited Oakland six months after the program's start, five new small parks were in the planning stage. Eleven community gardens were already in place in what had been vacant lots. One had been deep in rubble only two weeks before my visit. Some people in the neighborhood had heard about what TPL was doing, contacted Costa, and told him they wanted to develop a garden on an abandoned lot on 39th Avenue. Costa discovered that it was owned by Imperial Savings and Loan, one of the savings and loan associations that had agreed to cooperate in the program. The bank turned the lot over to TPL in two days time. Costa arranged for a company run by former convicts and drug addicts to clear the lot and till the ground (cost: $50). Water hookup was arranged ($25) and new pipe installed ($10). Fencing was purchased at half price ($15), by arrangement with a local store. Men, women, and children from 16 families in the block met several times to decide how to use the lot (they wanted it divided into 16 plots, each 10x10 feet square, with a small area in the back for a sand box and a place for babies and very young children to stay while their mothers were working in the gardens).

A community design school volunteered a student to help in landscape design. By the end of the second week, at a cost of less than $150, the 39th Avenue lot was a working community garden and a few seedlings were already poking green shoots through the dark soil. A year later, residents dug a 35-foot well and, with a grant from the National Center for Appropriate Technology, brought Oakland its first windmill in eighty years. It pumps water into storage tanks for the garden.

On East 9th Street I visited with a retired man as he worked with a neighbor in the new community garden. Frank Nunes proudly showed me his beets, radishes, turnips, broccoli, eggplant, and three kinds of beans. "My kids, my niece, they got no garden," he told me. So the new garden plot will supply food for all of them.

Costa took me to see the site that had presented the greatest engineering challenge to date. It was a hillside so steep and eroded that buildings had long ago caved in. It was such a tangle of weeds and other vegetation that it had been nicknamed "Jungle Hill." But it was an open area in a neighborhood that sorely needed a park, so with cooperation and planning ideas from the largely Mexican-American neighborhood, TPL went to work figuring out how to make it usable. Two lots on the hill were owned by savings and loan companies, two others were held by the county for unpaid taxes, and three lots were privately owned. TPL persuaded the savings and loan companies to donate their two lots, paid the $500 back taxes owed on two others, and bought outright the remaining three lots for $1,000. Other volunteers pitched in. The local chapter of the California Society of Engineers gave two hundred hours to make an engineering study and a plan for grading the site. A group of Navy Seabees who had organized a company called the Weekend Warriors did most of the grading work free. Several other groups joined with neighborhood volunteers to design and build a play area. A company donated trees. Soon Jungle Hill had become a park and playground worth $225,000. California Governor Edmund G. "Jerry" Brown, Jr. came to Oakland on Arbor Day 1978 to officially open the area, plant an oak tree, and give a talk which he admitted lasted longer than his State of the State address.

A nine-member board elected from the community directs a land trust which now holds title to the area. The Trust for Public Land has organized 33 of the Oakland parks and garden sites into nine neighborhood land trusts. Neighborhood leaders organize three or four area sites into some of the trusts. The neighbors elect members to a board of trustees who meet quarterly and make policy for their trust. Title has been turned over to these local trusts, although a reverter clause provides that the land goes back to the Trust for Public Land in case the local trust falls apart. In addition to owning a piece of their neighborhood, these Oakland people for the first time are having an opportunity to initiate and follow through with decisions about land use.

In a similar neighborhood land-trust program started in Newark, TPL has incorporated five trusts to hold title to 25 properties, mostly active play spaces in congested inner-city neighborhoods which lacked recreation areas.

Costa has found a gradual change of attitude toward the environment in the Oakland neighborhoods. Once a vacant lot has been made into a garden, some neighbors clean up their own yards, paint their houses, plant flowers. The children watch avidly as the plants grow, and they learn respect for the land. Residents having experienced the rewards of working together have gone on to deal with issues such as crime, housing, or education.

Education of another sort is paramount among the Trust for Public Land's activities. Its founder, Johnson, and Joel Kuperberg, who became president when Johnson was tapped in 1977 by Governor Brown to head the state's Department of Resources, have concentrated on building a new profession of land savers by teaching the techniques of land preservation so that others can practice in their own communities across the nation. TPL tries to teach not only the complexities of tax matters, financing, and law needed in this specialized new profession, but also the sociopolitical skills of community organization, group leadership, and fund raising.

The TPL staff reviews every transaction for the lessons that can be learned. Much of the information has been assembled in a two-volume, 800-page training manual. In addition, video tapes record sessions in which the participants in a transaction criticize their mistakes and analyze new knowledge acquired. A grant from the Rockefeller Brothers Fund enabled TPL to launch its formal training program in 1976. Those taking the training include Trust for Public Land student field representatives, volunteers from many parts of the nation (mostly retired business executives), as well as workers in conservation organizations, and city, state, and federal employees involved in land purchases and land acquisition.

Although the Trust for Public Land gives high priority to saving relatively small natural areas in or near cities, it devotes a large amount of activity to saving ecologically significant shorelands, wetlands, or mountains threatened with development. Joel Kuperberg himself has sparked some major land preservation in Florida, his native state, where he formerly served as director of the state land agency. In 1976 some 3,000 acres in the Florida Keys worth $3.1 million were obtained by Kuperberg and TPL for the Federal Great White Heron National Refuge at a cost of $1.3 million.

In 1974 Kuperberg set his sights on obtaining for the state's environmentally endangered land acquisition program two tracts owned by the largest community development company in Florida, the General Development Corporation. One of the tracts, a 7,000-acre area that included 22 miles of shoreline, adjoined GDC's large (20,000 population) development, Port Charlotte, near the Gulf of Mexico. The land Kuperberg had his eye on consisted mostly of mangrove swamps and wetlands that formed a breeding ground for many forms of marine life. His other target was on the eastern side of the state, 840 acres near GDC's smaller Port St. Lucie development. The land featured ponds, lakes, and marshes which are a feeding and nesting place for migratory birds and a superb bass fishing area. The Port St. Lucie land was a vital part of a long strip called the Savannas, which the state sought to purchase. Both areas were within the state's environmentally endangered lands acquisition program plan. But land could not be purchased unless there was a willing seller. If Kuperberg could convince General Development to go along, he then planned to get a legally binding agreement that the lands would be fully protected by the state and that citizen groups be allowed to participate in managing the two areas.

When Kuperberg approached General Development, he found an immediate ally in the company's vice-president for environmental affairs, Arthur Harper. But the chances for any kind of deal seemed remote. General Development was not in a position at the time to use the potential tax benefits to advantage. It had been protecting the land in its natural state for a number of years and had no current plans to develop it. And the company had some doubts about the ability of the state to protect the land over a long period of time. Company officials recalled that in the past, political maneuverings had resulted in the state's selling off large blocks of public land for development purposes.

The company raised the issue that if the state gave these lands preservation status, this might hinder GDC's ability to obtain permits for developing its remaining lands adjacent to the newly preserved tract. GDC would also need assurance that Kuperberg's proposal met with local citizen approval in the areas.

Environmentalists, naturally suspicious of developers, had to be sold on the proposal. Some of them thought that the company, unable to get permits to build on these wetlands, was just trying to use this good deed as political leverage so it would be able to do more building. And the Florida state cabinet would have to be persuaded to purchase the proposed tracts and agree to any restrictions placed on management of the lands.

What helped Kuperberg overcome these and multitudinous other difficulties that arose during the more than three years of negotiations was that the key individuals involved in the transaction—the conservation leaders, the management of GDC, and Florida Governor Reuben Askew—all had a sense of the environ-

mental ethic. They could see the necessity for preserving the areas
intact for future generations. Kuperberg's efforts finally paid off in
early 1978 when the Trust for Public Land bought the acreage from
General Development at one-sixth of its appraised value and
resold it to the state. The state accepted the land subject to 15 deed
restrictions which would assure that the lands would be kept in
wilderness status. TPL organized citizen land trusts in both areas to
oversee the management of the lands and act as an advisory
council.

Kuperberg gives much of the credit for the Port Charlotte and
Port St. Lucie land saving to Harper. General Development
Corporation has a better record than most Florida developers,
emphasizing home building and community development, not just
land sales. GDC has been opposed by environmentalists in the
past—especially because of its high-density housing, construction of
canals, and some practices that caused pollution. But in recent
years the company has been out front on a number of environmental initiatives. One year after Harper was hired as a lawyer to cope
with environmental regulations, he was made a vice-president, and
he extended his activities to include more than just coping with
government regulations.

In 1975 Harper and GDC engineers and biologists worked with
the Florida Audubon Society helping the state to draft workable
but tough regulations for control of dredge-and-fill pollution in
state-controlled wetland areas. In 1977 Harper testified before a
congressional committee urging stronger wetlands controls. Harper
worked with the company's home-site development department to
create an Environmental Quality Laboratory at Port Charlotte
(with 16 scientists and staff) which is responsible for water quality
and marine habitat control at all seven GDC communities and
does outside contract work for the state and federal governments.
And GDC has for eight years been developing a low-pressure
sewer system providing low-cost central waste treatment to avoid
septic system drain field sources of water pollution.

GDC does not have a written environmental policy, but its top
management philosophy provides for a strong sense of social
responsibility.

"I feel the company must have a responsibility to the customer,
to the public at large, to our employees, and to our shareholders,"

says GDC President William R. Avella. "Part of that responsibility is helping make the world a better place in which to live, and that means making every effort to preserve as much of the land as possible in its natural state."

The other element that made Kuperberg's Florida land-saving efforts successful was the assistance of Governor Askew, who supported TPL's proposals and helped to gain the Florida cabinet's approval for the state's purchases of the Port Charlotte and the Port St. Lucie lands. At the formal ceremony transferring the Port St. Lucie land to the state, Governor Askew spoke of saving land "to let the whole system of nature work. . . . When we save nature's little jewels—and that's what this Savanna area is—we can say to our children that the bass fishing will be as good for your children as it was for me, and a place for rare birds and aquatic life and plants. We know that if we do not grow in harmony with nature, if we do not preserve most of our valuable wetlands, we will not only degrade our immediate lifestyle and that of future generations, but we can also ruin our economic chances."

The man who started the Trust for Public Land, Huey Johnson, is one of the growing cadre of land savers whose life was changed by reading Aldo Leopold. Johnson is a pragmatic visionary who started his career selling food-packaging machinery before drifting around the world for three years looking for a purpose in life. Back in the United States, he got a job in the summer of 1962 at Lake Tahoe as a seasonal biologist for the California State Fish and Wildlife Department. One evening at dinner, his boss, Almo Cordone, quoted from Aldo Leopold's *A Sand County Almanac* and asked Johnson if he had ever read it.

"I had never even heard of Aldo Leopold," recalls Johnson of the incident. "But when I read it, and especially his essay, 'The Land Ethic,' my life was changed. The land ethic became my theme of life."

Johnson, who over the past fifteen years has participated in the preservation of several hundred endangered parts of America, believes that land saving is really an art form. "What do we remember from the Renaissance three hundred years later?" he asks. "How the police system worked, or the transportation system or political forums? No, we remember the art works which we can see today. I hope that three hundred years from now what will be remembered as the best of our age is the art work of the parks preserved, the natural areas, the green space of the city."

Johnson believes that the most important part of saving land takes place in people's minds, in finding ways to involve citizens so that the saving of land is a result of participating in the land ethic. "The child who donates a nickel to help save a piece of the wild may forever keep a commitment to that land which he may cherish years later. Sometimes the worst thing that could happen is to have private land donated for public purposes without any involvement of the people."

The people of Coeur d'Alene, Idaho, proved Johnson's point a few years ago. One day in 1972, some donation cans appeared at Coeur d'Alene's Borah Elementary School, bearing the label: "Help Save Tubbs Hill." The donation cans were a small part of lawyer Scott Reed's campaign to save a piece of land needed by his community.

The young lawyer and his environmental activist wife, Mary Lou, took sixty of the school children for an outing on Tubbs Hill.

"Any of you kids ever been here before?" asked Reed.

Every hand shot up.

"How many times?"

"Five ... ten ... twenty ... a hundred!" they shouted.

"I bet you thought the city owned the whole thing," said Reed. Heads nodded. He explained the threat to Tubbs Hill, where for generations the citizens had hiked the trails, scrambled up and down its steep slope, picnicked on its rocky ledges, and swum off its beaches in the invigorating cold water of Lake Coeur d'Alene.

The city already owned and protected much of the 135 acres of Tubbs Hill by purchasing the shoreline and a water supply area, explained Reed. Two homes had been built on one acre of the hill. The problem was that owners of the remaining 34 acres had recently sold a half-acre lot for home construction and formally requested a sewer extension from the city. Reed took the children to see the two homes already built on Tubbs Hill. If others built homes like this all over their favorite part of Tubbs Hill, where could they hike or swim or play, he asked.

The urbanization of Tubbs Hill had appeared inevitable when Reed started his campaign. While most of the townspeople weren't happy about the prospects of development on the hill, they took the attitude that it was a part of "progress," or they theorized that even if it hurt the town, a person had a right to do what he wanted with his own property.

When Reed started his campaign he sought advice and assistance from Huey Johnson, then just getting going with the Trust for Public Land. With neither the Reeds nor Johnson knowing just how they would raise the money, the Trust made an offer of $250,000 for the entire 34-acre parcel. Other environmental activists in Coeur d'Alene joined the Reeds in urging the city council to turn down the sewer request. They let it be known that they had a plan to purchase the entire acreage.

The city council voted against the sewer. Reed then persuaded the landowners to cancel their contract for the lot sale and accept the TPL offer. The owners gave Reed and TPL an option. Now all they had to do was find a way to raise a quarter of a million dollars.

Reed set out to raise $50,000 from Coeur d'Alene residents, and to get the city government to put up $75,000 to buy the land for a park. Then he hoped to get the State of Idaho to apply for matching funds from the Federal Bureau of Outdoor Recreation under provisions of the Land and Water Conservation Fund. He knew that some of this money, derived from offshore oil-lease sales, was available to help states purchase parks and open space.

The Coeur d'Alene city council doubted it could commit $75,000, but agreed to sign the federal grant application, with the stipulation that it could back out at any time. Just when the federal fund application was approved, however, the Coeur d'Alene police and fire departments organized to demand higher salaries. When the city council increased the salaries 16%, nothing was left for the Tubbs Hill purchase.

The owner of one of the two homes on Tubbs Hill started a campaign against the purchase. He wrote anti-Reed letters to the local paper. He even ran a paid advertisement showing an enormous space-needle building right on top of Tubbs Hill, which he claimed could be built as a tourist attraction, and which he said would bring $135,000 a year in taxes.

Reed met that argument by gathering data to show that residential development of Tubbs Hill would in fact lose money for the city. The cost of supplying services and schools would far exceed the income from taxes. The outrageous space-needle advertisement actually served to strengthen the convictions of some of the city council members that the area should be saved.

But one council member asked Reed: "How do we know how the people feel and think about Tubbs Hill—why don't you get a poll by some independent group?" Reed recalls that about that time he started thinking this was like the fairy tales where, if you want to marry the princess, you get this "little" task to do, like slaying a dragon. Then when you've slain the dragon and come back to claim your bride, her father gives you just one more "little" task, and so on.

Reed persuaded the local junior college to have a political science class conduct a poll. The students set up business in a downtown parking lot and interviewed 100 people: 90 said the city ought to acquire Tubbs Hill. But the city council member still wasn't convinced. "You haven't talked to enough people to make a valid determination." The mayor then suggested having the Chamber of Commerce poll the business community.

Reed feared that few merchants would opt for a park, especially if the funds to purchase it might result in a tax increase. To his amazement, however, 52% of the merchants voted in favor! So the mayor and the city council finally were convinced. They juggled the budget and found $72,000 for the purchase.

Now to raise the remaining $53,000. Reed and the Trust for Public Land had two options: seek larger contributions from a few wealthy "angels" or try to raise the money from local citizens. They decided they had to do both. Johnson worked on the large gifts; Reed tried to generate support in Coeur d'Alene.

As Reed campaigned, attitudes began to change. Even a lumber mill manager who frequently opposed Reed's environmental pursuits was heard to say: "As a matter of principle, anything Scott Reed is for, we've got to be against. But at this price, you can't pass up Tubbs Hill. It's too good a bargain."

Nearly everyone joined the battle. The Junior Chamber of Commerce sponsored bake sales and other fund raisers. The kids at the Borah school dropped their pennies, nickels, and dimes into the donation cans, and also collected empty bottles, tin and aluminum cans, and old newspapers in town and sold them for recycling, raising $60.

As more people got involved and publicity spread, contributions increased. The local camera club, which had built a trail on the hill, raffled off a painting of Tubbs Hill and raised $800 by selling $1 chances. A woman in a small California town wrote that she could remember playing on the hill as a child, and wanted to have a part in saving it. She sent $500. At a benefit luncheon, prominent local people pledged $8,000.

With town sentiment strongly favoring the purchase, Reed went to the owner of the land. "Would you consider waiving the interest payments for the benefit of the community?" The developer agreed, in effect reducing the price $9,000.

Meanwhile in San Francisco, Johnson, armed with some photographs and a presentation, approached George Frederick Jewett, Jr., a trustee of a family fund, the George Frederick Jewett Foundation. Jewett had grown up in Coeur d'Alene and was one of the owners of Potlatch Forest Industries, whose lumber mill is on the shore of Lake Coeur d'Alene, a few hundred yards from Tubbs Hill. Jewett (whose foundation has no direct connection with Potlatch) listened to Huey Johnson's pitch. He said he would think it over.

By this time, the Coeur d'Alene citizens fund had reached $17,000. On June 29, 1975, the front page of the *Coeur d'Alene Press* carried a story that the Jewett Foundation was donating $30,000. All the moneys were now in hand to acquire Tubbs Hill, with $3,000 to spare for operating funds!

On the day the article appeared, I was visiting Coeur d'Alene, and heard the details from Mary Lou and Scott Reed as we hiked the trails of Tubbs Hill.

"It was a lot of work, but I'm glad now that we didn't get all the money from one donor," said Reed. "This way, thousands of people in town participated in saving Tubbs Hill. Now they'll feel part of it and want to protect it."

As we walked down the hill along the lake, three youngsters scooted past us and negotiated a small rocky slope to the water's edge. A couple passed by with a two-year-old riding on his father's shoulders in a backpack. A teenage couple strolled along the trail hand in hand. To these Coeur d'Aleners nothing had changed. This always had been "their" park.

As we left, we walked past the two homes. I asked Reed if, with the purchase completed, it wouldn't be a good idea to buy them and the two remaining lots next to them.

"Keith Artz of the Trust for Public Land talked to the owner one
day," said Reed. "He wanted $60,000 just for the two lots. No way!
We'd much rather leave them as they are. Teachers can point to the
houses and say, this is what happens when people don't have an
environmental ethic, this is what it might have been like if a lot of
people hadn't realized how important it is to preserve open space
for the benefit of all the people."

13

A DIFFERENT WAY TO TREAD

Supportive of the environmental movement though not necessarily a part of it is another growing group of people who share the conservationists' goal of a better quality of life and who, by their outlook and actions, try to tread more lightly on the planet. They function in ways that most people consider unorthodox but they come from all walks of life, professionals and blue-collar workers, scientists and farmers, economists and public officials, rich and poor, black and white.

There are two paths along which this largely unorganized group is moving, and sometimes the two paths merge. One approach seeks to harness the juggernaut of technology and unbridled growth. It is called appropriate technology or, sometimes, alternative or intermediate or soft technology. Its followers believe we must stop looking for the answer to every problem in bigger, more advanced technological development with its unknown impacts and side effects. They preach and practice a smaller-scale technology, finding alternative technological applications, systems more appropriate to the times and not likely to create more problems than they solve. The widely varied adherents might accept the slogan popularized by the late E. F. Schumacher—Small is Beautiful—even though the particular solution to a need might be a large-scale alternative (but less harmful) technology, or perhaps no technology at all.

Working toward the same ends but by a different route are people dissatisfied with the "plastic society" that features conspicuous consumption of resources, the scramble for wealth and status, a society that is dependent on big business and big government for nearly every necessity. They seek a style of living that makes them at least partly self-sufficient. They look for work that gives satisfaction, often turning to services or crafts to find it. They make conscious efforts to cut down on use of fuel and electricity. They may practice recycling or organic gardening, partly for economic and health reasons, but also with the awareness that prevailing wasteful practices will limit the availability of resources for others or for future generations. And they usually express concern for their neighbors, try to share when possible, and work at building a sense of community.

If the people involved in these two approaches sound like revolutionaries, they do not see themselves that way. They regard themselves more as pioneers, dissatisfied with conventional ways and forging ahead toward better ways of living and working. Most of them have no interest in overthrowing the present social, economic, and political system, even though they are not in complete agreement with it. Rather, they are finding ways to do their own thing within the established system.

Though the number of people practicing these two approaches is relatively small, their efforts and experiences serve as examples of means and methods that have a distinctly gentle impact on the environment. A report of Stanford Research Institute's Business Intelligence Program claims that 5 million Americans—3% of the adult population—are fully practicing a lifestyle of "voluntary simplicity," that another 8 to 10 million are partial adherents, and from one-third to one-half the population are sympathizers. The report's authors, Duane Elgin and Arnold Mitchell, define voluntary simplicity as a way of life combining "frugality of consumption, a strong sense of environmental urgency, a desire to return to living and working environments that are of a more human scale, and an intention to realize our higher human potential—both psychological and spiritual—in community with others."

Of the five values the report says lie at the heart of voluntary simplicity—simplification of the material aspects of life, a preference for human-sized living and working environments, less dependence upon large, complex institutions, a sense of ecological awareness, and growth of the inner, nonmaterial dimension of life—ecological awareness is considered central.

Although I believe the authors have overestimated the numbers, they have spotlighted a trend that is significant and which I ran into throughout the country.

The Stanford Research Institute study's estimates are based on public opinion surveys. Many respondents to polls give answers based on how they would *like* to act. But their answers can be very different from their *actions*. For instance, the SRI study points out that a 1975 Louis Harris poll showed that 92% of Americans are willing to eliminate annual model changes in automobiles. Even if that were relevant to voluntary simplicity, the sales of automobiles do not indicate that this "willingness" is being carried into action. Far from it.

An expert observer, Michael Phillips, one of the founders of an urban experiment in a simpler lifestyle called the Briarpatch Network, says that the Stanford Research Institute estimate of 5 million Americans practicing voluntary simplicity is one hundred times too high. Phillips believes that the SRI people mistakenly read citizens' frugality in reaction to inflation, and the trends to natural food and fibers, as being the permanent changes in values that characterize true voluntary simplicity.

"Americans are both frugal and gross consumers at the same time," he says. "The money most families save by being frugal, by going to garage sales and having the wife work is used to buy motorcycles, campers, and a weekend home in the woods. The frugality doesn't end up as voluntary simplicity or ecological watchfulness. Money is saved to spend."

Phillips adds that what the Stanford study is pointing out to

businessmen may direct attention to market segments that haven't
had enough attention. But "we should not delude ourselves that a
large shift in values is going on in America," he says. "Changes in
important values are occurring in small groups of people, but the
movement is slow and the number is small, probably in the tens of
thousands."

Any effort to count the people actually practicing voluntary
simplicity is complicated by the difficulty in determining whether
the phenomenon is, as Phillips suggests, simply a temporary
reaction to inflation, fads, and a general dissatisfaction with society.
I did find, however, a pervasive *desire* for a simpler lifestyle.

One evening in Seattle I sat in on a meeting where about fifty
people of all ages had gathered to hear a talk about a self-sufficient
community being planned near Cottage Grove, Oregon. Those at
the Seattle gathering appeared to be of middle income, most of
them employed, a few retired, a few still in college.

After a short slide show and talk describing the planned
community to be called "Cerro Gordo," Doug Oyler, a young man
formerly from Seattle, explained that he was not trying to recruit
people for the planned community. Rather, he had organized the
meeting to see if there were enough Seattlites with a common
interest in a changed lifestyle to form a group to discuss their
values and seek ways to forward their own ideas in some practical
manner. Oyler suggested that they all place their chairs in a large
circle, introduce themselves, and say why they had come to the
meeting.

"I've been thinking for three or four years of doing something
that had more connection with real life," said Gwen, a young
woman who identified herself as a tool designer for Boeing Aircraft
Company. "Just designing tools and building airplanes isn't adding
to having a sense of community. What I want is to provide things
without being dependent on others for all my needs."

Miss Perry, an elderly woman, spoke of growing up in a small
town and working hard to get out of it. "But now I'm intrigued by
the idea of going back to that kind of life."

"What interests me is the possibility of having an urban-based
lifestyle away from the city, but not a farm or rural life," said Bill,
a graduate student at the University of Washington.

George, a construction engineer, expressed his disappointment at not knowing his neighbors. "I'd like to live in a small community where people know and help each other yet have some self-sufficiency so they don't have to be always getting things from big business."

On around the circle: an urban planner who wanted to be involved in a new community; a young couple who had been taking a hard look at themselves and finding out that happiness doesn't come from material belongings; a woman from Chicago who had thought Seattle would be a smaller, nicer place to live but found it too big and wanted to find a place where she could get around safely on a bicycle; and a general contractor who said he just had a yearning "to get close to the earth."

To find out more from some of those who already had made a commitment, I went to Cottage Grove to talk with Christopher Canfield and others who were starting the new community of Cerro Gordo. In 1972, the then 22-year-old Canfield, business manager of a small electronics firm in Santa Barbara, California, decided to seek others who might support building a new town based on a sense of community and living in harmony with the land. He distributed nationwide a prospectus describing a design for integrating village and natural environments, for a broad-based primary economy including crafts and light production industry, and with self-government by town meeting.

"Most importantly," stated the prospectus, "we seek more meaningful and fulfilling ways of living. We want a slower tempo that allows a deeper appreciation of people and nature." The 40-page prospectus went on to discuss potential townsites in northern California, ecological and community values, alternative methods of producing energy, transportation, and education. It ended with an invitation to those interested in the birth and growth of a new community like this to send $5 for a subscription to Town Forum publications.

Within a year, nationwide membership in Town Forum had reached 2,500. Meetings were held in Los Angeles, San Francisco, and Santa Barbara, and Canfield set out to find a site for the new community.

He did not find his dream property in northern California. But he ran into several possibilities in Oregon and there also met

Charles A. DeDeurwaerder, professor of landscape architecture at Oregon State University at Corvallis. DeDeurwaerder was studying new town development in the Pacific Northwest and agreed to help plan the new community.

While Canfield was searching for a site, consideration of values among Town Forum members continued. DeDeurwaerder toured a dozen U.S. cities talking to Town Forum groups, trying to show them how some of the values of a medieval village might be gained without the harmful environmental effects. Many of those who had professed interest in the new community approach, it turned out, really were more interested in a two-acre lot of their own in the country where they could continue most of their middle-class suburban high-consumption habits.

When Canfield found the Cerro Gordo site, DeDeurwaerder made an acre-by-acre ecological study and reported that the water and other resources would support no more than 2,500 people. The 1,150-acre, partially timbered tract, named after the "fat hill" that dominates the land, has fairly steep slopes and is not prime agricultural land.

Over the Thanksgiving weekend of 1973, four hundred families from many parts of the nation attended a meeting at Santa Barbara. When they reached agreement to purchase the land at Cerro Gordo they settled on a method of financing the purchase through memberships and loans. Participants at the meeting also tentatively decided on some of the values for the community. The main residential area would have clusters of single-family or duplex homes within a 115-acre section and there would be no streets so that the town would not be dependent upon the automobile. An area would be provided for organic agriculture. The community would be limited to about 2,000 people. Necessary energy would be generated from within the area as much as possible through devices such as solar collectors, windmills, and methane digesters. Buildings would be constructed to use wood and solar energy for heating. And at a later meeting a decision was made for all members to act as land stewards, owning the property jointly, leasing some areas, and giving property rights to home-owners only for the land under their buildings.

By the summer of 1975, about forty families had moved to the Cottage Grove area, although no one was as yet living at the Cerro

Gordo site. Most of them lived and worked in the city of Cottage Grove (population 6,000), 6 miles west of Cerro Gordo. It has been hard sledding financially for some. They met with animosity from a few Cottage Grove people who feared the newcomers would take their jobs, or who believed rumors that this was to be a hippie, hard-drug, free-love commune. But the animosity largely abated as the long-time local residents discovered that most of the newcomers were hardworking, decent citizens, intent only on a simpler, more satisfying way of life.

Chuck Missar, for instance, a Stanford University engineering graduate, had worked for eight years in planning and construction management and had a background as an environmental activist before joining the Cerro Gordo efforts. He was a charter member of Friends of the Earth, performed organic gardening research in northern California with Alan Chadwick, and was one of the three principal authors of the best-selling *Energy Primer* published by the Whole Earth Catalogue. He and his wife Dian moved to Cottage Grove early in 1975 and soon bought an 80-year-old house while waiting for the new community to be started. Meantime, he was appointed to the Cottage Grove city planning commission and then became the city's director of public works.

John Mowat was a physics professor at Auburn University in Alabama, who says he had ideas for a new community similar to those of Canfield but had no idea how it could be done. Mowat came to Cottage Grove to join the experiment at a time when he had just finished a book on quantum mechanics, was in the process of getting a divorce, and was getting fed up with his job. He and two other people have formed a solar consulting company and have also developed the experimental sand-filter waste-treatment facility for the first homes to be built at Cerro Gordo.

The building schedule was delayed when Lane County—which had no comprehensive land use plan—rejected the first Cerro Gordo design for a 50-unit cluster. The group scaled down their plan to comply, but it was mid-1978 before building permits could be obtained and financing arranged so that construction could start. The first cluster of homes and commercial buildings, being constructed by the Cerro Gordo Association's own crew, was scheduled to be completed by the fall of 1978.

Several families had left the group but new people had arrived with a core group of about eighty people living in the area. A crafts group, a firm that builds parts for model railroads, and two other small businesses have been started and will move to the new commercial buildings. Since use of private automobiles to homes is not allowed, each cluster of homes will have one shuttle vehicle available to serve it, but the vehicle will not be able to come closer than 200 feet from the building except in emergency. And no new roads or streets are being built.

While Cerro Gordo has a long way to go before becoming a successful new community, most of those who have made the move are achieving the objectives that brought them to the area: a sense of community and a life that is in harmony with the land.

"We're generating a community first and a town development second—one that's being designed by that community to meet its unique specifications," says Canfield. "The environmental ethic tends to be the first of those specifications."

No one knows how extensive the back to the land movement is and how much of it is attributable to a dissatisfaction with the quality of life in the cities and suburbs. A *New York Times* article in 1975 estimated that the "self-sufficiency" movement had attracted tens of thousands of people across the nation. New York, West Virginia, Colorado, California, all the New England and Southern states have seen a large drift toward people buying small plots and turning to organic gardening and crafts. How-to books and periodicals on rural living, heating and cooking with wood, generating power by wind, water, and sun, and sale of magazines like *Organic Gardening, Mother Earth News,* and *CoEvolution Quarterly* are gaining in popularity.

This hankering for simpler ways, along with a feeling for the land and a hunger for community also has been manifested nationwide in the commune movement. Their number has fallen off somewhat since the late 1960s, but those living on communal farms or urban households are still counted in the thousands.

The character of most current communal living arrangements is quite different from the free-living, hippie-style communes that abounded during the late 1960s and early 1970s, when they were havens for lonely, alienated young people. Many of today's communal households are organized on the theory that several families and/or individuals can live more cheaply together than separately. It takes less fuel to warm one house than several; the chores that go with an energy-efficient, more independent life—cutting wood, tending gardens, composting garbage, and recycling trash—are more easily accomplished by several people than by one or two. Staple groceries are cheaper when bought and prepared in quantity, and so forth. While only a few have the environmental ethic as their primary motivation, communal groups generally have a style of living that tends toward a much lighter impact on the earth and its resources than do conventional lifestyles.

Communal groups tend to be fairly short-lived. The most lasting and successful groups living and working together are usually those based on a sharing of philosophic or religious beliefs. One such group are the Zen Buddhists who live and work communally at the Green Gulch farm, a half-hour's drive from San Francisco near the shore of the Pacific Ocean. Green Gulch is basically a place where Zen students and their families can live in monastic simplicity, learn through study and practice how to abide by the Buddhist principles of "Right Practice, Right Attitude, and Right Understanding." The result is a highly productive, ecologically and environmentally ethical relationship to the land, resources, and animal life.

The 115-acre property stretches for a quarter mile down a narrow valley to the Pacific. It is surrounded by Golden Gate National Recreation Area. When the Zen Center acquired it in 1972 with the help of The Nature Conservancy, it was being used as a ranch for experimental breeding of English Herefords.

Guided by their respect for all living things, the Zen students began nurturing the soil. They plowed all animal and vegetable wastes back into it, allowing the soil and the waste elements to fulfill their productive purpose. When I visited Green Gulch in 1976, about 10 acres were under intensive cultivation, producing a bounty of superb-quality vegetables entirely without chemical fertilizers or pesticides. Their harvests feed the fifty or so residents, leaving a surplus that is avidly bought up by city dwellers at the Zen Center's store in San Francisco's Fillmore District.

At the time of my visit to Green Gulch the area was in its second year of serious drought. The stream that courses through the farm was all but dry. Still, the residents were able to sustain their crops. The June morning when I worked in the fields with the students we harvested a dozen crates of lush, dark spinach of a variety especially selected for its ability to withstand dry spells.

All students who are physically able spend a period each morning in the fields, and certain others do it full time. Manual labor along with horse and mule power are gradually replacing the farm's fossil-fuel-dependent motorized equipment. Every bit of chicken and animal waste is composted with vegetable waste and weeds so that their essential elements can be tilled back into the soil. The students' efforts toward the self-sufficiency that goes with their "Right Practice" include plans for harnessing the Pacific Coast breezes with a windmill to provide electricity. They are experimenting with producing methane gas from decomposing wastes. Woodburning stoves provide space heating and cooking, and the few flush toilets still used on the farm are being replaced by the composting type which use no water.

Ordained Zen Buddhist priest Yvonne Rand, who has been one of the leaders in the Green Gulch project, showed me the building projects under way. Students have learned a special construction method from Japanese craftsmen. It is extremely slow and painstaking, but it is exquisite, and is designed to last for centuries. And that, Mrs. Rand told me, is one of the distinctive views of Zen: "Although we treasure living in the reality of the present, we are in no hurry. We build in terms not of a generation or two but five hundred years or more."

Yvonne Rand is herself active in local environmental causes, but points out that the environmentally correct practices at the farm stem from Buddhist principles more than from environmental concepts. Their approach to the perennial scarcity of water, for instance, is to learn to do with less, not to ration it or build dams to reserve more. The stream, which had been channelized in the ranching days, is being returned to its natural meandering course. Instead of plummeting straight down the canyon, carrying good topsoil to the sea, the stream will slow down, providing natural habitat for flora and fauna along its way and allowing the precious water to help the land as it goes.

The principles applied at Green Gulch are not new and find followers in all the major religions and religious philosophies.

Buddha, Lao Tse, Moses, Muhammad, and Jesus all chose simple lifestyles emphasizing spiritual over material values, and so do some of their followers. The Amish and some Quakers are obvious American examples. They have for years practiced simple lifestyles with little dependence on materialistic consumption.

A recent movement among Christians urges "creative simplicity" or "simple living." Although not organized into one centralized group, and varying widely in its practice, the movement owes its genesis to two 1973 meetings of Christian religious retreat center directors and their staffs.

At the first meeting in Shakertown, Kentucky, they discussed overconsumption of the world's resources and acknowledged that their own lifestyles and those of most Americans were a large part of the problem. At a follow-up meeting at the Yokefellow Institute in Richmond, Indiana, the group agreed on a pledge they would take and commend to others, and which they named the "Shakertown Pledge" in honor of their first gathering place.

Included in the nine-point pledge are three key personal commitments: "to lead an ecologically sound life," "to lead a life of creative simplicity," and "to share my personal wealth with the world's poor." The original signers of the pledge have since disseminated it nationwide, although they have no national organization and no denominational ties. They have encouraged various religious communities to rewrite the Shakertown Pledge to reflect their own concepts.

"What the pledge envisions," says one of the founders, Adam Daniel Finnerty, "is not a wholesale renunciation of all material goods and a life of ragged poverty. We don't want people to feel guilty every time they go to a movie or eat a handful of popcorn. What we do want, though, is that all of us should look at our lifestyle in the light of our faith and the very real needs of the rest of the world."

An ecologically sound, creatively simple lifestyle is important, says Finnerty, so that people's lives can be freed from excessive attachment to material goods, so that more wealth can be shared with those who need the basic necessities of life, and so that a more just world standard of living may be achieved.

The Shakertown Pledge and adaptations of it have received a

good deal of attention in religious circles, although no count has
been made as to the numbers of those who live by the precepts. A
booklet called *Taking Charge,* published by two American Friends
Service Committee groups in the San Francisco area, gives tips and
background material on how to˙ practice simple living. And a
number of denominations have started training programs in simple
or creative living, reducing material consumption, saving energy,
and developing self-sufficiency and community.

Totally unconnected with any religious commitment, however, is
a unique, loosely organized group in the San Francisco Bay area
that focuses on business and employment. It is called the Briarpatch Network. Briars are individuals who in their business or
work are more interested in sharing resources and skills with
neighbors or the community than they are in acquiring possessions
and status. Money and profits are not ignored, but Briars do not
consider them of primary importance. The "briar" analogy is to the
briar bramble bush that can survive in the cracks—among inhos-
pitable environments—uses little water and soil, and flourishes
without being bulky.

Most of the 225 small firms or professionals in the network have
scaled down their monetary requirements, sometimes drastically, in
order to work at something satisfying and fulfilling. They do not
feel they are lowering their standard of living, even though
compared to others with their abilities and education, they have
considerably lower incomes, sometimes bordering on statistical
poverty levels.

The members (and membership is self-determining—if you say
you are a Briar, you are) include a small publishing company, a
printer, a landscape architect, insurance salesmen, film makers,
restaurants, an electrician, artists, architects, lawyers, a mathemati-
cian, a chef, a dentist, a toy rebuilding company, carpenters,
economists, an animal clinic, weavers, a bakery, child care centers
and schools, a cooperative auto repair shop, two solar technology
firms, and a bicycle repair business. Among other small businesses
in the network are a publishing company specializing in environmental education books, an ecology center near the San Francisco
financial district, a cooperative farm operating alongside and
underneath a major freeway interchange not far from San Fran-

cisco's Civic Center, and the New Games Foundation, a nonprofit organization that helps individuals and groups to initiate new types of recreation and play just for the fun of it, games that involve young and old, weak and strong, and that eliminate the stress on winning, gambling, and strict rules.

The only qualification for becoming a Briar is the acceptance of an unwritten rule that the member's business records must be available to anyone. If a customer asks to see how a member arrived at the price charged for a product or a service, this information should be given. Each issue of *CoEvolution Quarterly*, for instance, includes an itemized record of all expenses for producing the issue, the amount of income, the net profit or loss, and the balance on hand.

Social gatherings—usually pot-luck suppers once a month—are a main source of Briarpatch networking, that is, exchanging ideas and finding ways to get help or to help someone else. Some of these parties are held for a specific purpose like discussing crafts or exploring manufacturing and distribution ideas. Briars have held smaller workshop sessions on preparing financial statements, advertising techniques, bookkeeping, and legal matters.

One of the Briars, Howard Sutherland of Berkeley, makes bicycle repair accessories and has written a *Handbook for Bicycle Mechanics.* "The better the service given by a bicycle shop, the more bikes will be used," Sutherland says. "The more bikes are used, the healthier people will be. Less pollution, too. This is a small business and I'm pretty much an idealist. I'm willing to live on less money in exchange for being able to have an impact on the world I care about."

Only a few of the Briars are active in the environmental movement. Yet most of them understand the worldwide need to conserve energy and natural resources and consider that they are working toward that end and applying an environmental ethic in their efforts to cut down on their daily consumption of material things and to live more simply. Says Michael Phillips, "The most effective thing each of us can do for conservation is to reduce our income. If a person keeps the same income but spends less, which means saving more, then the effect can actually be negative. The reason is that the savings are used by banks, savings and loan companies, etc., to invest in economic growth. Thus reducing income in the first place is the only effective form of conservation."

A number of Briarpatch businesses or professions are oriented toward sound environmental objectives. In an old factory building in Berkeley, for instance, I met Tom Conlon, whose business is the design and manufacture of windmill motors, blades, and related equipment. Conlon built his first windmill as a necessity while living in the Santa Monica Mountains in Southern California—the local utility wanted to charge him $1,000 a pole for 21 poles to bring him power. He left a job as plant superintendent for a metal stamping company because he was just following numbers on printed forms and "wanted to do something that would provide a product that would help people."

In January 1976 he leased an abandoned Berkeley warehouse with 24,000 square feet of space, which he now shares as living, working, and office quarters with the owners and employees of two other small businesses. Although unfilled orders have piled up for two years, Conlon's firm, AeroPower, is just now starting production. Earlier motors were not good enough, Conlon felt, and he kept trying to improve them, refusing to sell any until he was satisfied with the product.

When I visited his warehouse, ten of his "production line" motors were completed. He also had a new tooling machine he was adapting to make wooden blades more accurately and more rapidly. He has made about a thousand of the blades and is also building generators and electric controls.

"We are creating high-quality products that we can offer at fair prices," Conlon said. "We don't sell something when it's not needed and not required." Conlon told me other Briarpatch people had helped him in business affairs, and he has been able to give some others advice on getting things manufactured.

In downtown Berkeley, a few blocks from the University of California campus, Jane Riordon was tending her small fabric store, Cottonfield. The 24-year-old proprietress, who started the shop two years earlier, deals only in 100% cotton fabric and has built her business around finding better ways to serve customers. She chose to deal in cotton fabric, she says, because its manufacture does not require nonrenewable resources (like petroleum for synthetic materials) and is more comfortable to the wearer. She keeps a free lending library of patterns. "Pattern companies operate on a system of total waste," she says. "Every few months the companies discontinue hundreds and give stores credit for throwing the old ones away."

Across San Francisco Bay at San Rafael, I toured the new solar heated building constructed to house ENECON, a business dealing in energy conservation. ENECON's founder, Charles Kessler, greets visitors with an exhibit he calls a "demonstration laboratory." A sign at the start says: "The key words in solar energy use are: collection, storage, distribution, and retention." And then visitors can see for themselves some of the systems for collecting, storing, distributing, and retaining solar energy and learn how they work. The display is a collection of what Kessler and his colleagues believe are the best methods for solving a variety of home and business energy conservation needs in the way that may be the most economical and appropriate for the potential user.

Kessler started the business to fill a need he discovered when he wanted to put some solar panels on the roof of his home. "I spoke with dozens of solar manufacturing companies; each of them said their product or system was the best, but none of them did installation," he says. "I had no way of knowing which was best for my needs. I wanted some service and I couldn't get it unless I went to a private contractor who was selling one particular line, knew only that line, and really didn't know what was best for me. So I decided to start a company that would help people know the various lines available, help them learn what solar energy really is, introduce them to other energy-saving methods, and find a way to meet their particular need."

He put all the savings he had accumulated during his years in investment work and restaurant and theater ownership into buying hardware so he could try it out. He found several experienced space-heating engineers and people interested in his objectives who joined his efforts.

Kessler says that although the types of equipment displayed in his showroom-lab—the heat pumps, solar panels, waterless composting toilets, fireplace boosters, warm air recirculators, insulating windows and shades—proved to be the best he and his associates could find, they are ready to accept new systems that do a job better. The most important thing the company offers, however, is not merchandise but education.

"Our whole purpose is to demystify the process so that people can understand it," Kessler told me. "And we try to figure out the economics of possible solutions and how long it might take for an investment in solar energy to pay back its costs. Many times it is not worth it, especially in old houses that have to be retrofitted—and we tell our customers so."

ENECON also holds seminars for real estate agents, builders, architects, and contractors, and schedules tours of the lab for schoolchildren. A local bank even sent its loan officers to EN-ECON to be better informed when dealing with loans for solar energy or conservation applications.

The Briarpatch businesses contribute small amounts each month to pay two coordinators who assist fellow members in the sharing of ideas and services. One of them, Charles Albert Parsons, explained how he had scaled down his own needs, simplified his lifestyle, and found satisfying work. He had spent 20 years as an employment counselor, the last 13 of them with state government. In 1975, he quit and opened his own office. After a while, when he found the office confining, he started scheduling employment consultations at a bench in Golden Gate Park close to his home and to a public parking lot. The outdoors consulting proved so successful that he closed the office entirely.

"The park environment, the grass and trees and birds, is a pure work environment," Parsons told me. "I suppose it puts off some people for an employment counselor to tell them to meet him on a park bench. But for me it is a screening process. The people who come, love it. The environment seems to create a focus for people who are looking for work that is going to be satisfying and that will utilize their human potential."

Parsons and Bahauddin Alpine, the other Briarpatch coordinator, spend every Wednesday visiting Briar businesses to see how they can furnish advice and to bring the Briar in touch with other Briars who can be helpful. Sometimes they are accompanied by Phillips, who furnishes free financial and business advice. He earns enough money for his own needs by writing and as comptroller for a small foundation.

"Why do we want to live on less, make do with fewer possessions, and live by sharing with others?" asks Phillips rhetorically. "Some of us do it for political reasons: we believe it is

A DIFFERENT WAY TO TREAD   185

necessary to use fewer resources if the world is to survive. Most of
us do it because living on less is rewarding in itself—we love it. The
Briarpatch is created by and for people who want to live simply.
Our small businesses can charge less because we want less income
for ourselves. Our services can be better because our enjoyment
comes from our work; we are not working to make money in order
to do something else. Our work *is* what we want to do, and we
design it to be that way. It's our hours, our location, our own
environment, and our source of enjoyment."

Briars and other advocates of simple living are among those
traveling the path away from standard technological systems
toward technologies that are more appropriate to their style of life.
They are part of the rapidly developing alternative technology
trend which is rooted in a desire to cut down on energy and
resource use and prevent environmental harm. Alternative, appropriate, or intermediate technology is being sought by people who
realize that many of the modern technologies they once welcomed
are now proving potentially harmful and inappropriate for the
present as well as for an uncertain future.

Appropriate technology, the term most commonly used, raises
the natural question: appropriate for what and for whom? The
answers are wrapped up in the issue of what are a people's values
and how best to use technology to achieve their goals. A technology
that is appropriate to an economy rife with unemployment might
emphasize labor-intensive instead of capital-intensive practices.
Where a community's economy is depressed and where transportation is costly and wasteful of fuel, it might feature small-scale
production and decentralized, locally owned business rather than
dependence on large-scale, centralized enterprise. In all cases it
emphasizes energy efficiency, recyclability, conservation of resources, and compatibility with the environment. Technology that
is appropriate promotes more meaningful and satisfying employment and community cooperation.

The most prominent spokesman for a more appropriate technology was E. F. Schumacher whose book *Small is Beautiful: Economics as if People Mattered* set many people to thinking along
new lines. Schumacher had for some years been chief economist
and central planner for England's Coal Board, a nongovernment

company which regulates Great Britain's coal industry. In his spare time he organized the Soil Association, a nonprofit group promoting research toward more environmentally sound agricultural practices. He put his people-oriented economics into practice in a research and consulting organization, the Intermediate Technology Development Group, to help developing nations find low-cost, small-scale technological methods of improving their economies without bringing about some of the harmful impacts that the "Bigger is always better" industrial philosophy has brought to much of the world.

Schumacher warned that the industrial nations are using up the "capital" of nature at a disastrous rate because of a misguided sense of values and wasteful, production-oriented economic systems. The resulting pollution and harm to ecological systems threaten life itself. He disdained the usual ways of measuring progress. Modern economists judge the standard of living by the amount of annual consumption, always assuming that a person who consumes more is better off than one who consumes less. Schumacher suggested that we should seek to obtain the maximum of well-being with the minimum of consumption. Modern economics does not distinguish between renewable and nonrenewable materials—the cheapest is automatically preferred. But Schumacher held that to use nonrenewable resources needlessly or extravagantly is an act of violence. "And while complete nonviolence may not be attainable on this earth," Schumacher said, "there is nonetheless an inelectable duty on man to aim at the ideal of nonviolence in all he does."

The Schumacher I met in 1974 during his first trip to the United States after he wrote *Small is Beautiful* was a compelling speaker and a delightful individual. I met him at a small Wall Street luncheon arranged by Hazel Henderson, the self-taught economist who has been a leader in showing how to redirect the American economy to produce a sustainable society and better quality of life. She had invited Schumacher to discuss his theories and activities with a few important people from the financial world, plus vice-presidents from American Telephone and Telegraph and Prudential Insurance, and a couple of writers.

My surprise at the slight accent from Schumacher's native Germany lasted only a moment. Before he had talked five minutes

I was on the edge of my chair. Here was somebody actually espousing and doing the kinds of things I had been searching for. Even the financial people appeared to be impressed with the simple logic of his message, though for them it seemed just another interesting theory. For me it was a revelation to hear someone describing economics in terms of practical works, not just theory or social philosophy.

Schumacher singled out four main enemies in his talk: the trend toward "giantism" in development ("Aren't we clever enough to make things small again?"); specialization and centralization ("Any damn fool can make a complicated thing even more complicated—it takes a couple of geniuses to make complicated things a bit more simple"); high-capital requirements ("Instead of always emphasizing big projects that are labor saving, we ought to help the little fellow with a little bit of capital at least get started"); and a violent technology that shapes man ("So can't we devote systematically some of our intelligence to achieving the highest possible degree of nonviolence toward nature?").

Schumacher told us about some of the things the Intermediate Technology Development Group was doing. Zambia's President Kenneth Kaunda had asked Schumacher to advise him on rural development. The country's economy centered around the Copperbelt, which was highly mechanized and provided few jobs, but 85% of the people lived in rural areas with little development. Touring the Zambian countryside, Schumacher came upon one situation that typified the fallacy of depending on unachievable, large-scale production. The country needed egg crates. Schumacher found egg producers with their product spoiling because the supply of imported trays had stopped.

"We thought that this was one problem that could be solved on a small-scale, local basis," Schumacher told us. "Surely it can't be beyond the wit of men to produce egg trays in Zambia so the country is not dependent on faraway suppliers."

It was not so simple. Returning to London, Schumacher discovered that most of the world's supply of egg trays came from one multinational company headquartered in Denmark. When told of the problem, the company offered to build a large factory in Lusaka at a cost of half a million dollars. Schumacher said Zambia not only could not afford this but had no means to transport crates from Lusaka. Instead, it needed several small factories in rural areas, not one big urban factory. The Danish company's smallest machine produced a million trays a month. And the whole of Zambia could use, at most, only a million in an entire year.

"Why don't you make a smaller machine?" Schumacher asked the company.

"We talked to our engineers. That would be uneconomic," was the reply.

Schumacher's Intermediate Technology Development Group went into action. They hired a bright young industrial design student and told him to do two things: (1) redesign the egg tray so it would be sturdy and would not require crating, which was expensive for poor countries; and (2) set up a small-scale production unit and devise low-cost machines capable of making a small number of trays.

"The young man took the problem to the Royal School of Arts in London, and in six weeks we had a perfect design for an egg crate, far better than that of the multinational company," Schumacher recalled. "Some other students at the University of Reading's engineering department then designed a production unit with 2% of the capacity of the previously smallest unit. And a company in Scotland found a way to manufacture the machine at 2% of the multinational's estimated capital cost.

"Today we have a large sale for this machine, not only in developing countries, but for some developed countries who want to produce their own egg trays. The countries are able to use local labor and the indigenous paper pulp and waste paper, and save on the energy and costs that would be required if eggs were transported to and from central packaging points far from the markets."

Schumacher's group devised small-scale, decentralized brickworks for Pakistan, small water-storage tanks for Botswana, a simple oxcart design and do-it-yourself kit for Malawi, where farmers with increased production had more than enough for their own subsistence but had no means of transport to get their surplus to market.

What impressed me most about Schumacher's philosophy was that he was dealing with many of the elements I had found missing in the decision-making process of government officials and business leaders. While he used the campaign for a small technology as his focus, Schumacher's main thrust was toward a shift of values away from emphasis on materialistic wants (that often in the long-term bring harm to humans and the environment) to an expanding of consciousness that seeks the more permanent and satisfying things of the spirit. This change in values will lead, he insisted, to a new style of living that does not make inordinate demands on resources and the environment, and carries with it' a concern for others, for the natural world, and for the future. And Schumacher's strongest plea was for the people in affluent industrialized countries to change their wasteful nonefficient lifestyle, which could not continue without drastic consequences for the environment and for future generations.

Schumacher's 1974 U.S. tour did not create much of a stir. His book, while selling well in college communities, was not being promoted by its publisher, and sales were slow. His lectures were only moderately well attended. Most of the business community kept aloof. And although low-level officials of the World Bank and the U.S. Agency for International Development met with Schumacher while he was in Washington, no changes were evident in their policies.

By 1977, however, when Schumacher came to America for a 14-state, six-week lecture tour, things had changed. More than 300,000 copies of *Small is Beautiful* had been sold. Many Americans, having learned a few lessons from the energy crisis of 1973-74, had begun to experiment in various types of self-sufficiency. Appropriate technology was becoming more than a fad, although still outside the normal activity of business and industry. Schumacher's lectures attracted overflow crowds. He appeared on the *Today* television show and was featured in newsmagazine articles. Registrants from 41 states and five Canadian provinces attended his seminars in New York, Chicago, Montana, and California. He had long private meetings with the governors of Montana, Colorado, Nebraska, and Minnesota. And California Governor Brown, who had spent a day with Schumacher on an earlier U.S. visit, invited four hundred state employees and members of the legislature for an evening of discussion during which Schumacher, with Governor Brown acting as moderator, fielded questions for more than two hours. And on the final day of his 1977 tour Schumacher was

invited to the White House. A scheduled 15-minute private
meeting with President Carter extended to 45 minutes as they
discussed energy conservation, environment, and small technology.

When I talked with Schumacher the night before he left the
United States, he seemed extremely pleased with the reception he
had received all across the country. He still believed that not
enough appropriate technology was actually being started in the
United States, especially by the business sector, and he felt a lack
of awareness in federal and state governments. But the significant
amount of independent local activity in development of appropriate technology was most encouraging to him.

It was to be his last trip to the United States. Schumacher died a
few months later while traveling in Switzerland, and the appropriate technology movement lost its most convincing worldwide
spokesman.

It is true that the federal government has been slow to move in
meaningful or creative ways to forward the concepts of appropriate
technology. The Department of Energy is showing some belated
activity by giving grants for small-scale technology experiments in
the energy and energy conservation fields. Congress enacted a law
providing for establishment of a National Center for Appropriate
Technology with headquarters in Butte, Montana. As part of the
U.S. Community Services Administration the center gives small
grants—mostly under $5,000—for community experiments and
demonstrations of solar energy for heating water, making windmills, rooftop greenhouses, and methane digesters, training of solar
technicians, home weatherization, and other activities. The center
emphasizes providing employment and introducing appropriate
technology in low-income urban areas, but some grants go to rural
and native American Indian communities.

The government entity which is giving the most visible support
for appropriate technology is the State of California, where in 1976
Governor Brown established an official state Office of Appropriate
Technology (OAT). One of the governor's part-time consultants,
Stewart Brand, publisher of *The Whole Earth Catalog* and *Co-
Evolution Quarterly,* had been urging the concept for some time.
The major force behind appropriate technology was Sim Van der

Ryn, whom Brown had appointed in 1975 as state architect. Van der Ryn for several years had been working with ideas parallel to those of Schumacher and had founded the nonprofit Farallones Institute at Occidental, California, to teach and conduct research in appropriate technology.

Visiting Sacramento in 1976 I found the new California State Office of Appropriate Technology operating quietly, mostly riding Van der Ryn's coattails, and with no independent budget. The governor's official order creating the office stated that it would "assist and advise the governor and all state agencies in developing and implementing less costly and less energy-intensive technologies of recycling, waste disposal, transportation, agriculture, energy, and building design."

One of Van der Ryn's first projects lay within his own province as state architect, planning an energy-efficient new state office building in Sacramento. He had succeeded in blocking a previously approved plan for a traditional, square, high-rise building so that he could consider alternative types of energy-saving construction.

Van der Ryn felt that California, with its six or seven very different climate zones, should not habitually construct high-rise office buildings everywhere. He decided this new structure in Sacramento, where summers are very hot and winters are mild, should get the maximum benefits from the climate, use natural lighting as much as possible, and provide an open-space work environment.

The resulting design, being worked on when I visited, called for integrated use of a passive solar system in a four-story terraced building. It is designed so that solar heat can be used 80% of the time and the building can be opened up during Sacramento's cool summer nights for cooling. It will use about 25% as much energy as a traditional building would use. And although the price tag for construction with this use of the natural climate is $1 million higher than for a conventional building, it will save in energy outlays an estimated $19 million over the fifty-year life of the building.

As we sat in his office I asked Van der Ryn about the reports I had heard that the Office of Appropriate Technology was mostly a public relations job by the governor. He admitted that his only staff then was a consultant, Jerry Yudelson, but said that this low-key beginning was what he wanted. Priority should be given to removing legal barriers standing in the way of decentralization, change, and small-scale, self-reliant enterprise, he said. Existing state and county laws and standards favor big technology, and government often subsidizes large-scale, standardized activity at the expense of diversified local enterprise. He hoped to achieve results by reason and education.

"It's better to entice people into doing something that is right than to criticize them for doing something wrong," he said. "And we feel we can convince most of the decision-makers, when we have the opportunity, that the alternative technologies can save costs and be more efficient."

When he discovered that the Department of Parks and Recreation was planning a $600,000 sewage treatment plant for Angel Island State Park, Van der Ryn got a few people from the California State Parks System and some state waste treatment experts to make a visit with him to Angel Island and explore the possibilities of using an alternative system that would be less environmentally harmful. The park is across the bay from San Francisco and accessible by ferry, and has become excessively popular with hikers and bicyclists. Van der Ryn's task force discovered on their first visit that sewage from septic tanks in a heavily used area could be pumped 600 feet to an inaccessible spot at the top of the island. There, through spray irrigation and holding ponds, nature would digest and treat the sewage.

The parks people were interested. A management study commissioned by Van der Ryn showed that this appropriate technology system could save $500,000 in capital construction costs and could be operated with far less fuel and more cheaply than could a new treatment plant.

The parks officials agreed to use the waste-water reclamation system. And they also decided to reexamine plans for sewage treatment at other state parks to find out if septic tanks or pit privies might be more appropriate than costly and ecologically disturbing sewage plants.

State and local building codes in California and many other states are geared to metropolitan areas and work against the efforts of people in remote areas who want to use waste treatment systems such as composting toilets and other water-saving and soil-building methods. Van der Ryn had been working with the state housing director toward easing the laws or getting building code exemptions.

When I returned to Sacramento in the spring of 1978, the Office of Appropriate Technology was still a small-scale operation, but had proved itself to be far more than the short-lived public relations gimmick that some observers had at first labeled it. Although organized as a part of the Governor's Office of Planning and Research, the Office of Appropriate Technology had a small building of its own, a budget of $800,000, and a number of programs. Sim Van der Ryn chaired a six-person steering committee to direct policy and the OAT had a full-time director, Robert Judd, and a staff of 25.

The OAT has purchased 75 bicycles, which have been assigned to state agencies in Sacramento. For trips around the city, employees are encouraged to check out a bicycle instead of taking a taxicab or trying to get a state car. All state buildings now have bicycle racks.

Many small communities in coastal and foothill areas of California face difficulties meeting federal and state water quality standards. On-site sewage disposal had proved unsatisfactory and a source of pollution in those locations, and large, centralized systems were prohibitive in cost as well as wasteful of water, which is always in short supply. The Office of Appropriate Technology made a study of alternative technologies that would make decentralized treatment systems acceptable. OAT developed a proposal for management districts that could assure efficient maintenance of the small decentralized systems, then helped prepare legislation which was passed by the legislature. Now public entities in California have the option of operating small on-site systems rather than constructing costly central sewage treatment systems.

OAT helped the state architect's office train 18 people to construct solar water-heating systems and, as part of the training, installed solar systems on three state apartment buildings. A seven-member design group has been established in OAT to work with state agencies to design innovative systems that conserve resources. A mobile exhibit, "The New Possibilities Show," visits schools, community centers, fairs, and public gatherings throughout the state to inform people of various ways they can conserve energy and resources and improve the quality of life. OAT has a community gardens coordinator, Rosemary Menninger, who helps people in the more than eighty towns that have community gardens to tap into state resources for help. OAT cooperates with the state's Department of Water Resources in operating a large model drought-tolerant garden in downtown Sacramento to demonstrate water and energy conserving horticultural practices.

An atlas of community resources written in English and Spanish was compiled for California's South Central Valley area. The atlas lists community-based sources of self-help information. And the Office of Appropriate Technology has brought speakers from around the country, including Schumacher, Ivan Illich, Buckminster Fuller, Paolo Soleri, Hazel Henderson, Wendell Berry, and Scott and Helen Nearing, to help educate state employees on aspects of appropriate technology.

Another approach to appropriate technology has been carried out for several years on Cape Cod, where marine biologists John Todd and William McLarney, with goals similar to Schumacher's but with a scientific rather than an economic basis, run the New Alchemy Institute. On a 12-acre experimental farm they conduct research aimed at developing systems for energy-efficient, cheap, and environmentally sound ways of producing food and energy for domestic and agriculture applications.

The New Alchemists are not trying to turn lead into gold. They take another meaning of the word "alchemy": the ancient tradition of conducting research through the combined studies of science, philosophy, and the arts. From early May through October, biologists, zoologists, engineers, and ecologists work at the institute alongside musicians, philosophers, poets, and artists. This blending of educational backgrounds and experience promotes new ways of looking at science, values, and the environment. The participants do not live at the institute but commute from surrounding towns and communities. Though they spend a good deal of time in discussion, their primary activity is the creation of food-producing ecosystems that emulate nature and are scaled for use in places such as urban alleys, city rooftops, vacant lots and backyards, or on small, rural plots.

Their most widely known experiment is the backyard fish farm, which can furnish low-cost protein in an urban setting. They have

developed plans for simple types of fish farms that can become
self-perpetuating, or more sophisticated models using solar energy
and wind power.

The fish farms' success is based on understanding biological
cycles and ecological relationships. They run on clean, renewable
energy and call for fish that eat only vegetable matter. Fast growing
vegetarian fish did not exist in North America, so the New
Alchemists brought the tilapia (St. Peter's) fish from Africa. It feeds
primarily on algae and aquatic plants and grows to an edible size in
only ten to twelve weeks.

To simulate the necessary tropical environment, the New
Alchemists first designed a pool lined with plastic and covered with
a geodesic dome to trap and store the sun's heat. Later they
developed more elaborate designs involving water-pumping windmills and solar water heaters. To make these miniature food
producing ecosystems entirely self-contained, they developed biological waste filtering systems. Frogs, turtles, and spiders control
pests in the ponds. And in the more sophisticated greenhouse-
aquaculture complexes, shells and aquatic plant beds filter and
cleanse the waste waters.

The New Alchemists also work on ecologically sound alternatives to today's large-scale monoculture farming that relies on
energy-intensive machinery and petroleum-based chemical fertilizers. Crops and seed strains are chosen to encourage natural soil
enrichment and pest resistance, and safe, naturally sustaining,
small-scale strategies are applied to food production.

Todd and McLarney started their institute in Southern California in 1969. Dissatisfied with just talking about an impending
worldwide environmental apocalypse, as was popular at the time,
they decided to start an organization that would work on human-
scale solutions to scientific and ecological problems. Located on
Cape Cod since 1971, the New Alchemy Institute has attracted
such nationwide attention that it is besieged with visitors. Visits
have been restricted to Saturdays, when guests may share a potluck
lunch, observe what is going on, and even take a hand in the work.

"What we'd like to do in the broadest terms," says Todd, "is to
move society from one that is exploitive to one that's nurturing,
and to begin to design on the things that we have freely—the sun
and the wind and living organisms."

The New Alchemists hope the acceptance of fish farms and

small-scale, environmentally sound farming practices will make people familiar with the ecological concepts of recycling, energy conservation, and biological diversity and stability. Through this process they seek to teach stewardship and an understanding of the working of the larger natural world.

Todd believes that their demonstration of ways of living in harmony with nature is only the first step toward restoring landscapes and reuniting human ties with nature. "Ecology in abstract terms can tell us how the world works," he says. "But it doesn't become real until a little piece of the world works for you." He does not foresee an exodus from the city to the countryside, but he does believe that by tending a backyard fish farm, a rooftop garden, a windmill, or a solar heating device, urban dwellers can begin to experience stewardship of the earth.

In Berkeley, California, the Farallones Institute's Urban House is trying to demonstrate how alternative technologies can work in homes right in the middle of the city. Four college students live in the renovated Victorian style house on a small lot in West Berkeley. Under the direction of Helga and Bill Olkowski, the students conduct experiments and perform research in addition to running well-attended Saturday afternoon tours.

What I saw when I took the tour were practical examples of what any family could do to become more self-sufficient. Except for the expensive Clivus Multrum composting toilet, all the innovations were low-cost, simple, do-it-yourself designs. Other types of composting toilets, which can save the average family more than 10,000 gallons of water a year, can be built for less than $200, we were told. The house featured an aquaculture hatchery where crayfish, blackfish, and perch were being raised, a greenhouse, a solar collector for heating water, a solar grill, and a woodstove.

In the small yard every inch of space was in use, but not for lawn. Neat rows of vegetables, herbs, and strawberries flourished near mulberry trees being raised for silkworm production. A beehive, composting bins, and pens housing rabbits and chickens were unobtrusive. Driveways and walkways were surfaced with wood chips instead of cement or asphalt, the wood allowing moisture to carry nutrients to the soils beneath it and also providing habitat for useful insects.

The experiments are all monitored to record the amount of crops produced, growing times, and the presence of diseases or pests. No pesticides or other chemicals are used, and the soil is nurtured by the tops of plants, weeds, and garbage composted with chicken and rabbit wastes. The students were installing a methane digester that would tap the gases generated in the composting toilet and compost bin for possible use in cooking or heating.

The hundred or more people who take tours during the weekend are seldom merely curiosity seekers. Of all ages, the visitors ply the guides with searching, intelligent, practical questions based on an avid interest in trying some of these resource-saving and money-saving ideas.

The most extensive practical training being given in appropriate technology is the annual summer program in Alternate Energy and Agriculture, part of the Institute for Social Ecology at Goddard College, Vermont. Murray Bookchin, one of the pioneer American advocates of appropriate technology, directs the twelve-week program in which students earn academic credit and actually design and construct small-scale wind and solar-powered energy units. The courses include composting, aquaculture, architecture, solar systems, wind generators, organic horticulture, alternative energy, and social ecology, which is Bookchin's teaching specialty.

He is concerned about the increasingly technocratic emphasis being applied to appropriate technology. "There is a tendency to abandon values and think only in quantitative terms—not just how much energy can you save, but how many dollars you can make, without regard for ecological values," he says. "And unless we think of these technologies within the social and moral context it becomes meaningless.

"I emphasize in my courses the technology and the arts of self-sufficiency, but also that we permeate what we do with what I call the appropriate society and the values that should go along with it. Technology tends to dominate nature. So it is the responsibility of those who want to build an ecological society that's in balance with nature to not only develop these appropriate technologies, but to develop the social relationships and values that will bring them into harmony with each other."

14

PATH TO
THE PRESENT

The search for an environmental ethic cannot be confined to the present, for today's attitudes and values have roots deep in the past. Along with looking into current practices in business, government, and contemporary life, I delved into history to discover some of the major influences contributing to the environmental ethic.

Various kinds of ethics have affected American motivations over the years, accompanying the eras of colonization, development, westward expansion, and industrialization. America's earliest settlers brought with them values and attitudes rooted in European traditions. Their rudimentary knowledge of natural laws had eliminated much of nature's mystery as well as its sacredness. Their value system made it a virtue to own and develop land as a necessity for human well-being. And when they found a harsh wilderness before them instead of the balmy shores they had anticipated, they felt driven by the need to conquer the land and make it productive to support their civilization and growing population.

Historians and philosophers have traced two threads running through the fabric of Western civilization's attitude toward nature. One is man's dominion—the utilitarian concept of using nature for man's benefit; the other is the principle of stewardship—that mankind has certain responsibilities in relation to all living things and the land, water, and air, and should seek to avoid unduly disrupting them.

Both threads have support from the Old Testament, whether it be the exploitation theme "Be fruitful, and multiply, and replenish the earth, and subdue it: and have dominion over the fish of the sea, and over the fowl of the air, and over every living thing that moveth upon the earth" (Genesis 1:28), or the stewardship principle "the Lord God took the man, and put him in the garden of Eden to dress it and to keep it" (Genesis 2:15).

The new settlers' attitudes toward nature clashed with those of the native American Indians. Reverence for the land and for nature was the creed of the Indians, who lived in comparative harmony with the natural environment. The Indians looked to the earth as the source of all life. They saw themselves as a part of the biotic community. But the colonists regarded themselves as superior to the natural world and set apart from it. In line with their Christian tradition they believed in man's dominion over nature and that nature's purpose was to serve man. Nevertheless, their European heritage also included seeds of an environmental ethic which had been slowly germinating over the centuries. Many colonists practiced limited forms of conservation, including, for instance, restrictions on deer hunting in some areas. And William Penn wisely decreed that for every five acres of land cleared, one must be left forested. Thomas Jefferson and many of his affluent peers practiced a benign control over property and nature, seeking to assure continued productivity by good land practices. They enjoyed "improving" upon nature by coaxing it into an esthetically pleasing and orderly landscape. They also saw land as more than a utilitarian source of goods and wealth; they regarded property ownership as conferring dignity and status, giving the owner responsibility and a stake in his country.

Benjamin Franklin also expressed a concern about man's interference with the order of nature.

> Whenever we attempt to amend the scheme of Providence, and to interfere with the government of the world, we had need be very circumspect, lest we do more harm than good. In New England they once thought blackbirds useless, and mischievous to the corn. They made efforts to destroy them. The consequence was, the blackbirds were diminished; but a kind of worm, which devoured their grass, and which the blackbirds used to feed on, increased prodigiously; then, finding their loss in grass much greater than their saving in corn, they wished again for their blackbirds.

Most American colonists, building on the philosophy of John Locke, considered stewardship of the land to be equivalent to stewardship of capital. Under Lockean ethics the owner could convert the land to increase capital in whatever way necessary. This Lockean view of land as private property has led several centuries later to today's prevailing attitude which encourages stripmining, subdivision, or whatever else will bring the highest dollar return.

Seventeenth- and 18th-century Europe saw the growth of science and a mechanistic view of nature, propounded in the 17th century by Newton, Descartes, and others who sought to explain all things in terms of laws of physics. This view held that there are no aspects of living organisms that cannot be explained by these laws. The actions and interactions of the parts of the universe were probed, but the view of the whole was largely ignored.

Meanwhile, however, in Europe, philosophers, artists, poets, landscape designers, and musicians took refuge from the Industrial Revolution by turning to romanticism. Jean-Jacques Rousseau exalted nature and celebrated man's oneness with nature because it would produce a better society and the spiritual improvement of man. "Nature never deceives us; it is always we who deceive ourselves," he wrote. William Wordsworth showed how the love of nature leads to love of man. He believed in a dynamic man-nature

· relationship. "Come forth into the light of things, Let Nature be your teacher," he wrote. Or again,

> One impulse for a vernal wood
> May teach you more of man
> Of moral evil and of good,
> Than all the sages can.

In the young and growing America's rush for development, however, nature more often presented obstacles to be overcome than a haven for the soul. The seeming abundance of natural resources encouraged practices that emphasized technological efficiency and speed of development with little thought for the effects on the future of the land and resources. The quicker the development, the greater the benefit and prosperity for the individual and society, it was believed. In this heady atmosphere, loggers stripped the forests with little regard for impact on the watershed, and gold miners destroyed mountainsides and river valleys with their hydraulic mining and dredging.

Nevertheless, a few of those 19th-century Americans warned of the need to preserve the land for future generations. Artist-explorer George Catlin noted in his journal that the abundant buffalo and their habitat in the wilderness of South Dakota could become extinct. "Many are the rudenesses and wilds in nature's works which are destined to fall before the deadly axe and desolating hand of cultivating man," he wrote in 1832. The buffalo and the wilderness might not disappear if they were

> preserved in their pristine beauty and wilderness, in a *magnificent* park, where the world could see for ages to come, the native Indian in his classic attire, galloping his wild horse ... amid the fleeing herds of elks and buffaloes. What a beautiful and thrilling specimen for America to preserve and hold up to the view of her refined citizens and the world, in future ages! A *nation's park,* containing man and beast, in all the wild and freshness of their nature's beauty.

Forty years later, when Congress established Yellowstone National Park in 1872 as the world's first wild park to be set aside for the public, the action went largely unnoticed. It resulted mainly from the lobbying of a few enthusiasts and the fact that no one else, least of all the miners, timber interests, and cattlemen, yet appreciated the potential of the land included in the park. The land was inaccessible and hostile Indians roamed the area. The water power resource of the Yellowstone River was not yet recognized.

Some efforts at conservation and preservation were evident during the 19th century in America. Under the impetus of Frederick Law Olmsted, New York authorized Central Park in 1853, and Olmsted designed and built it. The City Beautiful movement of the 1880s and 1890s was an effort to bring the beauty of "nature" to the city. A number of states took early measures to protect their resources: California banned hydraulic gold mining soon after statehood and established Yosemite Valley as a state park in 1864. New York established the large Adirondack Forest Preserve in 1885. And in 1891 Congress passed the Forest Reserve Act permitting the president to create forest reserves by withdrawing land from the public domain.

A landmark in the development of an environmental ethic and a call for a sense of responsibility for man's actions on the land was the publication in 1864 of George Perkins Marsh's book *Man and Nature*. Marsh had been a Vermont farmer and American minister to Turkey and to Italy, and after seeing the devastation of the land by bad farming and logging practices in Europe and in his native Vermont, he sought to bring about change in these practices in America. He gave detailed examples of the land abuses and their impact. Marsh viewed the earth as a whole in which man was an intruder who failed to understand the laws of nature or the consequences of his actions which threatened nature's balance. He optimistically concluded that adherence to a better understanding of nature, the promise of science, and the applications of technological innovations would enable man to redeem himself and restore the balance of nature.

Although Marsh was in effect the first American to engage in what amounted to ecological analysis on a large scale, there had been an ecological element in English naturalist Charles Darwin's *Origin of Species* (1859). Darwin described the fragile and complex interactions of a species with its environment and also the process of natural selection, which, he suggested, may apply to man as well. A German, Ernst Haeckel, coined the word "ecology" *(öcologie)* in

1866 in a sketch about a new science he said was concerned with "nature's economy." He derived the term from the Greek *oikos* meaning "household or home or place to live," and he defined ecology as the "relation of the animal to its organic as well as its inorganic environment." While his sketch concerned how organisms interact or compete for food, the term ecology is now usually defined as the study of the relationship of all living things including man to their environment. Those views of the natural world as a living process sensitive to the actions of man ran counter to the popular belief that the natural world was something for man to possess and control.

The American version of transcendentalism that had been articulated by Emerson and Thoreau was gaining strength and followers. The transcendental attitude valued a resort to wilderness, a renewing of the human spirit in solitary communion with nature. John Muir was introduced to transcendentalism while a student at the University of Wisconsin and became its far western prophet and the leading exponent of wilderness values, especially those of California's Sierra Nevada.

Muir possessed powerful abilities as a writer, and the beauty of his prose, imbued with a strong sense of the environmental ethic, contributed a great deal to public understanding of the value of the natural world and its creatures. Echoing Thoreau's famous phrase "In wildness is the preservation of the world," Muir once wrote: "In God's wildness lies the hope of the world—the great fresh, unblighted, unredeemed wilderness. The galling harness of civilization drops off, and the wounds heal ere we are aware."

Muir as a political activist was instrumental in getting Yosemite Valley and the surrounding mountains made into a national park in 1891, and he was the prime mover in establishing the Sierra Club in 1892 to help preserve wilderness values.

The Sierra Club was only a part of the citizen movement that gained strength in the latter part of the 19th century, largely in reaction to the exploitation of natural resources. The American Forestry Association was started in 1875, the Appalachian Mountain Club in 1876, the American Ornithologists Union in 1883 (in addition to numerous Audubon societies), the Boone and Crockett Club in 1887, and hundreds of sportsmen's and natural history clubs.

The 1890s and early 1900s saw the surge of a utilitarian

conservation movement. This approach differed radically from that of the preservationists. Though both had the general aim of protecting and controlling natural resources, the utilitarian approach was to make the wisest use of resources for the greatest number of people while still stressing a form of conservation. This meant *use,* not preservation in wilderness or in unbroken stands of timber. One of utilitarian conservation's early exponents was John Wesley Powell, foremost explorer of the Grand Canyon, who was a sponsor of large federal reclamation and irrigation projects to bring water into the arid regions of the West.

Gifford Pinchot, the first American professional forester, who coined the word "conservation" in 1905, became the principal exponent of the Progressive Conservation movement. Pinchot wanted to protect, preserve, and renew natural resources. But he insisted that "the first principle of conservation is development, the *use* of the natural resources now existing on this continent for the benefit of the people who live here now" (italics added).

For a while Pinchot and Muir were friends, Pinchot the utilitarian, working for careful use of resources, and Muir for the esthetic and ethical values of preserving the land intact for present and future generations. Soon after the turn of the century, however, the fundamental and radical difference between Muir's preservationist ideal and Pinchot's utilitarian conservationist approach led to a sharp conflict between the two men. They became bitter enemies over an effort supported by Pinchot to build a reservoir in the pristine Hetch Hetchy Valley of Yosemite National Park, in order to supply water for the city of San Francisco. The dam became a national issue, and Muir wrote:

> That any one would try to destroy Hetch Hetchy Valley seems incredible. ... These temple destroyers, devotees of ravaging commercialism, seem to have a perfect contempt for Nature, and, instead of lifting their eyes to the God of the mountains, lift them to the Almighty Dollar. Dam Hetch Hetchy! As well dam for water-tanks the people's cathedrals and churches, for no holier temple has ever been consecrated by the heart of man.

The battle continued for a long time and was finally decided in favor of Pinchot in 1913, when Congress with the backing of

Interior Secretary Franklin K. Lane, a former attorney for the city of San Francisco, approved the Hetch Hetchy Dam. Losing this battle broke Muir's heart and he lived only a short time longer. Before his death he wrote that through Hetch Hetchy "the conscience of the whole country has been aroused from sleep." In one way he did have the last word. Despite several attempts over the years, no other dam has ever been built within a national park.

Earlier, Congress had passed the Antiquities Act of 1906 permitting preservation as national monuments those federal lands having unusual scientific, natural, or historical significance. The National Park Service was established in 1916 and expanded under the leadership of Stephen Mather and Horace Albright. States protected natural areas as parks and forest reserves. New citizen organizations such as the National Audubon Society, the Save-the-Redwoods League, and the Wilderness Society were formed. Wilderness areas were set aside within national forests by administrative action and given special protection against logging or development, and a system of national wildlife refuges was established.

The label "conservation" was given to activities that included establishment of the U.S. Bureau of Reclamation, the building of many large dams and irrigation projects, and widespread flood control programs of the U.S. Army Corps of Engineers. Massive efforts at soil conservation were started, especially after the dust bowl of the early 1930s, culminating in the establishment of the Soil Conservation Service of the U.S. Department of Agriculture. Regional planning and multiple use of resources were objectives of the huge Tennessee Valley Authority to improve the environment of a large region. The Taylor Grazing Act of 1934 gave the federal government control of use of public lands in the West.

Some experts have suggested that the success of the utilitarian conservation movement, while providing many benefits to the economic interests of the nation, was at the expense of the expansion of the preservation interests. Part of the achievement of the utilitarian conservationists, says historian Susan L. Flader, "lay in capitalizing on the pre-existing moral fervor for resource protection and channeling it into support for their programs of scientific resource management. The result was certainly a stronger

base for federal resource management agencies, especially the
Forest Service, but this co-opting of the citizen movement may well
have sapped its vitality and led to the fractioning of interests, petty
squabbles, and minimal influence characteristic of the movement
down to recent times."

In the first half of the 20th century people began to give thought
to social concerns rather than seeking only to conquer the land. But
it was not until the 1940s that the stirrings occurred which resulted
in today's broadly based environmental movement and its concern
for quality-of-life issues.

A profound influence on growth of the environmental ethic
began with publication of Aldo Leopold's *A Sand County Almanac*
(1949). Leopold learned only one week before his death in 1948
that a publisher had agreed to print it. Though it had few readers
at first, *A Sand County Almanac and Sketches Here and There*
became well known twenty years later when it was "discovered" by
the general public during the popular environmental movement of
the late 1960s and early 1970s.

Leopold's acute curiosity and powers of observation, combined
with a delightful literary style, carry the reader to discoveries in
both the natural and ethical realms. Inappropriate as its title seems
for a work of such power, the book's main part is indeed an
almanac—a lyrical, revealing account of natural observations
month-to-month at Leopold's Wisconsin property. The last half of
the book is devoted to philosophical essays including "Thinking
Like a Mountain" and "The Land Ethic," which have influenced
and inspired countless environmentalists and writers.

Leopold's ideas underwent a constant refining throughout his
life. After graduating from Yale with a degree in forestry, Leopold
worked for the U.S. Forest Service in New Mexico. By the age of
26 he was supervisor of the Carson National Forest, managing a
billion board feet of timber and a million acres supporting 200,000
sheep. He was attracted to the fish and game management aspects
of Forest Service work and later became the "father" of professional wildlife management in America. At first he was interested
in protecting game animals from predators to provide a shootable
surplus. But influenced by the science of ecology his concept
evolved into one of preserving ecological diversity, not for the sole

purpose of protecting game but to maintain a natural balance among plants and animals. A reorientation also took place in his thinking from a historical and recreational justification for wilderness to a predominantly ecological justification. And in 1935 he became one of the founders of the Wilderness Society.

In his later years Leopold felt more and more the need for an ecologically based ethic. But it was not until the final year of his life that he completed a revised version of his seminal essay "The Land Ethic." This essay set forth the concept of individual responsibility for the health of the land. Leopold wrote that a system of conservation based solely on economic self-interest is hopelessly lopsided.

> It tends to ignore and thus eventually to eliminate many elements in the land community that lack commercial value, but that are (as far as we know) essential to its healthy functioning. It assumes, falsely, I think, that the economic parts of the biotic clock will function without the uneconomic parts. It tends to relegate to government many functions eventually too large, too complex, or too widely dispersed to be performed by government. An ethical obligation on the part of the private owner is the only visible remedy for these situations.

Just before publication of *A Sand County Almanac,* another book helped to show the international dimensions of the growing environmental dilemma. *Our Plundered Planet* was written by Fairfield Osborn, president of the New York Zoological Society and founder of The Conservation Foundation. The book was widely read and aroused many people to recognize the harm being done to the world's natural resources and of the limits to these resources. Osborn painted a striking picture of land being destroyed because of the absence of planning and the harmful agricultural practices that led to erosion, depletion, and loss of productivity. He also warned that the world would face certain disaster unless population growth was curbed. He concluded the book:

> The tide of the earth's population is rising, the reservoir of the earth's living resources is falling. Technologists may outdo

[""]

themselves in the creation of artificial substitutes for natural subsistence, and new areas, such as those in tropical or subtropical regions, may be adapted to human use, but even such recourses or developments cannot be expected to offset the present terrific attack upon the life-giving elements of the earth. There is only one solution. Man must recognize the necessity of co-operating with nature. He must temper his demands and use and conserve the natural living resources of this earth in a manner that alone can provide for the continuation of his civilization. The final answer is to be found only through comprehension of the enduring processes of nature. The time for defiance is at an end.

Rachel Carson's eloquent writings on the need for protecting nature, and her courageous crusade to warn the nation of the potential harm from pesticides and toxic substances, played an important part in the building of an environmental ethic.

Carson had been a lifelong lover of the outdoors and was a born wordsmith. She entered college planning to become a writer, but her encounter with required biology courses drew her into studies that led to bachelor's and master's degrees in zoology as well as postgraduate study in genetics and other ecologically related subjects. But her writing talent refused to lie fallow. Working for the U.S. Fish and Wildlife Service by day, she wrote articles and books in her spare time. One of them, *The Sea Around Us,* plunged her into national prominence in 1951.

In the late 1950s Carson was troubled about the growing threats to the environment being posed by advancing technology. She had become increasingly aware that a growing list of chlorinated hydrocarbon pesticides were affecting fish and wildlife. The pesticides had appeared to serve mankind well by wiping out some insect-carried diseases, but the poisons' long life in the environment was having a devastating effect on wildlife. Carson's troubled ethical sense was finally shocked into action when she heard of songbirds dying after neighboring land was sprayed with DDT. She felt compelled to alert the public. And this time she abandoned her quietly lyrical style and, in *Silent Spring* (1962), painted a calculatedly shocking picture of the process by which DDT worked its way up the food chain from plankton through fish to birds in ever-increasing concentrations until it proved fatal to the birds and produced a silent spring. She gave case study after case study to drive home the point. And though it was uncharacteristic for her to go beyond the scientifically proven, she warned that man was next in the food chain—although there was not yet evidence of impact on man.

The wide readership and resulting discussion of *Silent Spring* were significant among the accumulating factors which by the 1960s were beginning to make Americans conscious that the old saying "What you don't know can't hurt you" might not be true after all. Rational people began to think about unknown and unforeseen consequences and side effects of new technological, scientific, or medical discoveries, when in the past we would have accepted their benefits without question.

Rachel Carson dedicated *Silent Spring* "To Albert Schweitzer who said 'Man has lost the capacity to foresee and to forestall. He will end by destroying the earth.'"

Schweitzer is not ordinarily considered a part of the environmental movement, but his ethic of a reverence for life has influenced many people throughout the world. Although Schweitzer recognized that on occasion it would be necessary to injure or destroy some forms of life in order to preserve human life, he preached what he called "an absolute ethic."

> The ethic of reverence for life recognizes no relative ethic [Schweitzer wrote]. It considers good only the maintenance and furtherance of life. It brands as evil all that destroys and hurts life, no matter what the circumstances may be. It keeps no store of appropriate compromises between ethics and necessity ready for use. Again and again, and always in some original fashion, the absolute ethic of reverence for life brings a man to terms with reality. It does not rid him of conflicts, but it forces him to decide for himself in every case how far he can remain ethical, and how far he must yield to the necessity of destroying and harming life and suffer the ensuing guilt. A man does not make moral progress by being instructed in compromises between the ethical and the necessary, but only by hearing ever more clearly the voice of the ethical, by being ruled ever more strongly by a longing to preserve life and to promote it, and by withstanding

ever more stubbornly the necessity for destroying and injuring it.

Coincident with the rising tide of the environmental movement in the late 1960s and early 1970s a number of scientists and citizen leaders were adding facets to an environmental ethic.

The wilderness preservation ethic of John Muir found an enthusiastic advocate in David R. Brower, a native Californian who picked up the Muir theme during many hiking trips into the Sierra during his youth. Just as Muir led the way in awakening the nation's environmental conscience during the Hetch Hetchy fight of the early 20th century, Brower, as executive director of the Sierra Club for 17 years, played a major role in rousing nationwide support to keep two large dams out of Grand Canyon. And in one sense Brower was more successful than Muir—the dam projects were defeated in 1968, as were proposals in the 1950s for two dams within Dinosaur National Monument, another campaign on which Brower worked. He was a leader in the fight for the North Cascades National Park and worked on countless other preservation projects. He also started the series of handsome picture-text "exhibit format" books which attracted the attention of many people who might not otherwise have become interested in environmental causes. More than half a million of these books have been sold. In 1969 Brower organized a new international organization, Friends of the Earth. By 1978 it had 50,000 members in 16 countries and was working on both national and international environmental issues. In recent years Brower and Friends of the Earth have been involved in seeking a soft energy policy, a conserver society, opposing nuclear power development, and encouraging citizens to participate politically in environmental causes.

No attempt has ever been made to measure the influence American painters and photographers have had on the development of an environmental ethic. The artist with the most direct influence, especially in helping to build support for preservation of national parks, has been Ansel Adams, whose majestic black-and-white photographs have been inspiring people for more than fifty years. A soft-spoken but imposing, Muir-like figure, Adams has played a significant behind-the-scenes role in preservation politics. He has been a major force in the Sierra Club and was a member of its board of directors for 37 years. As far back as 1936, Adams was lobbying Congress with his portfolio on Kings Canyon, which later was made a separate national park in 1940. And a visit at the White House with President Ford in 1975, and later correspondence with him, played a part in Ford's 1976 campaign pledge to increase funding and personnel for national parks. Although most identified with Yosemite National Park, the Adams "images" have recorded the grandeur of America from Maine to Alaska. And while his photographs have overshadowed his writings, Adams nevertheless has exerted influence through his prose, both in prolific personal correspondence and in the text accompanying his published photographs. For instance, in *My Camera in the National Parks* (1950) he wrote:

The national parks represent those intangible values which cannot be turned directly to profit or material advantage. It requires integrity of vision and purpose to consider such impalpable qualities on the same effective level as material resources. Yet everyone must realize that the continued existence of the national parks and all they represent depends upon awareness of the importance of these basic values. The pressures of a growing population, self-interest, and shortness of vision are now the greatest enemies of the national park idea. The perspectives of history are discounted and the wilderness coveted and invaded to provide more water, more grazing land, more minerals, and more inappropriate recreation. These invasions are rationalized on the basis of "necessity." And this necessity may appear quite plausible on casual examination. People must have land, and land must have water. Cattle and sheep must have forage. With the establishment of reservoirs—great man-made lakes often reaching far into the wilderness domain—come diverse human enterprises, roads, resorts, settlements. The wilderness is pushed back; man is everywhere. Solitude, so vital to the individual man, is almost nowhere. Certain values are realized; others destroyed. The dragons of demand have been kept at snarling distance by the St. Georges of conservation, but the menace remains. Only education can

enlighten our people—education, and its accompanying inter-
pretation, and the seeking of resonances of understanding in
the contemplation of nature.

The writings of microbiologist and ecologist Garrett Hardin,
especially his 1968 paper "The Tragedy of the Commons," have
done much to alert people to the ethical dilemmas of a laissez-faire
system operating in a world of limits—although Hardin's proposed
solution has been controversial among environmentalists. The
University of California at Santa Barbara professor of human
ecology is an ardent advocate of population control, and his
"Tragedy of the Commons" is based on an 1833 pamphlet on
population which draws an analogy with the village common
(pasture) which has a large but limited carrying capacity. Hardin's
use of the analogy assumes that each villager has the right to graze
as many cattle as he wishes. In the beginning this seems to work, as
long as tribal wars, poaching, and disease keep the numbers of
both man and beast below the carrying capacity of the land. But
each herdsman realizes, even when he sees limits to the capacity of
the commons, that if he has ten cattle and adds one more, he would
have eleven only slightly leaner beasts rather than ten normal ones.
And thus it is in his own self-interest to add another.

The rational herdsman concludes, states Hardin,

> that the only sensible course for him to pursue is to add another
> animal to his herd. And another; and another . . . But this is the
> conclusion reached by every rational herdsman sharing a
> commons. Therein is the tragedy. Each man is locked into a
> system that compels him to increase his herd without limit—in a
> world that is limited. Ruin is the destination toward which all
> men rush, each pursuing his own best interest in a society that
> believes in the freedom of the commons. Freedom in a
> commons brings ruin to all.

The ethical implications of the tragedy of the commons are that
a villager who recognizes the limitations and scrupulously avoids
adding to his herd does not prosper, whereas the villager with only
immediate self-interest in mind profits, at least until eventual ruin
comes to all. Hardin modernizes the village analogy by relating it
to current problems, not only in population but in overwhaling of

the seas, or overuse of the national parks, limited in size but open to a growing population without limit. "Plainly," says Hardin, "we must soon cease to treat the parks as commons or they will be of no value to anyone."

Hardin does not believe that an environmental ethic can solve the world's food, resource, and pollution problems soon enough to avert disaster. In his "Tragedy of the Commons" essay he suggests that the solution to the irresponsible self-interest that ruins the commons is to impose social arrangements that coerce people into responsible behavior. These arrangements are something short of prohibitions. He calls them "mutual coercion mutually agreed upon." An example is the use of parking meters, agreed upon by citizens, which limit the time the driver may park but do not prohibit parking altogether, a restriction imposed in order to reduce traffic congestion. If the driver acts irresponsibly and overparks, he is ticketed and fined. If his behavior continues, his fines increase. Laws designed so that penalties for breaking them become increasingly expensive, or undesirable in other ways, in effect coerce the public into compliance, Hardin argues.

Barry Commoner, labeled by *Time* magazine in 1970 as the "Paul Revere of Ecology," has done perhaps more than any other contemporary scientist to draw public attention to the environmental ills caused by technology. Commoner and his colleagues at Washington University's Center for the Biology of Natural Systems, which he heads, are constantly working on research which Commoner uses in headline-making attacks—on milk supplies contaminated by strontium 90, for example—or his claim that hamburgers cooked improperly are a potential health hazard. His popular 1971 book *The Closing Circle* claimed a relationship between pollution and profits. Commoner charged that the processes of manufacturing and farming have been displaced by more profitable new technologies which, without appreciably enlarging the per capita consumption of food, shelter, clothing, and transportation, have brought human activity increasingly outside the balance of nature.

Commoner has also popularized what he calls the laws of ecology: everything is connected to everything else (the ecosystem consists of multiple interconnected parts which act on one another); everything must go somewhere (there is no such thing as waste); nature knows best (any man-made change in a natural system is likely to be detrimental to that system); and there is no such thing as a free lunch (anything extracted from the global ecosystem by human effort must be replaced or paid for later).

One powerful spokesman for the ethic who is often overlooked by environmentalists is a French internationalist who with his own inimitable flair has brought environmental concerns to popular attention over the last two decades. Those who might consider Jacques-Yves Cousteau as only an oceanographer, television producer, and underseas adventurer are mistaken. Within him is a deep sense of the environmental ethic. As explorer, as scientist, as philosopher, as politician, he endeavors to communicate a message that all citizens must bear a responsibility for the oceans, the waters that go into them, and the entire biosphere.

When I met Cousteau at a conference on problems of offshore oil drilling, I discovered that he was in the midst of a campaign to rekindle some of the 1970 spirit of Earth Day. He did so by staging "Involvement Days" at major cities around the nation during 1976 and 1977 under the auspices of the Cousteau Society, a nonprofit organization with 150,000 members in the United States. Cousteau, with the cooperation of local environmental organizations, took over a civic center or auditorium and for an entire day and evening presented events similar to those held on Earth Day. A typical involvement day was held at the Seattle Coliseum in October 1977. Local environmentalists organized 120 exhibits in one large hall in which they showed slides and explained their work. The day's activities included speeches by Paul Ehrlich, Amory Lovins (of Friends of the Earth), and Cousteau, with question-and-answer sessions. There were forums discussing major issues of interest to the region, such as oil tankers in Puget Sound, nuclear power plants, and the plight of whales, and there was also a film festival and musical entertainment. About 15,000 people attended the Seattle involvement day. Cousteau staged other such events, some of them with different formats, in Anaheim, California; Lakeland, Florida; Milwaukee, Houston, and Boston.

Cousteau's basic message rests on two pillars: Without a healthy water system no life is possible on the planet, and any kind of pollution ends up in the sea. He writes:

The ocean is the sewer for the entire planet; rain, streams, and rivers drag into the sea toxic particles from the smoke of the factories or of the incinerators, lead compounds from the exhausts of automobiles, pesticides from farm and domestic sprays. Radioactive waste is dumped into the Atlantic. Any irreparable damage done to the water system is an unatonable crime; any human enterprise that might bring about such permanent scars must be withheld until it is proved harmless. The permanent damages that have already been done must be publicized as examples of mistakes to be avoided in the future.

Mass slaughter of whales, incessant scraping of the North Sea's bottom with heavy trawl nets, killing of porpoises and dolphins in tuna purse nets, ravages of coral reefs by spear-fishermen, oil drilling in unsafe offshore areas—these are examples of how a distorted image of progress can lead to a shameless rape of the sea. With increased production as the only goal of national governments, the responsibility to the environment and to future generations is abandoned. Today the word progress is used as a synonym for growth, and growth gets out of hand.

To whom can we turn to obtain an unbiased evaluation of the risks we can accept, not only for ourselves but also for our children, our grandchildren, and the hundreds and thousands of generations to come? The answer is obvious: the average citizen can rely only on his own judgment; his civic duty is to give utterance to that judgment by all means and as loud as he can.

Cousteau presents the environmental ethic as using two basic criteria: first, that no risk at all should be taken when survival of the human species is at stake or when the quality of life of future generations may be threatened; and second, that no chance should be taken on issues that could bring about irreversible damage to the environment in which we live.

"There are good reasons to believe the public is beginning to be aware of these criteria," Cousteau says. "Facing today's environmental emergencies, people are armed with faster and better information than ever before. From the heart of the people a new concept of happiness will emerge, based on a better evaluation of the renewable and non-renewable resources of the planet, on a selfless desire to share these resources more equitably, on respect and love for nature and for life, as well as on the development of new and higher moral standards. If 'quantity' cannot be increased indefinitely, 'quality,' on the contrary, can grow forever."

The Limits to Growth (1972) set forth a compelling picture of the consequences of unchecked growth applied to limited resources. The book, written principally by Donella H. Meadows, was based on work done by a Massachusetts Institute of Technology team headed by Dennis L. Meadows. They wrote the book as a report for The Club of Rome's Project on the Predicament of Mankind. The team used mathematical models to look at the present growth trends in world population, industrialization, pollution, food production, and resource depletion. If the trends of exponential growth continue unchanged, the report concluded, "the limits to growth on this planet will be reached sometime within the next 100 years. The most probable result will be a rather sudden and uncontrollable decline in both population and industrial capacity."

It is possible to alter these growth trends and to establish a condition of ecological and economic stability that is sustainable far into the future, the report said. And if the world's people decide to strive for the latter outcome, "the sooner they begin working to attain it, the greater will be their chances of success."

The importance of starting to attain stability as soon as possible was illustrated with dramatic simplicity by use of a French children's riddle that illustrates exponential growth (doubling, i.e., 1-2-4-8-16-32-64-128 . . .) and the apparent suddenness with which fixed limits can be reached.

> Suppose you own a pond on which a water lily is growing. The lily plant doubles in size each day. If the lily were allowed to grow unchecked, it would completely cover the pond in 30 days, choking off the other forms of life in the water. For a long time the lily plant seems small, and so you decide not to worry about cutting it back until it covers half the pond. On what day will that be? On the 29th day, of course. You have one day to save your pond.

The report went on to show that the limits of some resources can be predicted if knowledge of the rate of their use is known. Severe problems arise, however, in such areas as the upper limits for the exponential growth of some pollutants. How much carbon dioxide or heat, for instance, can be released into the atmosphere without disturbing the natural ecological balance of the earth and producing irreversible changes in the earth's climate? Or how much radioactivity, lead, mercury, or pesticide can be absorbed by plants, fish, or human beings before the vital processes are severely interrupted? The gathering momentum of exponential growth is such that when the upper limits come into view there may not be enough time left to do anything about correcting the situation before tragedy occurs.

In a separate paper, Donella Meadows and Jørgen Randers, two members of the MIT Limits to Growth team, discussed "The Carrying Capacity of Our Global Environment: A Look at Ethical Alternatives." They pointed out that present human behavior is guided by the general idea that all people alive *today* are equally important and that the objective function is to maximize the total current benefits for all these people.

If we choose to adhere strictly to the objective of maximizing the short-term rewards of the present generation [Meadows and Randers wrote], there are in fact no long-term environmental tradeoffs to be made. . . . The question about use or non-use of DDT, for example, would be easily resolved. The fact that 1.3 billion people today can live in safety from malaria due to DDT would strongly outweigh the costs—for instance, in the form of inedible fish—inflicted upon future generations through our continued use of the chemical.

We are basically facing only one ethical question in the impending global crisis. Should we continue to let our actions be guided by the short-term objective function, or should we adopt a longer-term perspective? . . . We feel that the moral and ethical leaders of our societies should adopt the goal of increasing the time-horizon implicit in mankind's activities— that is, introducing the longer-term objective function which maximizes the benefit of those living today, subject to the constraint that it does not decrease the economic and social options of those who will inherit this globe, our children and grandchildren. .... People in general feel some responsibility for the lives of their children, and the long-term objective function seems to be the value implicit in the actions of conservationists. However, ultimately it must be present in *all* our activities.

The solution suggested by Meadows and Randers for the approaching collision between growing societies and the physical limits of the earth is to achieve a "global equilibrium," a steady state in accordance with the globe's physical limits.

The basic philosophy of a steady state economy is not really new—it was discussed in the 19th century by John Stuart Mill.

It is scarcely necessary to remark that a stationary condition of capital and population implies no stationary state of human improvement. There would be as much scope as ever for all kinds of mental culture and moral and social progress; as much room for improving the Art of Living and much more likelihood of its being improved.

Modern-day advocates are led by economists such as Kenneth Boulding and Herman Daly. A steady-state economy and sustainable society do not imply an end to all forms of growth, but simply a sharp limit upon forms of growth that damage our life setting. Steady state may be defined as a stable population that takes from the environment no more each year than is grown in a year, reduces to a minimum its use of raw materials that once used cannot be replaced, and reduces to a minimum all pollution and waste that must be discarded into the environment. To achieve these goals the stock of productive capital goods is stabilized and what is produced is made to be much more durable, able to be repaired and eventually recycled.

Under the present measure of growth—the gross national product (GNP)—bigger is generally accepted as better. The GNP does not consider whether or not the growth is harming the environment or the extent to which it drains nonrenewable resources. But the steady-state economists would require measuring the *real* costs of growth, and determining when the costs outweigh the benefits.

The extension of ethics to embrace man's relation to land and the animals and plants which grow upon it, propounded by Aldo Leopold, has been expanded upon and developed in recent years by a number of scientists, historians, and theologians in their efforts to awaken citizens to the need for an environmental ethic.

Roderick Nash, professor of history and chairman of environmental studies at the University of California at Santa Barbara, has developed the most thorough extension of the basic Leopold philosophy. To explain the evolution of ethics, Nash uses a diagram in the shape of an inverted pyramid. Starting at the narrow bottom point with self, it then broadens to include, step-by-step: family, tribe, nation, race, mankind, mammals, animals, plants, life, and at the top, environment—or "the rights of rocks."

What most concerned Leopold was the possibility of evolving beyond a definition of ethics that halted with *Homo sapiens* [writes Nash]. The upper tiers of the ethics diagram represent this enlargement.... The transition from the human level in the ethical pyramid to all life, and then the transition from life to non-life pose major philosophical problems. Person-to-person ethics is based on mutualism.... There is a practical pay-off to being moral, namely security.... Animals, plants, bacteria, and rocks do not have the capacity for moral mutualism with human beings.... Leopold is clearly on the side of those who feel that rocks and oak trees and wolves are valuable for themselves, regardless of the human interest that might adhere to them. He explicitly rejects self-interest, however enlightened, as the proper rationale for conservation. Self-interest always priorized life and things according to their value to man and not its value to the ecosystem and to itself.

Man, whom technology has made a new god in terms of power to modify the earth, must evolve a god-like ethic that is all-inclusive rather than anthropocentric [adds Nash]. With such an ethic would come the perception that exploitation of the earth is just as wrong as exploitation of one's neighbor. Conversely, with environmental ethics a reality, the entire life community and the rocks as well will be perceived as man's neighbors as in fact they are.

The land ethic demands that we be concerned about the

condition of the environment not because it is profitable or beautiful and not even because it promotes our own survival as a species but because in the last analysis it is right.

The extension of some types of rights to nonhumans was recognized by Justice William O. Douglas in a major Supreme Court suit—*Sierra Club* v. *Morton* (1972)—concerning a proposed Walt Disney ski resort in a California national forest area which would have required a concrete access highway to be built through Sequoia National Park. Although the Sierra Club's "standing" to sue the secretary of the interior to refuse permission for the road to go through the national park was denied in a 4-3 vote, Justice Douglas wrote an eloquent dissent, which stated in part:

> Contemporary public concern for protecting nature's ecological equilibrium should lead to the conferral of standing upon environmental objects to sue for their own preservation. . . .
>
> The voice of the inanimate object should not be stilled. . . . before these priceless bits of Americana (such as a valley, an alpine meadow, a river, or a lake) are forever lost or are so transformed as to be reduced to the eventual rubble of our urban environment, the voice of the existing beneficiaries of these environmental wonders should be heard. . . .
>
> Those who hike the Appalachian Trail into Sunfish Pond, New Jersey, and camp or sleep there, or run the Allagash in Maine, or climb the Guadalupes in West Texas, or who canoe and portage the Quetico Superior in Minnesota, certainly should have standing to defend those natural wonders before courts or agencies, though they live 3,000 miles away. Those who merely are caught up in environmental news or propaganda and flock to defend these waters or areas may be treated differently. That is why these environmental issues should be tendered by the inanimate object itself. Then there will be assurances that all of the forms of life which it represents will stand before the court—the pileated woodpecker as well as the coyote and bear, the lemmings as well as the trout in the streams. Those inarticulate members of the ecological group cannot speak. But those people who have so frequented the

place as to know its values and wonders will be able to speak for the entire ecological community.

The "rights" of nature have been considered not only in the legal realm, but among thinkers and scholars in philosophy, biology, history, anthropology, theology, literature, and political science. They were the subject of a book by Christopher Stone—*Should Trees Have Standing?* (1975)—and of a major conference in 1974 at Claremont, California, where it was discussed (although with a wide diversity of viewpoints) by an international group including Charles Birch from Australia, John A. Livingston from Canada, Native American Indian writer Vine Deloria, Jr., Pulitzer Prize-winning poet Gary Snyder, Garrett Hardin, Roderick Nash, John Lilly, Paul Shepard, Joseph W. Meeker, John B. Cobb, Jr., and John Rodman.

Rodman, professor of political studies at Pitzer College and the Claremont Graduate School, who organized the conference says:

"The environmental movement is in some danger of being torn between two points of view. On the one hand are the 'Enlightened Egoists' who claim to calculate that it is useful and necessary to save the California Condor or the Furbish Lousewort in order for the human species or human civilization to survive. On the other hand are the 'Nature Moralists' who would insist we have a duty to save, or at least not to exterminate, condors and louseworts because they have a right to exist. Both Enlightened Egoists and Nature Moralists occupy niches within the overall ecology of the environmental movement. The danger is that their paths will diverge radically and that the contemporary movement will split like the earlier movement split into conservationists and preservationists. This is why it is important to recognize a third and more comprehensive dimension of the emerging environmental ethic— what I call 'Ecological Sensibility.' Ecological Sensibility involves an awareness that the individual self and the politically organized society, as well as the biosphere, are ecologically structured— composed of diverse elements interacting to maintain what is normally a relatively steady state condition."

A somewhat far-out institutional solution has been proposed by an MIT researcher, Newell B. Mack. In a 1972 paper which has appeared only in a volume of congressional subcommittee hearings, Mack delved into the problem of the rights of future generations.

Our choices help shape the earth on which future generations will live [Mack wrote]. But their needs seldom guide our decisions. Should the needs of distant generations weigh in our choices? [he questioned] And, if so, how can we limit one generation's impact (felt centuries later as radioactive wastes, modified climate, etc.) so as to enforce the rights of later generations?
Because no distant generation pushes its will on us, we are not forced to recognize any "right" it may have to limit our power. One motivation we have for considering the future effects of our actions is *our* concern for "grandchildren" many generations hence. A different motivation might be to regard *them* as having some sort of claim to the earth they will inherit. Do *they* have rights, quite independent of how far in the future *we* emotionally care about the consequences of our actions? In short, do grandchildren have rights?

If it is judged that grandchildren do have rights, then working toward a steady state society is necessary, Mack concludes. But "those who would benefit most from a sustained society, our grandchildren, are powerless," he writes. "Their weight is not felt in the tug-of-war which produces decisions."
Mack's unorthodox idea was to draft a bill for Congress to implement the wording of section 101 (b) of the National Environmental Policy Act, which states that "it is the continuing responsibility of the federal government" to act so that the nation may "fulfill the responsibilities of each generation as trustee of the environment for succeeding generations." Mack proposed a Grandchild-Rights Amendment to the Constitution providing: "Equality of rights under the law shall not be denied or abridged by the United States or by any State on account of generation."
Other legislation would establish a Grandchild Protection Agency ("to examine our generation's options, and lobby for the choice which it feels a later generation might want us to pick"). And the bill would require Grandchild Impact Statements to

estimate the consequences (depleted resources, modified climate, etc.) of our decisions for our grandchildren, written from our *grandchildren's* point of view, *not ours.*

A spoof? No. Mack's suggestions are a "thought experiment" rather than a proposal for specific legislation, but he feels that nongovernmental groups could lobby—now—as surrogates for future generations. And he believes the concept of explicitly considering future generations in our decision-making deserves eventually to be institutionalized in the government.

Elements of an environmental ethic are suggested by Lewis Mumford in his book, *The Pentagon of Power* (1970).

> Reformers who would treat the campaign against environmental and human degradation solely in terms of improved technological facilities, like the reduction of gasoline exhaust in motor cars, see only a small part of the problem. Nothing less than a profound re-orientation of our vaunted technological "way of life" will save this planet from becoming a lifeless desert. And without such a wide-ranging preliminary alteration of personal desires, habits, and ideals the necessary physical measures for mankind's protection—to say nothing of its further development—cannot conceivably be carried out. . . .
>
> For its effective salvation mankind will need to undergo something like a spontaneous religious conversion: one that will replace the mechanical world picture with an organic world picture, and give to the human personality, as the highest known manifestation of life, the precedence it now gives to machines and computers.

Although René Dubos is controversial among some preservationists for his beliefs in a Benedictine ethic toward the earth—a creative stewardship in which humans interact with nature and improve it—he has been a major influence in alerting the public to the need for an ecologically ethical approach. The French-born microbiologist has been an advocate of environmental causes such as preserving Jamaica Bay, Long Island, from development, improving the quality of life for residents of the inner city (he headed the first national Conference on the Urban Environment), opponent of growth for growth's sake, and waste of energy, and a strong supporter of biomass conversion and other uses of solar energy. It is in his writings, however, that he has been most widely known, especially in his Pulitzer Prize-winning book *So Human an Animal* and in *A God Within,* and for an article "A Theology of the Earth," published in *Audubon* Magazine in January 1972.

The problems of poverty, disease, and environmental decay cannot be solved merely by the use of more and more scientific technology [Dubos wrote in his *Audubon* article]. Technological fixes usually turn out to be a jumble of procedures that have unpredictable consequences and are often in conflict with natural forces. Indeed, technological magic is not much better than primitive magic in dealing with the fundamental issues of human existence, and in addition, it is much more destructive. In contrast, better knowledge of man's relationships to the Earth may enable us to be even more protective of the natural world than were our primitive forebears; informed reason is likely to be a better guide for the management of nature than was superstition or fear. We do know scientifically that the part of the Earth on which we live is not dead material but a complex living organism with which we are interdependent; we also know that we have already used a large percentage of the resources that have accumulated in the course of its past. The supply of natural resources, in fact, presents a situation in which the practical selfish interests of mankind are best served by an ethical attitude. . . .

While the living Earth still nurtures and shapes man, he now possesses the power to change it and to determine its fate, thereby determining his own fate. . . . The Biblical injunction that man was put in the Garden of Eden "to dress it and to keep it" is an early warning that we are responsible for our environment. To strive for environmental quality might be considered as an eleventh commandment, concerned of course with the external world, but also encompassing the quality of life. An ethical attitude in the scientific study of nature readily leads to a theology of the Earth.

The need for something like a spontaneous religious conversion was developed in more detail by E. F. Schumacher.

The problem posed by environmental deterioration [he wrote] is not primarily a technical problem; if it were, it would not have arisen in its acutest form in the technologically most advanced societies. It does not stem from scientific or technological competence, or from insufficient scientific education, or from a lack of information, or from any shortage of trained manpower, or lack of money for research. It stems from the lifestyle of the modern world, which in turn arises from its most basic beliefs—its metaphysics, if you like, or its religion.

The whole of human life, it might be said, is a dialogue between man and his environment, a sequence of questions and responses. We pose questions to the universe by what we do, and the universe, by its response, informs us of whether our actions fit into its laws or not. Small transgressions evoke limited or mild responses; large transgressions evoke general, threatening, and possibly violent responses. . . .

It is unlikely that the destructive forces which the materialist philosophy has unleashed can be "brought under control" simply by mobilizing more resources—of wealth, education, and research—to fight pollution, to preserve wildlife, to discover new sources of energy, and to arrive at more effective agreements on peaceful co-existence. Everything points to the fact that what is most needed today is a revision of the ends which all our efforts are meant to serve. And this implies that above all else we need the development of a lifestyle which accords to material things their proper legitimate place, which is secondary and not primary.

Justice William O. Douglas discussed the environmental ethic in *The Three Hundred Year War, A Chronicle of Ecological Disaster* (1972). He called the book "a plea to all men to follow Aldo Leopold's ethic and enlarge the boundaries of the community to include soils, waters, plants, and animals, or collectively, the land."

As a people we have no ecological ethic [Douglas wrote]. We talk much about Law and Order and we mean it when we say that burglaries, street crimes, holdups and the like must cease. But in a deeper sense we have a basic disrespect of law—unless the law restrains the other group, not our own.

The corporate world—every pressure group—is always looking for means of avoiding or even evading environmental regulations. One of their techniques is to control the agency entrusted with protection of the public interest. . . .

Critics say that a "no growth" society would be repudiated by the poor as a conspiracy to rob them of the material things others have already acquired. Yet it is clear that the ravaging and raping of the earth that has gone on must stop. New amenities toward the less fortunate among us must be cultivated, as vast restructuring of society is needed. But there is no reason why the Good Life may not be enjoyed when we are in a state of equilibrium instead of in an era of roaring growth. . . .

Our priorities have been an overseas war, not the Three Hundred Year War at home. Population pressures mount; littering and pollution remain a scourge; the powerful lobbies seem bent on destroying our last few sanctuaries.

For things to change [Douglas concluded] there must be a spiritual awakening. Our people—young and old—must become truly activist—and aggressively so—if we and the biosphere on which we depend are to survive.

15

"WITHOUT LEAVING ANY TRACK"

Reviewing the impressions collected over the ten years since I became aware of the environmental ethic and started looking for it in places where decisions are made, I find some conclusions forming in my mind as to how the ethic is faring in the three branches of government and in business, in labor, in education, and in religion. These are the areas where I feel that its presence can have the greatest effect on the quality of life.

How is the environmental ethic faring in the three branches of the federal government?

Congress intended to furnish an institutional framework for bringing environmental concerns into executive branch decision-making when it enacted the National Environmental Policy Act of 1969, with its environmental impact statement process. Despite considerable foot dragging by the agencies, which have tended to prepare impact statements after decisions have been made, the process itself has at least given environmental concern a place in many agencies. More than 8,000 environmental impact statements have been filed, and most agencies have hired scientific and environmental experts to prepare them. It is to be hoped that the addition of these experts as permanent staff members may help to influence future actions.

In a number of instances agencies have abandoned environmentally harmful projects after environmental assessments were made, although most agency officials are reluctant to say how many have been dropped or to specify which ones. Quite a few federal projects have been canceled or modified or delayed as a result of lawsuits filed against government agencies by citizens or environmental legal groups such as the Environmental Defense Fund, the Natural Resources Defense Council, and the Sierra Club Legal Defense Fund.

Laws such as those enacted to control air and water pollution or provide additional parks and wilderness have also produced environmental compliance from the agencies, though the compliance is often grudgingly given. The Department of Energy has created the position of assistant secretary for environment. So has the Department of State, although the post has had little influence. The Department of Transportation added an assistant secretary for environment and urban affairs in 1969, but later eliminated the post. The work of these and other units and the presence of an impact statement for letting environmental concerns be heard along with economic and technological factors do not guarantee an environmentally sound approach, however. The agency decision-makers are still free to disregard these inputs—and they do all too often.

In mid-1978, with President Carter's approval, the Council on Environmental Quality took a significant step to force agencies to build the environmental concerns into their planning processes early, before decisions are made. After holding extensive hearings, CEQ set forth the following new regulations:

• Impact statements should be prepared early enough so that they can serve as an important contribution to the decision-making process "and shall not be used to rationalize or justify decisions

already made." Also environmental documents and appropriate
analyses must be circulated and reviewed at the same time as other
planning documents.

• Impact statements should identify the environmentally preferable alternative and the reason for identifying it, as well as the
agency's selected alternative if it is not the environmentally
preferable one.

• Each proposal should contain relevant environmental documents, comments, and responses as it goes through the agency
review process in order to allow agency officials to use the
statement in making decisions.

• In all cases requiring environmental impact statements, the
agency must prepare a concise public record of the decision, giving
the reason why the environmentally preferable alternative was not
followed and the reasons why other specific considerations of
national policy overrode those environmental alternatives.

Bureaucracy being what it is, some federal executives will still
find a way to get around these provisions. But the new regulations
should go a long way toward closing the present decision-making
loopholes.

The National Environmental Policy Act also has fallen short of
accomplishing fully Congress's objective of providing the president
with an institution—the Council on Environmental Quality—which
could give him regular environmental advice to be weighed with
other factors in the decision-making process. As noted earlier,
Presidents Nixon and Ford did not use the council directly for
environmental advice. While President Carter does not meet with
the council or its chairman regularly on environmental matters, he
does make it possible for the council to send its suggestions to him.
And it receives his own written comments in return—a proof that at
least the council's ideas are getting to him for consideration.

A president necessarily draws upon many sources in addition to
the Council on Environmental Quality for advice on environmental issues. And he should be expected to weigh the economic,
political, and social factors along with the environmental. President
Carter's well-developed personal sense of environmental commitment was more evident in his first year in office than at mid-term,
when practical political considerations were demanding more
weight than at the beginning. However, he has appointed well-

qualified people as members of the Council on Environmental Quality, and the administration has hired so many environmental activists that it has taken a considerable toll on conservation organizations, which have lost some of their best workers to the administration.

Gus Speth, Carter appointee to the Council on Environmental Quality and a vigorous critic of government actions when he was a lawyer for the Natural Resources Defense Council, observes that the degree to which environmental considerations are involved in executive branch deliberations varies greatly from year to year and from issue to issue.

"We are very far along in having environmental concerns institutionalized in the executive branch. With some exceptions, environmental considerations are now factored into the day-to-day decisions of federal agencies, largely because of the existence of a series of powerful laws enacted by Congress during the past decade," Speth told me. "Environmental impacts are regularly weighed with economic and other factors in making agency decisions. This routine incorporation of environmental factors, however, does not mean that the bureaucracy is now heavy with environmentalists or that environmental concerns are always paramount. Far from it. Indeed, our economic and energy troubles and a more acute awareness of some of the costs and constraints of environmental programs have *decreased* support for environmental protection in some quarters, in and out of government," Speth said. "Environmental gains today are hard fought and much more difficult than in the immediate past. The degree of concern over the economy and energy, the leadership provided by particular administrations, the support for the environment in Congress, and other factors all seem to affect the amount of sympathetic support environmental concerns receive in the executive branch."

One example of how environmental concerns are being dealt with by federal agencies and the difficulties these considerations create is illustrated by the Army Corps of Engineers. Although in the past it had earned from environmentalists the name "Public Enemy No. 1," the corps has made efforts over the past several years to change its anti-environmental image.

Since 1970 the Corps of Engineers has appointed a citizen board of environmental advisers, filed more than 1,500 environmental impact statements, and modified one out of every three projects being planned or already under construction when impact statements showed the need to reduce adverse ecological or social effects. The corps halted 46 projects or studies because of potential environmental harm. It has hired 450 natural and social scientists to assist in environmental work, and several hundred military and civilian employees have taken special environmental training courses. The corps's preparation of environmental impact statements and review of other agencies' statements is generally considered good. The corps dropped considerations of a site for the Hartland Dam on the Arkansas River in Kansas to avoid destruction of bald eagle and golden eagle wintering areas, abandoned a hurricane barrier project at Stratford, Connecticut, because it would harm an extensive wetland, and eliminated a proposed dam at Big Pine Lake near Attica, Indiana, because it would have meant the loss of esthetic, scientific, and educational values in the Fall Creek Gorge. The corps's official policy for flood control now lists finding a "nonstructural" alternative as the first priority. This means that rather than considering only a dam or other construction, the corps should try to correct flooding problems by purchase of land in flood plains or through other solutions that depend on correct use of the land. The corps has also made progress in restoring marshes, protecting wetlands, and preventing many harmful dredge and fill operations.

"The corps has always had concern for environmental affairs, but this concern had a much lower priority than primary objectives assigned it by Congress," Chief of Engineers Lt. Gen. John W. Morris told me. He acknowledged that the environmental movement and the groundswell of citizen pressure forced the corps to change its priorities and procedures. "It took a while to get this cranked up," Morris said. "We had a 30,000-man organization and we had to reshape ourselves with only a few added people. We had a large load of projects that had been conceived in a different era and under different conditions. We had inertia in some places, and some of our people didn't want to lean toward the environment. We had environmental lawsuits against us—and they were needed. But what we have accomplished environmentally in a few years will seem in the span of history almost an overnight change."

The corps still has a long way to go before General Morris's environmental objectives are reflected in the field. One of the difficulties is a lack of an adequate structure to enable environmental concerns to be built into decision-making at a high enough level. For instance, one of the corps's best environmental sections is the one in Seattle. Under the direction of Steven Dice, a 25-member Environmental Resources Section has been assembled, including a number of biological and social scientists. The unit, however, operates at a third echelon in the organization, reporting to the chief of planning, who reports to the chief of the engineering division, who reports to the district engineer. As a result, the environmental resources section has a difficult time influencing policy.

Most of the citizens who have opposed the corps for many years admit it has made some progress but complain that the major problems still exist. Some district engineers, influenced by old-line civilian public officials, still resort to environmentally harmful solutions. Also, neither Congress nor the Office of Management and Budget has been in any hurry to approve and fund nonstructural projects, and in practice the nonstructural approach has not so far been a viable alternative to building a new dam or channel.

At the 1978 "damfighters" conference of the American Rivers Conservation Council, most of the 200 delegates from 13 states, representing 70 environmental and civic organizations, had complaints about the corps. They were especially vocal about the corps's efforts to perpetuate projects such as the Trinity River Channel in Texas, Locks and Dam 26 at Alton, Illinois (which could lead to dredging a wider channel on the Mississippi River), and the Tennessee-Tombigbee Waterway (ten locks and dams to move toll-free barge traffic along a 232-mile waterway from the Tennessee River through Mississippi and Alabama to the Gulf of Mexico). Tenn-Tom costs have risen from $289 million to the present $2-billion estimate. To maintain a favorable benefit-to-cost ratio, the corps has been allowed by Congress to maintain the discount rate of 3¼% that existed when the project was first authorized. Under the current discount rate of over 6%, which is more than double the original, the Tenn-Tom would be an economic failure and probably would have to be dropped. Critics also have alleged that the corps, without approval from Congress, has expanded the width of the Tenn-Tom from the authorized 170 feet to 300 feet so that it will accommodate wider barges and allow heavier traffic. When asked why it continues with these old projects the corps answers that Congress has approved them and that (like good soldiers) corps officials are only following orders.

Brent Blackwelder, chairman of the board of the American Rivers Conservation Council and water resources lobbyist for the Environmental Policy Center, says that he is not convinced that the corps has turned over a new leaf. "We have stopped more than fifty dams in the last ten years, saving taxpayers about $4 billion," Blackwelder told me. "But I'm working harder than ever now in battling against corps projects. The same civilian corps employees who have always controlled things in the past in the districts are still there, pushing to start construction on a huge range of environmentally damaging projects which already have been authorized. The same people are in control of the public works and appropriations committee, and the corps military people go along with what the committee members want. The corps is doing a good job in the areas in which it has regulatory authority, such as wetlands and dredge-and-fill operations. But while we may find occasional excellent examples of nonstructural flood control projects that the corps has produced, I can count them on the fingers of one hand."

The Corps of Engineers has not yet earned the plaudits of environmentalists. And until something happens to change the system in which powerful congressmen get authorizations and funds appropriated for the controversial projects, no one should expect too much more of an environmental ethic to emerge in the Corps of Engineers.

Looking at the legislative branch of the federal government, I have found that many members of Congress—with some notable exceptions—have maintained a record of concern for the environment and a degree of understanding of environmental issues. Individual members are of course subject to many political pressures affecting the way they shape and vote on legislation. Environmental lobbyists have made their presence felt in the halls of Congress even though they have been vastly outnumbered and outspent by the lobbyists of the development interests. The small staffs of the Sierra Club, Friends of the Earth, the Environmental

Policy Center, and other organizations have performed extensive research into the issues and made their cases in a responsible manner that has impressed many members of Congress.

Despite occasional slowness, Congress has managed to pass a large number of environmental laws during the past decade. And the backlash against the environment has not resulted in a significant change in legislation, probably because members of Congress realize that environmental issues remain important to their constituents.

Early in 1977 the Senate shuffled its hidebound committee structure for a number of reasons, one of which was to deal better with environmental matters. The new system is somewhat better structurally, but improvement in dealing with environment has not been greatly evident so far. In the House of Representatives attempts at reorganization failed except for the division of duties of the disbanded Joint Atomic Committee among several committees.

The committee system of the House and Senate is not geared to looking at long-term, comprehensive solutions to environmental problems. Instead, committees tend to deal with current issues one at a time. They rarely focus on why today's crisis occurred and what it indicates about the identity and dimensions of tomorrow's crises. And while the environment has received a comparatively good reception in the 1970s, this may in large measure be attributable to the fact that environmental concerns had not yet run into direct competition with energy development, jobs, and the economy, and the costs in dollars and limitations on growth that will be involved in achieving cleaner air. As that happens, the strength of the environmental movement will be severely tested.

The ability of members of Congress to deal with environmental issues has been greatly aided by the establishment and growth of the Environmental Study Conference. When Representative Richard L. Ottinger of New York returned to Congress in 1975 after a four-year absence, he sensed that there was danger of losing the environmental gains of recent years. With ten other members of the House he formed the Environmental Study Conference. At first it was similar to weekly breakfast sessions he had arranged in 1969-70. The concept grew, a professional staff was hired, costs were shared among congressional members, and a weekly bulletin was published giving members detailed background, pro and con, on all of the environmental issues involved in legislation the House would be considering. The conference spread to the Senate in 1976, and by 1978, 70 of the 100 Senators and 230 of the 435 members of the House had joined. Five former newspaper reporters have been hired to do the type of research and writing that provides objective analytical reports for the weekly bulletin. The writers also prepare special studies on upcoming subjects of interest. Weekly breakfast discussions with prominent guest speakers, and briefings related to news events or new scientific or technological work, keep the conference members informed on environmental issues.

A second means of helping members of Congress make wise decisions related to the environment is the Congressional Clearing-house on the Future, started by Rep. Charlie Rose of North Carolina. As chairman of the House task group on computers, Rose was interested in having the data that were being accumulated in the private sector concerning futures issues made available to Congress. The Clearinghouse effort is led by 23 members of the House and 4 Senators. It distributes a monthly newsletter and arranges discussions with leaders in the field, such as Margaret Mead, Herman Kahn, Arthur Clarke, John Kenneth Galbraith, Isaac Asimov, Buckminster Fuller, Elizabeth and David Dodson Gray, and the late E. F. Schumacher. Trends in several subject areas are being monitored by 130 congressional staff people who review books and periodicals on a volunteer basis and point out to members of Congress places where change is expected to occur.

Most surprising of the three branches of government in its ability to deal with the conflicts arising from the environmental movement has been the federal judiciary. Some environmentalists feared that their lawsuits would place important decisions in the hands of conservative judges who had no knowledge of environmental values. Contrary to these predictions, the courts have proved to be a major factor in carrying out the intent of the new environmental laws and have elaborated upon them in a way that has led to fuller environmental protection. This does not mean that most judges are environmentalists or that the environmentalists have won most of the cases. In fact, the environmentalists lose the majority of cases they file. A study of litigation under the National Environmental Policy Act showed that in cases where lawsuits had been filed

against federal agencies over their environmental impact statements, the court decided in favor of the agencies in five out of
every six cases. Yet on most of the important cases that would
strengthen or weaken new environmental legislation, the courts
have ruled to bolster the statutes—in laws covering air and water
pollution, pesticide registration, nuclear licensing, and endangered
species; in supporting state and local land use laws, and interpreting the National Environmental Policy Act with regard to areas
such as oil leasing, grazing on public lands, clear-cutting of timber
in national forests, the Alaska pipeline, highways, dredge-and-fill
activities, wetlands protection, dams, wilderness, and strip mining.

Why have the courts—particularly at the federal appellate level—
taken these positions, especially inasmuch as few judges are
outspoken environmentalists? Two factors may help to explain.

One is that the courts have been involved in an informal
administrative reform movement, and it happens that environmental lawsuits have played an important part in the process through
which the courts have closely reviewed the actions of the federal
agencies. In the late 1960s a number of individuals had been
complaining that the courts were allowing the government to be lax
in enforcing civil rights, consumer protection, and other laws
dealing with citizen concerns. Government agencies often were
arrogant when dealing with complaints. Then along came the
environmental movement which found that the government was
not only casual about enforcing laws and regulations but also was
itself one of the chief culprits in harming the environment through
building highways or dams or giving permits for pipelines or
dredging operations, or clear-cutting timber.

The environmental movement also had in its forefront a number
of people not accustomed to getting a quick brushoff from
government, and the movement included skilled lawyers who were
environmentally concerned and willing to donate their time and
services to environmental causes. Their solid, well-prepared, and
legally persuasive arguments have been a major factor in the
courts' responsible decisions.

The environmental impact statement provision of NEPA opened
the way for many lawsuits against the government. Aided by
liberal rulings on "standing" from the Supreme Court in nonenvironmental areas, citizens were able to bring environmental cases

into the courts. With the new environmental laws as catalyst, the courts by and large interpreted the laws to make the agencies more responsive.

Another reason for the decisions' appearing to reinforce environmental legislation might be that most judges are upper middle class, politically sensitized, and, as a group, personally concerned about the quality of life and threats to environmental quality. For whatever reasons, the courts, in most cases, have forced government agencies to administer and enforce the law more adequately and take cognizance of citizen complaints.

In a number of the environmental cases of the 1970s, even though procedural (as opposed to substantive) issues were being argued, some judges showed clear evidences of an environmental concern in their rulings or dissenting opinions.

Supreme Court Justice William O. Douglas's environmental view came through strongly in a number of court situations before he retired in 1975. For instance, in a California dam construction case in which the environmental impact statement was alleged to be faulty but the District Court had refused to stop the building of the dam, Douglas wrote in 1974:

The tendency has been to downgrade this mandate of Congress [The National Environmental Policy Act] to use shortcuts to the desired end, and to present impact statements after a project has been started, when there is already such momentum that it is difficult to stop. There are even cases where the statement is not prepared by a government agency, but by a contractor who expects to profit from the project. One hesitates to interfere once a project is started, but if the congressional mandate is to be meaningful, it must be done here.

And when the Supreme Court refused to accept a case in which a freeway in San Antonio would have taken 250 acres out of Brackenridge-Olmos Basin Parklands along the San Antonio River, Douglas wrote a 1970 dissent, saying:

Is not the ruination of a sanctuary created for urban people an "irreversible and irretrievable loss" in the meaning of 102 [Section 102 (2) (c) of the National Environmental Policy Act]?

I do not think we will have a more important case this term. Congress has been moving with alarm against the perils of the environment. One need not be an expert to realize how awful the consequences are when urban sanctuaries are filled with structures, paved with concrete or asphalt, and converted into thoroughfares of high speed modern traffic.

In the Mineral King case, Justice Potter Stewart, in writing the majority opinion that denied standing to the Sierra Club, still acknowledged that:

> Esthetic and environmental well-being, like economic well-being, are important ingredients of the quality of life in our society, and the fact that particular environmental interests are shared by the many rather than the few does not make them less deserving of legal protection through the judicial process.

And in a dissenting opinion on the same case (along with Justice Douglas), Justice Harry A. Blackmun said:

> The case poses—if only we choose to acknowledge and reach them—significant aspects of a wide, growing and disturbing problem, that is, the Nation's and the world's deteriorating environment with its resulting ecological disturbances. Must our law be so rigid and our procedural concepts so inflexible that we render ourselves helpless when the existing methods and the traditional concepts do not quite fit and do not prove to be entirely adequate for new issues?

Justice Blackmun also referred to a pertinent observation and warning of the 17th-century English poet and clergyman, John Donne:

> No man is an Iland, intire of itselfe; every man is a peece of the Continent, a part of the maine; if a Clod bee washed away by the Sea, Europe is the lesse, as well as if a Promontorie were, as well as if a Mannor of thy friends or of thine owne were; any man's death diminishes me, because I am involved in Man-

kinde; And therefore never send to know for whom the bell tolls; it tolls for thee.

[Devotions XVII]

Judge Skelly Wright of the U.S. District of Columbia Circuit Court of Appeals, in the landmark 1971 Calvert Cliffs case, required the Atomic Energy Commission to revise its rules governing consideration of environmental issues.

> We do not impose a harsh burden on the Commission. For we require only an exercise of substantive discretion which will protect the environment "to the fullest extent possible." No less is required if the grand congressional purposes underlying NEPA (the National Environmental Policy Act) are to become a reality.

In another landmark case, *Zabel* v. *Tabb* (1970), the U.S. Circuit Court of Appeals reversed a district court which had ruled that the Army Corps of Engineers could not refuse on environmental grounds to allow a trailer park developer to dredge and fill land in Boca Ciega Bay near St. Petersburg, Florida. Stated Chief Judge John R. Brown in his opinion:

> We hold that nothing in the statutory structure compels the Secretary [of the Army] to close his eyes to all that others see or think they see. The establishment was entitled, if not required, to consider ecological factors and, being persuaded by them, to deny that which might have been granted routinely five, ten, or fifteen years before man's explosive increase made all, including Congress, aware of civilization's potential destruction from breathing its own polluted air and drinking its own infected water and the immeasurable loss from a silent-spring-like disturbance of nature's economy.

State court judges have also made some significant environmental decisions, especially in land-use cases, upholding laws protecting natural areas. One of the outstanding decisions was reached in

Wisconsin when property owners started dredging their lakeshore land to develop it, in defiance of a Marinette County shoreline zoning ordinance. When the landowners sued the county, claiming they were being deprived of the right to develop their own property, the Wisconsin Supreme Court backed Marinette County. Said the court:

> Swamps and wetlands were once considered wasteland, undesirable, and not picturesque. But as the people became more sophisticated, an appreciation was acquired that swamps and wetlands serve a vital role in nature, are part of the balance of nature and are essential to the purity of the water in our lakes and streams. Swamps and wetlands are a necessary part of the ecological creation and now, even to the uninitiated, possess their own beauty in nature. . . . The shoreland zoning ordinance preserves nature, the environment, and natural resources as they were created and to which the people have a present right. The ordinance does not create or improve the public condition but only preserves nature from the despoilage and harm resulting from the unrestricted activities of humans.

How is an environmental ethic faring among the state governments?

A number of states have made progress in looking at environmental concerns. Eighteen states and Puerto Rico have passed laws or issued executive orders requiring environmental impact statements. Florida and California have been the most outstanding in their environmental commitment.

When Reuben Askew became governor in 1970, he realized that Florida faced impending crises in two environmental areas—availability and quality of water, and loss of natural areas and resources to development. He did not himself know what to do to avert the crises and, with an elected cabinet, his power to act administratively was severely restricted. So one of his first actions was to call a water management conference of citizen leaders from business, labor, environment, land developers, and public officials. Askew directed them to work out solutions and draft a legislative program, and they did. A permanent citizens committee helped to draft legislation and, with strong citizen support, four major laws were enacted: a land and water management act, a land conservation act, a water resources act, and a comprehensive planning act.

Voters supported a $240-million bond issue to enable the state to buy up critical areas, and many parcels ripe for development have already been saved. For a state dominated by a "growth at all costs" attitude for most of the 20th century, with little regard for environmental protection, Florida has shown remarkable progress in conservation, although the development pressures are still strong and the new legislation has not been implemented as vigorously as its proponents had hoped.

"Florida will grow," Askew told me during an interview. "We should not fear that growth. But we should make sure that it is in the right place at the right time and that we can manage it. We will need compromises consistent with our goals. But the benefit of the doubt must always be reconciled in favor of the environment. You can't come back and undo the changes made in nature. We don't own the land. We are only passing stewards, and we will be known to future generations for what we pass on to them."

California has a long record of citizen environmental concern that has produced some unique accomplishments. After a citizen brought suit against a developer for not filing an environmental impact report in compliance with the California Environmental Quality Act, the courts interpreted the law as requiring impact reports not only on major state actions but on large-scale commercial developments as well. When special interest lobbyists succeeded in defeating passage of legislation to protect coastal areas, citizens forced onto the 1972 ballot a proposition for coastal zone protection, and it won 55% of the vote. California air quality standards and pollution requirements for automobiles and trucks are higher than federal standards. And Governor Brown has appointed people from the environmental movement to a number of key positions in state government.

Brown's director of planning and research, Bill Press, organized an unusual conference in February 1977 on the subject of the land ethic. One hundred and fifty people were invited to explore the system of values by which state government makes land-use decisions and to adopt a land ethic for the state. The participants represented small and large-scale agriculture, real estate, major developers, railroad and timber companies, native American

Indians, environmental groups, state and local government, banks, and utilities. They listened to talks by Roderick Nash, E. F. Schumacher, and Governor Jerry Brown, and, after breaking into small discussion groups, they assembled to consider translating a land ethic into policy. And the participants agreed to support, in their own ways, the following ethic:

> First, the land is the basis of all life. Second, that land is a very valuable, a very limited, and an irreplaceable resource. Third, that we as temporary stewards on the land have a responsibility to care for the land, to nurture it, and to turn it over to those who follow us in better condition than we found it.

Governor Brown has strong views on the need for an environmental ethic:

> It is not enough just to pass laws to protect the environment. The law has to reflect the feeling of the people in a society. The natural resources of our state—and the nation—affect all the people and their children. We need caring and commitment to draw on the natural resources in a way that is sustainable over the long term, that has concern for future generations. The people who will come after us don't have someone speaking for them unless we do. And that has to become part of the ethic of our culture.
>
> Very few cultures have had the ability to take care of their own and to make the sacrifices and the commitment to preserve and enhance the quality of life threatened by the subtle changes to the land, whether erosion, destruction of natural species, loss of timber or agricultural land or wetlands. I would hope that the idea of protecting the resources can permeate business, labor organizations, banking institutions, and universities as well as the political process. This is not something that can be left to the few. We have to move the ethic out to the people and draw their support so we protect tomorrow's decisions with today's decisions.

One example of the attempt to institutionalize environmental concerns took place during the eight years in which Evelle Younger was attorney general of California. To fulfill a campaign promise, Younger established a ten-person environmental unit shortly after his election in 1970. He told the unit's director, Nicholas Yost, that instead of acting primarily as attorney for the state agencies, as is a normal function of the Attorney General's Office, Yost's unit should consider the people as its clients and respond directly to citizens' environmental complaints. Assistant attorney generals in the unit, all of whom were environmentalists, were instructed not to wait for other agencies to refer cases of environmental violations but to identify problems and environmental abuses by their own investigatory work. The environmental attorneys were to seek solutions through litigation, legislation, administrative proceedings, or out-of-court agreements. A citizen advisory committee was also formed to assist the unit.

"We hired people with fine legal abilities—but we also sought a demonstrated environmental commitment," Yost told me during a visit to his San Francisco office. "We wanted lawyers who show evidence of having initiative. Many lawyers wait for someone to walk into the office and say: 'Here's my problem, solve it.' We expect our lawyers to go to meetings of citizen groups, visit the areas involved, and take on problems in an affirmative way and translate the problems into something which, as lawyers, they can act upon.

"We consider the environment more than just the parks and trees and lakes and rivers, more than the natural resources and rural habitat. The human habitat in the cities is just as important. We especially try to help citizens or organizations who have no other place to turn, or places in which problems were not being handled properly," Yost said.

For instance, it was common knowledge that the Los Angeles County Air Pollution Hearing Board was granting variances to almost everyone who applied. But citizens felt helpless to do anything about it, and the state had no authority to move in. Yost's unit, however, drafted legislation to reconstitute the hearing board and tighten procedures, and then lobbied in Sacramento to help get it passed.*

Unlike public interest law firms, which cannot lobby because

* In 1977 Yost left the Attorney General's Office to become general counsel of the federal Council on Environmental Quality.

244 FOOTPRINTS ON THE PLANET

they would lose their tax-exempt status, the environmental unit has proved extremely effective in helping to pass new legislation. Attorney General Younger often wrote letters to key legislators suggesting that new laws be passed. The unit's attorneys followed up by personally contacting the legislators to give them more information. The unit tackles small problems along with the large. When the residents of a neighborhood in Torrance discovered that a public utility planned to line their street with gigantic transmission poles and lines, the citizens thought they were powerless to stop the action. They complained to the Attorney General's Office. The environmental unit took up the cause and prepared a court case. The utility changed its plans and located the lines on a commercial thoroughfare.

The unit intervened on another occasion when the supervisors of Mendocino County received an application for a zoning change to allow construction of a large motel on the Pacific Coast shore within the famous Pygmy Forest Ecological Staircase. This area, 150 miles north of San Francisco, consists of five elevated terraces carved by the sea. The lower terraces are about 100,000 years old, and the highest and oldest terrace is possibly a million years old. Students and researchers frequent the staircase and visitors are drawn to its unique canyons, terraces, ancient dunes, tall redwoods, and dwarf pines and cypresses.

An environmental impact report prepared by a consultant to the developer, and approved as its own by Mendocino County, concluded that the development of the 80-unit motel on 12 acres along the coast was the worst of seven possible alternatives. But the county supervisors went ahead despite this conclusion and approved the zoning change for the motel.

After receiving complaints from citizens, the environmental unit joined a lawsuit previously filed by a woman living adjacent to the proposed motel. The citizen had won a temporary injunction because no environmental impact report had been filed. Deputy Attorney General Louise Renne of the environmental unit argued in support of the appeal being made to the state court of appeals. "The basic issue is: Once an adequate environmental impact statement is prepared, is the responsible agency free to disregard it, rendering the whole decision-making process a meaningless exercise in futile paper production? The answer must be 'no.' Otherwise, as a practical matter, the [California Environmental Quality] Act will have little effect."

The appellate court overthrew the lower court ruling. And the Pygmy Forest Staircase was spared from the encroachment.

What about the status of an environmental ethic in business and industry and in the financial world?

Some of the examples reported in this book would indicate that the seeds of an environmental ethic are at work. But they may be a long time sprouting. For the predominant ethic of business, centered around short-term results and a narrow identification of its interests, largely overlooks environmental concerns. The cases where some corporations are making efforts to include the environmental impacts in decision-making are greatly in the minority, and even those few examples were difficult to find.

Some economists may argue that it is wrong to expect business to include environmental concerns other than those required by law, because to do so would eat into profits. That would be altruism, which is not legitimately a part of the business ethic. Some go so far as to argue that it is morally unethical for a business executive, entrusted with the funds of stockholders who expect the maximum profit, to practice any form of altruism.

Other economists argue that corporations have a responsibility to serve the social good of the community, that historically charters under which early American corporations were formed encouraged private capital to promote ends regarded as serving the public interest. Harvard Business School Professor George Cabot Lodge advocates that the federal government should charter the 2,000 or so large, publicly held national and international corporations to make certain that the corporations serve as public entities which act in the public interest.

The corporation must be seen as part of the several communities it touches and essential to the design and development of the communities in which it is actually located [wrote Lodge in his book *The New American Ideology* (1976)]. The charter must consider it [the corporation] an integral part of the political, economic, social and cultural life of each community, one that affects its housing patterns, transportation system, education needs and more. Through the charter itself, therefore, the community must have a fundamental say in the corporation's being.

In the financial world the common position of most executives I met was that they had no right to condition loans on whether the individual or corporate applicant planned to use the funds for environmentally harmful practices. I remember the expression of shock on the face of a vice-president of a major insurance company when I asked if his company had an environmental policy concerning loans and investments. He seemed indignant that anyone could expect such a thing and told me that corporations had no right to delve into anything except the financial soundness of the company or individual requesting the loan. And as a corporate official, he had a responsibility to stockholders and clients to give the highest possible return on the dollar. I wonder if his company has ever considered that the policyholders themselves might want their company to have a policy concerned with the long-term interests of the community. The holder of an annuity, for instance, if given the choice, might be very interested in what kind of living environment would be available twenty years hence when he received the income from the annuity, and perhaps would agree to a slightly reduced profit by the company, if necessary, in the interests of the long-term welfare of the environment.

This kind of approach, however, I found largely absent from the business and financial world. The leaders seemed to be waiting for the shareholders or the general public to demand a change in policy on behalf of greater environmental concern before the company leadership would even consider it. In the one place that might be best suited to supporting enlightened environmental policies—the trade associations—I could find no signs of concern for industry-wide or trade-wide adoption of an environmental code of ethics (except for the unsuccessful Maine Bankers Code reported in Chapter 11). Trade associations seem to be so concerned with lobbying for corporate advantages or to head off unwanted laws that they haven't the time or inclination to make any significant effort to coordinate agreements among members to support the public interest in the environmental area.

My biggest disappointment, however was to find so few companies with an adequate institutional structure for environmental decisions, other than a unit charged with pollution control matters. In most large corporations today the chief executive officer's personal conviction for—or bias against—environmental responsibility sets the policy for the company. Rare is the company that includes in its corporate structure a system that allows for the environmental impacts of all major decisions to be brought to the attention of top management where options can be presented for less environmentally harmful alternative solutions.

How has organized labor dealt with environmental concerns? Is an environmental ethic evident among labor leaders, or in the rank and file?

It is hard to generalize about organized labor because no unified position exists among the more than 130 national and international unions based in the United States. All of the organizations are, of course, interested in those environmental conditions in the workplace that affect workers' well-being. In addition, a few large unions were active in the "Breathers' Lobby" that fought for clean air legislation, and in the 1969 Citizens' Crusade for Clean Water which pressured Congress into increasing federal funding from $214 million to nearly $800 million for the construction of sewage treatment facilities. Environment was seldom a priority for the national union leadership, however, even at the height of the popularity of antipollution activities in the late 1960s and early 1970s. During the 1974-75 recession, support for environmental causes was virtually nil among the national and local unions.

In recent years, however, the labor movement has found that environmental concerns can sometimes be in its best interests. Labor organizations helped environmental groups in lobbying for a toxic substances control bill and also in working for a strip mining law and for energy legislation. Some unions even supported a bill for expansion of the Redwood National Park.

A Citizens-Labor Energy Coalition was formed in 1978 with plans to take on issues such as opposing deregulation of natural gas, providing increased employment opportunities, developing energy self-sufficiency through conservation, and promoting non-inflationary and environmentally-sound alternative energy technologies. One-third of the sixty organizations making up the coalition are from organized labor, and it is chaired by William Winpisinger, president of the International Association of Machinists.

Several years ago environmental advocates formed a Washington-based organization, Environmentalists for Full Employment, seeking to bring labor and environmental groups together, and especially trying to show environmentalists why they need to work with labor. The effort has resulted in the recent phenomenon of environmental lobbyists working the offices of Congress, urging support for the Humphrey-Hawkins full-employment bill and the labor reform act.

Although the environmental and labor movements can share common interests on occasion, it would be wrong to overestimate their solidarity. In the Redwood National Park situation, the AFL-CIO lobbyists at first worked against the addition to the national park because they believed it would destroy lumber industry jobs. Only when the bill was amended—providing a $40-million package for retraining and transitional assistance to loggers, and new maintenance jobs in the park—did the AFL-CIO reverse course and help pass the bill. Labor leaders naturally pursue policies linked directly to wages and employment security, and environmental considerations are usually those involving worker health and safety. For their part, environmental leaders have not been able to rally their memberships to display enthusiasm for labor causes. The priorities of many environmental group members remain with wilderness, parks, and wildlife, just as the average union member's primary concerns are wages, job security, and working conditions.

Even when national and international union leaders have supported environmental causes, local unions have not always gone along. This is especially evident when an industry threatens to shut down a plant or lay off workers unless state or federal environmental control regulations are eased and workers believe that their jobs are endangered. Some locals have joined with the business-sponsored organizations formed to oppose genuine environmental causes. These "environmental balance" organizations—such as the National Environmental Development Association, California's Council for Environmental and Economic Balance, the Environmental Balance Association of Minnesota, the

New Jersey-based Society for Environmental and Economic Development (SEED), and the Oregon-based Western Environmental Trade Association—have lobbied in states and Congress to delay or weaken pollution control laws.

The union that has taken the most environmentally responsible stance is the United Auto Workers (UAW), the nation's second largest union. In the past decade it has made major strides toward setting a national environmental policy for the union and has tried to persuade its local leaders and membership to act in the interests of the environmental good of all society as well as for a better-quality work atmosphere. This policy emerged from the foresight of Walter P. Reuther, longtime UAW president, who persuaded his union's International Executive Board in 1967 to approve the establishment of a UAW Department of Conservation and Resource Development. He gave strong leadership to the union's environmental activities until his death in an airplane accident in the spring of 1970.

I first became aware of Reuther's environmental commitment when I heard him speak at a February 1970 pre-Earth Day conference at the University of Michigan. I was amazed at his sense of social responsibility and fearlessness. As the head of a union whose workers' jobs depended on a thriving auto industry, Reuther attacked the industry for not developing a nonpolluting engine and for failing to meet its public responsibility ("They've been more concerned about the level of their sales, the level of their profits, than they have been concerned about environmental problems of human beings"). He also called on the auto industry to join with the government and with other industries in developing a modern mass transportation system all over America. ("It is asinine to have hundreds of thousands of people all going to the same place at the same time for the same purpose and all of them dragging two tons of gadgets with them. We've got to put traffic under the ground in our great urban concentrations.")

In an Earth Day speech at Oakland University in Rochester, Michigan, Reuther went even further, advocating an Environmental Bill of Rights amendment for the federal constitution, and a new governmental instrument, a National Environmental Protection Commission. The commission, Reuther proposed, should have the power to stop an industry from building a factory on a site if it threatened the environment, to allow a product to go on the market or stay on the market only so long as it can be proved to be compatible with man's living environment, or to shut down a polluting industry until the pollution was corrected. Said Reuther:

> Unless man takes affirmative action to stop the reckless use of technological power, which does violence to man and violence to man's environment, we shall not survive. We have used our technology with total disregard of its impact upon man's environment. Our problem is that we are more concerned about the quantity of our goods than about the quality of our goals. We are more concerned about the volume of our gadgets (and the automobile is perhaps the worst of those gadgets) than we are about the quality of life. We have been corrupted, and we have been brainwashed by the Madison Avenue hucksters who have made too many Americans believe that the quality of American life is determined by the brightness of the chrome on the new Cadillac. But that has nothing to do with the quality of life.

After Reuther's death his objectives were carried on by UAW's Department of Conservation and Resource Development under Vice-president Olga Madar and her successor, Odessa Komer. The environmental activities staff led by John Yolton worked with local unions and citizen environmental organizations and lobbied in Washington. And Frank Wallick, editor of UAW's *Washington Report,* gave strong support to environmental activities.

In the summer of 1970, UAW and the United Nations cosponsored a symposium on the impact of urbanization on man's environment. More than 125 participants from 23 countries attended the meeting held at the UAW Family Education Center at Black Lake, Michigan. Later that year UAW put on a conference at Black Lake for 300 college students and community environmental group leaders. The goal of the conference was to redefine strategies and tactics through which environmental and labor coalitions could work at local levels for environmental improvement.

At almost every major environmental meeting I attended UAW's Yolton often was the only union representative present. I knew about UAW's support of environmental causes such as new Alaska parks and wildlife refuges, land-use control legislation, saving the Big Cypress area near the Florida Everglades and the Indiana Dunes National Lakeshore. From Yolton I learned that the UAW resource department had helped to establish environment or conservation committees in most of the UAW locals, conducted environmental education workshops for four hundred UAW members and their families on water pollution, energy, and land use, and conducted week-long conservation workshops for local union leadership in several parts of the nation.

In the period 1973-76, UAW's environmental advocates found it difficult to get cooperation from local unions because of fears that environmental costs might take away jobs. And the UAW leadership did not push environmental activities boldly during this time but concentrated on promoting energy conservation activities. By 1976, the economic climate had improved and Komer and Yolton organized another conference at Black Lake. More than three hundred local and national labor officials, environmental activists, and community leaders met to discuss "Jobs and the Environment." UAW President Leonard Woodcock called for a new alliance between labor and environmentalists to thwart "environmental blackmail" by industries and to hasten full employment. As an outgrowth of the conference, the Environmental Protection Agency supported more than twenty regional workshops on environment, jobs, and the economy. And several labor organizations, including the UAW, participated. In 1977-78, the UAW also continued its environmental education work and promoted development of jobs in solar energy. UAW President Douglas Fraser served on the organizing board of Sun Day, 1978, as did the heads of the Machinists and Sheetmetal Workers unions.*

UAW's national leadership, and especially the locals, are not always on the right side of environmental issues, of course. When the auto industry was fighting to delay air pollution control regulations, for instance, the UAW leadership supported this delay.

Apart from the limited efforts of national or local unions in working on environmental causes, what about the rank and file workers—are they showing evidence of an environmental ethic?

* Fraser succeeded Woodcock, who retired in 1977 and was named U.S. representative to the People's Republic of China.

Outside the workplace, union members appear to have about the same level of concern for the environment and for nature and wildlife as do business executives or professionals. Members of the labor force, however, may not feel free to express their convictions on how job-related activities affect the environment.

One incident of an environmental ethic at work did get some national notice several years ago. In 1969, Gilbert Pugliese, a millwright at the Cleveland plant of the Jones and Laughlin Steel Corporation, refused to carry out orders to push a button that would have sent several hundred gallons of waste oil into the Cuyahoga River. Pugliese was suspended for five days, but the company reinstated him even though he still refused to carry out the disposal orders. Two years later, when a foreman again insisted that Pugliese discharge oil into the Cuyahoga, he again refused, risking 18 years of seniority. He was supported by his local union, and in the face of publicity and embarrassment, Jones and Laughlin relented and started a procedure to use drums and pumps to dispose of the waste oil.

For the most part, though, workers faced with the choice of doing a job as ordered or protesting the potential harm to the environment, take the path that protects their jobs. Statistics can be quoted all day long to show how many more jobs are created by environmental controls than are lost in plant closings actually forced by added environmental costs, but the arguments do not override workers' fears if they feel their own jobs are threatened.

How is environment faring in American education?

It was the hope of many conservationists that the nation's schools and colleges would be able to imbue students with the understanding and awareness of the interconnectedness of humanity with the world of nature that underlies an environmental ethic. Interest in the environment tends to follow popular trends or perceived threats to personal welfare. After the wave of enthusiasm surrounding Earth Day activities in 1970—with students in schools and colleges forming the backbone of the public interest—many people just took it for granted that environmental education would speedily grow. They expected it would gain acceptance in the schools and that curriculums would expand to fill the need. But those hopes have not been fulfilled.

There have been many obstacles. Educators have not settled on a basic definition or method of teaching environmental education. Environment has been taught as a special subject, as part of biology or other science courses, as outdoor recreation, or a part of social studies, so it has not had a single strong base of support in the education hierarchy. Educators differ over whether teachers of all disciplines should weave it into all of their courses, whether environmental education is a separate discipline, or whether schools should leave it to nonschool organizations. Most of today's teachers have been trained in a system that did not include getting enough of an understanding about environmental issues to be able to teach them in their own disciplines. And teacher-training programs and curriculum materials are expensive and have been developed slowly, while funding has been minimal. In those cases where experimental environmental education programs have been developed locally with federal funding assistance, the programs often die with the end of the subsidy. These programs have rarely been evaluated, and even when they are, there has been no adequate means to spread programs which were successful to other schools. It is always hard for a new subject to gain a place in the educational hierarchy, especially without a sharp focus and strong constituency. Environmental education has been somewhat of an orphan.

Despite these difficulties, environmental education is needed to help children and adults understand how the natural world works and the relationships of one part to another. Children and adults need to discover, whenever they are known, the impacts on nature of humanity's actions. They need to learn to deal with the tradeoffs that may be necessary among the environment, energy, and the economy in order to make wise choices among the alternatives available to them, and to demand alternative solutions as problems arise.

The environmental education picture is not all negative. Environmental concepts are finding their way into standard curriculum materials. Several outstanding textbooks have been published on environment. Once the state departments of education geared themselves to the task, they gave a considerable measure of attention—though not much funding support—to the environment. Many local school systems used federal assistance to develop environmental ideas, and a number of excellent programs are under way in schools across the country.

One example is Project KARE (Knowledgeable Action to Restore our Environment), sponsored by the public and parochial schools of a five-county area in southeastern Pennsylvania and the Philadelphia Model Cities Program. KARE shows schools how to set up local action programs in which students take on a specific environmental problem in the community and deal with it. For instance, two high schools in Berwyn and Malvern, Pennsylvania, cooperated on a local action program to study the effects of development on a 5-square-mile rural community drained by Birch Run, a small tributary of a drainage system that flows into the Schuylkill River, a major Pennsylvania waterway. The students analyzed water samples that indicated that Birch Run was not badly polluted. But their study of the land's composition suggested that for various reasons the area was unsuitable for further development. The students reported their findings to the town planning commission with the result that new zoning ordinances were written, based at least partly on the students' studies. The young people not only learned about ecology but found out how to work within the political structure to protect the environment. And the activity brought into play their skills in English, mathematics, and social studies, as well as other skills.

One of the most widely adopted environmental programs at elementary and secondary school level is Project ECOS (an acronym for Environmental Education Community Opportunity for Stewardship), launched in 1971 by the combined school districts of Westchester and Putnam counties in New York. The ECOS idea is now being used in varying ways in dozens of schools across the country. Instead of imposing environmental education on the already crowded curriculum as a separate subject, ECOS shows teachers how to integrate environmental concepts into their regular subjects. Teachers who attended ECOS traveling work-shops in many parts of the nation soon found that environment could be an aid in teaching. A French teacher who attended gave her students articles from newspapers in France that dealt with pollution, population, and land-use problems in that country. Students in English classes at one school took a course in which science fiction was the means of considering real issues of land development, sewage disposal, and other environmental problems. After field trips they presented reports and held discussions, then wrote short stories about what might happen to the environment, good or bad. In the same school, teachers used a study of rock music to teach both harmonic principles and environmental concepts by having students pick out ecology themes presented in much of today's popular music. In another city a social studies teacher had ninth grade students compare pollution problems on Egypt's Nile with those of the Great Lakes and other American waters. They looked at plays, short stories, and films in their study. And a school in the Southwest invited homeowners to come to the school and let the students show them how to test the quality of their water. Although these experiences may be superficial, they help to awaken in many students an interest and concern for stewardship that may one day grow into an environmental ethic.

The pioneers of environmental education have been the national and regional conservation organizations. For instance, the Massachusetts Audubon Society (founded in 1896) has since 1939 sent teachers into schools to teach conservation and ecology. Currently fifty Audubon teachers are working in about sixty Massachusetts schools. In addition, Massachusetts Audubon Director Charles E. Roth has on his staff three people working full time on in-service training of teachers.

"Increasingly now, we are working with schools over a three-to-five-year period," says Roth. "We work with teachers of all disciplines and all grades, trying to address the relationships between ecology and economics and all the other subjects."

The organization has been working for more than twenty years with the schools in three major cities, Worcester, Pittsfield, and Lowell, as well as in parts of Boston, to get environmental concepts to urban children. In addition to in-school programs they run eight day camps, one resident camp, and several touring camps in the summer, and 13 wildlife sanctuaries which are staffed to conduct environmental training.

Most of the national and regional conservation organizations are active in various phases of environmental education, producing periodicals, books, and teaching aids, making their nature areas and sanctuaries available for study, and using them for educational programs. In 1973 a group of people from some of these organizations formed the Alliance for Environmental Education to coordinate the activities and exchange of information among the conservation organizations and others involved in environmental education.

Colleges and universities responded dramatically to the surge of student and faculty interest in ecology in the 1960s and college curriculum offerings now include many environment-related courses. A few colleges and universities even offer interdisciplinary majors in environmental studies. Students can study such subjects as economics, natural and political science, and the arts and humanities and relate them all to environment. The University of Wisconsin-Green Bay focused its entire curriculum on environment when it opened in 1969. The College of the Atlantic, a small institution in Bar Harbor, Maine, has as its central theme the study of human ecology. The college catalog describes its purpose: "to study the various relationships which exist between humans and their environments, including both the natural world which supports our existence and the society and institutions which we have created."

Among a number of environmental graduate study programs throughout the country, the University of California at Los Angeles (UCLA) is involved in two particularly innovative activities. In one, teams of students from architecture and urban planning, the graduate school of management, and environmental sciences conduct practical projects in urban areas and natural resources. For instance, they looked at all the potential transportation alternatives for the greater Los Angeles area, analyzing energy conservation, impacts on air quality, and effects on minority groups. In another project they assessed development and population growth near Mammoth Lakes, in California's High Sierra, and studied the impacts of these activities on wilderness quality, air quality, and water purity and availability. Linked to this program is another for doctoral candidates in environmental sciences and engineering, which seeks to develop highly qualified professionals and give them the ability to solve technological problems with minimal impact on environment. Candidates, who must have a master's degree in some field of science or engineering, take environmental and other courses for a year to broaden their background. They spend their second year working on one or more of the multidisciplinary teams involved in practical problems of the Southern California area. Then the candidates intern for a year or more with large private companies; ordinarily, each has responsibility for a corporate project. Finally, the candidates return to UCLA for at least one academic quarter to write reports on their work and participate in another multidisciplinary team study so that what they have learned can be disseminated among others. Richard Perrine, chairman of the Department of Environmental Engineering, is encouraged by the progress being made in these two programs, although he admits that the environmental approach has not made great strides among the entire UCLA engineering school of more than 2,000 students. I asked Perrine how many students obtain an understanding of the ecological approach. "We're lucky if we can get one hundred a year to even look at this side of engineering," Perrine replied.

Miami-Dade Community College created a thirty-week general course called Man and Environment, and packaged it to be presented as a high quality television series. The acceptance by students who took the TV course for credit and by other television viewers was so enthusiastic that Miami-Dade has now made it widely available. It has been presented in more than thirty cities and an accompanying text, *Man and Environment,* has been published.

Is an environmental ethic finding a place in religion?

Although most of the world's religions have ethical codes or creeds which relate to an environmental ethic, the followers of a particular religion may not recognize or practice it as such. For instance, one who follows Jesus's teachings, "Love thy neighbor as thyself" or "All things whatsoever ye would that men should do to you, do ye even so to them" (the Golden Rule), would refrain from polluting or harming the environment or—by extension—the people, wildlife, and land that depend on a healthy environment.

The churches have given little recognition to environmental ethics. Individual members, however, have formed small groups to study ways to practice elements of the principles set forth in the

Shakertown Pledge (Chapter 13), or creative simplicity, or ecological justice. The American Friends Service Committee's San Francisco group puts out a newspaper on simple living and has published *Taking Charge,* a guidebook to simple living that includes the Shakertown Pledge. More than 60,000 copies are in circulation, and many local religious organizations use it as the basis for study groups. As a result of religious teachings, many followers of Zen Buddhism and other Eastern religions also practice a lifestyle that is in harmony with nature.

There have been several attempts to get church organizations nationally involved in supporting environmental and energy concerns, as they did with civil rights. In 1975 a coalition of nine national Christian and Jewish religious bodies sought to start a program "to engage the American religious community in an organized manner with the environmental-energy-resource crisis, focusing its substantial educational, institutional, and ethical resources upon the task of helping human society achieve a dynamic equilibrium with its environment."

A task force of the United Church of Christ tried to launch a national program on a Christian lifestyle and ecology, a program that would promote "an ecological consciousness, simplicity of life, and more moderate consumption by the affluent, and a just redistribution of global resources." The 186th General Assembly of the United Presbyterian Church in 1974 recommended that Presbyterians "examine societal and individual lifestyle patterns, seeking ways to alter lifestyles in order to reduce energy dependence." And the following year's General Assembly recommended a program "to implement strategies for living that respond creatively to the ethical issues of conservation and use of natural resources." None of these, however, has resulted in a national program.

In 1978 the National Council of Churches of Christ completed a two-year Energy Study Project and proposed a policy statement on "Ethical Implications of Energy Production and Use." The draft statement of the policy explored the basis for a new ethic of ecological justice:

Must not the classical Judeo-Christian understanding of "neighbor" now be radically expanded to encompass all

humans in past, present, or future generations, as well as to
include all the rest of non-human creation? Today the world
faces such a biblically unknown threat as nuclear contamination of indefinite extent and indeterminate duration. Can such a
horrendous threat to all survival be adequately met with an
ethic that deals only with the rights of human beings who are
presently alive? Are not all people called to move on to
embrace an ethic of ecological justice that takes into moral
consideration the claims of those involved and endangered
"neighbors" who, in the present energy debate, are necessarily
voiceless? Are not all people called to expand the human
understanding of time and space in order to defend those
victims who are voiceless because they do not yet exist, or
because they exist in the non-human creation? Ecological
justice is an ethic inspired by Christian hope for the fulfillment
of God's promises.

Since 1970 the Interfaith Center for Corporate Responsibility
(ICCR) has coordinated activities of 22 Protestant groups and 150
Roman Catholic orders in seeking to make corporations responsive
to the concerns of the churches as shareholders. The ICCR grew
out of a study during the Vietnam War which showed that
although many church organizations were speaking out against the
war, they were at the same time investing in corporations that were
supplying major implements of warfare. The interfaith religious
group extended its concerns to other social issues such as equal
rights for minorities, investment in South Africa, strip mining of
coal, building of breeder nuclear reactors, and other environmental
and energy activities of corporations. The ICCR staff members
negotiate with management about the issues, they introduce
litigation before the Securities and Exchange Commission, prepare
resolutions to be introduced at corporation annual meetings, and
vote blocks of church stockholdings. Church coalitions or the board
of ICCR also suggest and promote issues and stock resolutions.
Although these resolutions usually get only a small percentage of
the vote at the annual meeting of a corporation, ICCR's activities
have been influential in getting some companies to reexamine their
policies. In 1977 and 1978 there were very few environmental
resolutions because other priorities were ascendant among church

groups and because ICCR staff had been cut in size. Its one
environmental success of 1977 was a resolution asking EXXON to
produce a report on coal strip mining in the West and Midwest.
The resolution was backed by corporate management and received
98.5% of the vote. Corporate management opposes most ICCR
resolutions, and a 4% to 6% proxy vote is considered high, although
some nonenvironmental church resolutions in recent years have
received 10% or more of the vote due to support from banks,
pension funds, and mutual funds, which in the past have backed
corporate management.

There is a small cadre of Christian ministers and lay religious
leaders who have adopted the environment and conservation of
natural resources as part of their field of ministry. David and
Elizabeth Dodson Gray, for instance, are a theologically trained
couple (he is an ordained minister) who some years ago turned to
the earth's environment and limits to growth as the major focus of
their ministry. They now direct the Bolton Institute and promote
environmental concepts through research, writing, teaching, working with congressional committees, and within academic, religious,
and other organizations. Through the Boston Industrial Mission
two clergymen, Scott Paradise and Norman Faramelli,* worked for
a decade ministering to executives and researchers in Boston-based
high-technology industries. The Mission helps executives, scientists, and researchers to explore the ethical implications—environmental, social, Christian—of their business and technological
practices.

From 1965 through 1974, the Faith-Man-Nature group under
the leadership of Philip N. Joranson held meetings and conferences
and published papers as a partnership of theologians and church
people with environmental scientists as well as with representatives
of other disciplines and vocations. The writings of Paul Santmire,
chaplain of Wellesley College, have stimulated efforts to link
theological concerns with environmental concerns. In his book,
Brother Earth (1970), Santmire argued that a need existed for a
theology of nature, because without it nature would inevitably be
treated as existing only for human use, having no rights of its own.
He also urged the concept of having the church become involved in

---

* In 1977 Norman Faramelli became the director of environmental affairs for the
Massachusetts Port Authority.

inner-city environmental problems and that ecological justice should become part of the organized church and be incorporated in preaching, in liturgy, and in policies. Other environmentally oriented ministers and concerned lay people teach at colleges throughout the nation, helping a generation of college students to become more sensitive to value issues involved in environmental and energy choices.

Aldo Leopold wrote more than two decades ago: "No important change in ethics was ever accomplished without an internal change in our intellectual emphasis, loyalties, affections, and convictions. The proof that conservation has not yet touched these foundations of conduct lies in the fact that philosophy and religion have not yet heard of it."

Religion appears to have heard of it by now. But not the churches.

This review of an environmental ethic in government, business, labor, education, and religion indicates that although there are scattered instances of an ethic being accepted and applied, they are rare. The many good state and federal laws are not fully effective. Most business, industry, and government agency decision-makers seem to feel they have done enough if they simply stay within the letter of the law, and some of them evade, resist, or seek to delay compliance with environmental laws. Understaffed state and federal government pollution control agencies are unable to enforce their own laws adequately. Some government officials, under the pressure of reelection and changes in administrations, find it hard to look beyond the immediate future. And some corporate managers, believing that their own careers may depend on short-term gains, avoid accepting responsibility for the long-term environmental consequences of their products or processes. As for the general public, polls continue to show that the majority of Americans give a high priority to environmental values. When confronted with choices that affect their immediate self-interest, however, many of these same people opt for environmentally harmful courses of action. The evidence indicates that although an environmental ethic does exist, it hasn't enough strength at present to produce a real difference in the choices of most people, especially those who make the big decisions that affect much of the nation.

I did find in government, as well as in corporations and other entities of the private sector, a few organizational structures through which environmental effects could be factored into decisions before actions were taken. But those structures proved effective only when some individual in the organization was sufficiently imbued with an environmental ethic to give force to environmental concerns—an individual business leader, a lawmaker, a public official, or a local citizen activist who cared enough to lead the way.

Wherever I encountered these environmentally caring decision-makers I found that their actions resulted from a kind of *enlightened* self-interest. Instead of acting only for "me" (their own restricted, personal interests), they were considering "us" (their neighbors, their community, and the natural world) in their decisions. And they had widened their span of interest from a preoccupation with "now" to consideration of a "now that includes the future." They were practicing what might be called "environmental citizenship." Considering the impact of their decisions and living as responsible members of nature's system amounts to environmental citizenship much the way abiding by the law, voting, paying taxes, and acting responsibly toward the community constitute political citizenship.

Relatively few decision-makers, however, are practicing environmental citizenship. Those who are doing so have a personal sense of values that is essentially different from the prevailing value system. This sense of values makes them willing to go against the power structure of their community or town or company or legislative body or government agency. Environmental citizenship will not be widespread, therefore, until a major shift in values takes place.

During my research and interviews, as I posed questions about the existing basis of decision-making, I encountered a good deal of skepticism over environmental goals as well as over the significance of an environmental ethic and the need for a shift in values. Here are some of the arguments I heard:

• *"You talk about the need for energy conservation that may require sacrifices or changes to less energy-consumptive lifestyles.*

Why should we deny ourselves because of an energy crisis that doesn't really exist? The United States has enough oil and natural gas for years and years. And besides, by the time our supplies are gone we surely will have some new technological solution—nuclear fusion or solar energy at cheap prices—that will satisfy everyone's wants."

This argument can be answered from several bases. It is obvious that our escalating energy consumption is already exceeding the domestic supply. The economic price of imported oil is increasing and so are the political risks and uncertainties of dependence on foreign oil. A nation that values its political freedom cannot allow its foreign policy to be shaped to accommodate demands of oil-rich countries. And how long will it be before Arab nations, whose religious beliefs demand concern for future generations, realize the short-sightedness of an economic and political policy that allows the draining of their own energy sources just to satiate a wasteful American energy consumption? Ethical considerations are important in the energy picture. No one yet fully knows what environmental price we will have to pay for the technological "fix" on which we depend for future energy supplies. The methods of producing fusion power may also present waste disposal hazards, thermal pollution problems, and unknown other side effects. Dependence on large-scale solar energy facilities will bring plant siting dilemmas like the ones we already face in trying to find environmentally acceptable locations for coal-powered or nuclear-powered plants.

And we cannot ignore the ethical problem of a nation (the United States) with only 6% of the world's population, consuming each year one-third of the total nonrenewable energy resources produced by all the countries in the world. Don't we have a responsibility to find ways to curb our energy excesses if they are enjoyed at the expense of depriving other peoples? As individuals most of us don't continue to spend more money than we earn, and we try to save a little for the future. Should we spend the world's energy supply with less forethought? Without firm knowledge that the technological solution will be available to provide sufficient energy for our needs—as well as for people in other countries—don't we have an ethical responsibility to seek less energy-consumptive ways of living?

When we extend our concern beyond our own shores to the

entire planet and its human and nonhuman occupants, the environmental consequences of present actions take on much greater dimensions and present an even greater need for the universal application of an environmental ethic. For instance, scientists studying loss of farmland due to harmful agricultural practices in many parts of the world say that unless environmentally sound practices are instituted soon, perhaps as much as one-third of the world's farmland will become desert by the year 2000. Also, forecasters say that increased timber cutting, especially in tropical forests, if continued at present rates without proper reforestation and watershed protection, would bring about severe flooding in those areas and climatic changes that would have worldwide consequences.

• *"Why should we worry about losing a small percentage of the country's agricultural land each year to development or the loss of topsoil by erosion? We still have plenty of farmland."*

In the United States we lose 2 million acres of farmable land each year to highways, airports, subdivisions, surface mining, or other development. Another million acres a year are converted into reservoirs or ponds through public works projects. With a total cropland base of 400 million acres plus 24 million acres of reserve immediately convertible to cropland, an annual 3-million-acre loss is disturbingly significant if we broaden our concern to include the increasing need for food here and abroad, or if we think of the needs of future generations. With this broader outlook we should question urbanization taking place on prime agricultural land when nonagricultural land is available. Shouldn't a developer or highway builder be required to prove that no other site exists before being allowed to use prime agricultural land? Shouldn't the proposed project's benefits to the public be weighed against the potentially greater benefits of keeping the land as it is? Also, topsoil destruction is a result of bad agricultural practices on the part of the farmer who misuses topsoil that may have taken thousands or millions of years to accumulate. Shouldn't some restrictions be placed on agricultural practices that deprive future generations of productive use of the land?

• *"Why do we need all the species of wildlife when there are so many? After all, we lost the dinosaur and the carrier pigeon and countless other species and humanity has survived without them."*

No one can say with certainty that humanity today is worse off for the loss of these species. But I can point to the fact that since the Pilgrims arrived in 1620 a total of 45 species of mammals and birds have become extinct in the United States; 107 species are currently threatened, and 1,850 plants have been proposed for endangered listing. One worldwide study estimates that by the year 2000, habitat destruction and alteration and conversion of wild lands to other purposes will lead to a total loss of from 500,000 to 600,000 species of animals and plants. Although no one can predict what the loss of a single species can mean, each and every life form is a link in an ecosystem, a link whose significance may not be discovered until years after the species has disappeared. We may find out much too late what its value was. But even if it should prove not to be vital to humanity's survival, should we knowingly destroy the species—as we may do with the snail darter—when there are alternative courses available that would allow both humanity and the endangered species to survive and even flourish?

• *"But doesn't each individual organism act for the most part in its own self-interest? Then why shouldn't we?"*

Each species does act in its self-interest but the effect is action that benefits the entire group, in accordance with the evolutionary process. That is the so-called balance of nature, and it produces the diversity that creates stability in the ecosystem. Humankind enters the picture with a predominant focus on self-interest. Humans have the power to choose to live in harmony with *or* greatly damage an ecosystem because they are impelled by conscience rather than instinct. A snail darter—or a lion—does not have such a choice, so does not need an environmental conscience. There is great need for humanity to have such an ethic.

• *"Why should you expect an environmental ethic to be given such high priority? Aren't you putting environmental values above human values?"*

An environmental ethic is essential in decision-making. But it certainly should not interfere with a social ethic—our social responsibility or obligations toward fellow humans and their needs and rights. An environmental ethic must be integrated into our overall systems of beliefs and coordinated with our economic system; it should not displace or override these beliefs and systems. The environmentalist who becomes so single-minded about defending the community as to act with a tyrannical puritanism that ignores social values such as justice, compassion, and equity is bound to fail. Environmental advocates need to consider the full consequences of their objectives just as they demand of others the consideration of the environmental consequences of *their* objectives. Those concerned primarily with ecological justice must be certain that they do not gain it at the expense of social justice. And those seeking human justice should avoid gaining it at the expense of harm to the ecosystem. It makes no sense to preserve the environment at the cost of national economic collapse. Nor does it make sense to maintain stable industrial productivity at the cost of clean air, clean water, parks, and wilderness.

Our society harbors a belief that technology can solve all of our problems. This belief is incompatible with both an environmental ethic and a social ethic. Technology that does not provide adequate protection against environmental and social impacts may bring more problems than solutions. We have seen time and again in recent years that what looked like technological panaceas have brought with them unforeseen and undesirable side effects and as yet unknown future consequences. Uncertainty about the effects of humanity's activities is one of the reasons for treading lightly on the planet. In the face of this uncertainty we need above all to act with a sense of humility. This applies equally to those of us for whom the environment is of prime concern. What we may believe is the environmentally correct way of acting may itself bring unforeseen consequences in the future. There is no more excuse for arrogance on the part of environmentalists than among technocrats. Thus the several key values and beliefs need to be given their due weight and woven together into a balanced whole.

• *"You advocate a wide-scale shift in values. Basic values are handed down from generation to generation. Isn't it unrealistic to expect the kind of values you talk about to be adopted?"*

Certainly values do not shift easily or quickly. Yet prevailing values do change—usually subtly, and occasionally quite radically.

Values sometimes undergo change as a result of laws. In the case of civil rights laws, for instance, Congress hoped that the legally imposed change of behavior would eventually produce a change in racial outlook. Similarly, the authors of the National Environmental Policy Act believed that the legal requirement for environmental impact statements would produce a change of values in government decision-making. Judging from the results of these laws to date, this method alone has not had a particularly strong effect on values.

A crisis and the large-scale corrective action following the crisis can result in value change. The so-called energy crisis of 1973-74 was a situation that with perceptive political leadership could have led millions of people to seek less dependence on products based on scarce petroleum and discover the satisfactions of a quality of life based on values other than ever-increasing material consumption. Because the national political leaders did not perceive the long-term nature or implications of the problem, they declared that the crisis had ended although the long-term danger remained and was not dealt with. Yet many people did undergo some subtle changes in their outlook and lifestyle practices.

A slow but lasting shift in values can come through education, within or outside the formal systems of schools and colleges. Education can convey principles and facts that help to shape the personal system of values. Practice of an environmental ethic comes more naturally and readily to one who has been taught to understand humanity's effects on the holistic system of which we are a part and that system's effect on us. And when this ethic is rooted in knowledge rather than emotion it can produce balanced and compassionate actions.

Value changes also come about through example. As a few people demonstrate the satisfactions and success an environmentally ethical approach can bring to business or government or modes of living, an impression is made on the public. It may take time for the example to be widely recognized and emulated. Many people may take note of an experiment, admire it, identify with it, yet not be willing at first to take part in it. But as they see its success, they may support and join it. The speed with which an example may affect the general value system may be greatly accelerated when the mass communication media "discover" the example and publicize it.

The sense of values leading to environmental citizenship will be increasingly important as population pressures, material growth, resource depletion, and the effects of technology carry the threat of ever more destructive impacts on the planet. The presence of an environmental ethic in our everyday decisions could be more important than we realize. Our decisions as individuals—at home and at work, as citizens, workers, professionals, or corporate or public officials—taken together, determine the hopes and quality of life for everyone. In all walks of life we are presented with ethical choices.

• For instance, what would you do if you were a loan officer for a large bank: A prominent local developer and builder comes to you for a $2-million loan to construct a new shopping center. The 10-acre site he has purchased includes 5 acres of wetland along an estuary on the outskirts of town, and he plans to fill the wetland and build on it a large parking lot and satellite business buildings. The builder's credit is good. He has been promised permission from the local planning board for a change in zoning, and other public agencies have assured him that he can get the necessary permits. He considers the land worthless to the community in its present form. Some environmentalists complained to the newspapers when his plans leaked out, but the builder feels that since he owns the land he has the right to do with it whatever is in his best interests financially. Also, the project will generate business for the bank and create jobs in the community.

As a bank loan officer, you have been trained to consider primarily the builder's ability to pay back the loan. Do you also have a responsibility to the community the bank serves and plans to continue to serve for many years in the future? If so, do you seek the opinion of respected ecologists and public officials about the potential impact on the community from the filling and paving of the wetland? You might find that the wetland performs the function of naturally treating wastes, that it is a source of food supply for fish and birds, provides a resting site for migrating birds, and for years has been of esthetic value to the community as a lovely vista to look out on from nearby roads. Do you thus have a responsibility to weigh these environmental and public values along with the financial values involved in your responsibility to the bank?

But is it the place of the bank to act as an environmental arbiter? Or should these considerations be left to government? The loan for the proposed project would benefit the bank's shareholders and the project would give an economic boost to the community in added employment and tax revenues. How do you weigh these against the potential environmental hazards to the community? Should you approve the loan or turn it down?

• What would you do if you were an architect in the same community: The builder of the proposed shopping center has commissioned you to design the center to accommodate a maximum number of patrons. You know the wetland's ecological value. To save it, you work out two possible solutions. One calls for a reduction in the size of the project. The other requires building a large parking structure, adding considerably to the cost. The developer says both plans will diminish his potential profits, and insists on going ahead with his original concepts. Do you refuse the commission?

• What would you do if you were a wheat farmer who owns several parcels of land: Most of it is good, flat farmland, but one-third is steeply sloped. To make the best immediate profit you could plant wheat on all of the land, including the slopes. If you do, the cultivation will cause heavy erosion, and over a period of 20-30 years most of the topsoil will wash away. Do you opt for the added wheat acreage? Or should you preserve the slopes for pasture?

You are faced with another choice: You have a barely adequate supply of groundwater, just enough to irrigate your entire wheat crop over several years, and the groundwater table recharges slowly. Using it for your entire crop will cause the water table to recede, thereby reducing your neighbor's water supply as well as your own. If you irrigate only half of your wheat each year, the normal recharge rate will maintain the groundwater at a constant level. An unirrigated wheat field yields only one-third to one-half as much wheat as an irrigated field. Should you irrigate all of your land?

• What would you do if you were an office worker living in a suburb 10 miles from your job downtown and you drive to work each day alone: The Environmental Protection Agency says that if 40% of the workers now driving their own cars alone to work would carpool or use public transportation it would help your city meet the air pollution standards it is now violating. No public transportation is available. But you could join or form a carpool with people in your neighborhood who work near you. You like the convenience of driving your own car, and the independence and quietude of being alone. To join a carpool would cost you that privacy and convenience. But it would save you money and would eliminate much of the stress of having to drive in rush hour traffic each day. Do you continue to drive alone or carpool?

• What would you do if you owned a home near the waterfront where a developer wants to erect a huge condominium on the site of an abandoned wharf and has requested a zoning variance: The zoning board is holding a public hearing. If you attend you could present arguments that the waterfront area should not be intensively developed. On the other hand, perhaps you ought to stay out of the controversy. If the development takes place it will open the area to widespread commercial development and your own property would increase in value. But the neighborhood would lose much of its quietness and residential qualities. Do you attend the hearing and oppose the zoning change?

Faced with dilemmas such as these, any of us could understandably decide either way. With the predominant values in society weighted toward narrow self-interest, the role of those who seek the environmentally ethical route is difficult and often unpopular. Yet if we do not make our choices on the side of the environment now, our options will narrow rapidly as the pressures of population growth, resource depletion, and pollution irreversibly alter the quality of living on the planet. Each of us, individually, can look for ways of making fewer demands on nonrenewable resources. We can seek to live in harmony with the natural order. We can replace a self-only, short-range outlook with universal, long-term values. And we can bring environmental considerations into our decisions, from the smallest to the greatest. Our enlightened self-interest can evolve into an environmental ethic that will work toward protecting and enhancing the quality of life for all of us. As we seek to share John Muir's vision,

> we all dwell in a house of one room—the world with the firmament for its roof—and are sailing the celestial spaces without leaving any track.

SUPPLEMENTARY READING

Adams, Ansel. *My Camera in the National Parks.* Boston: Houghton Mifflin, 1950.

Allen, Rodney F., Carmelo P. Foti, Daniel M. Ulrich, and Steven H. Woolard. *Deciding How to Live on Spaceship Earth: The Ethics of Environmental Concern.* Winona, Minn.: St. Mary's College Press, 1973.

Barbour, Ian G. *Western Man and Environmental Ethics.* Reading, Mass.: Addison-Wesley, 1973.

Barney, Gerald O. (ed.). *The Unfinished Agenda: The Citizen's Policy Guide to Environmental Issues.* New York: Crowell, 1977.

Berry, Wendell. *The Unsettling of America: Culture and Agriculture.* San Francisco: Sierra Club, 1977.

The Briarpatch Book: Experiences in Right Livelihood and Simple Living. San Francisco: Glide/Reed-Addison House, 1978.

Brown, Lester R. *The Twenty-Ninth Day: Accommodating Human Needs and Numbers to the Earth's Resources.* New York: Norton, 1978.

Carson, Rachel. *Silent Spring.* Boston: Houghton Mifflin, 1962; rev. ed. New York: Fawcett, 1973.

Commoner, Barry. *The Closing Circle: Nature, Man, and Technology.* New York: Knopf, 1971.

Dasmann, Raymond F. *Environmental Conservation.* New York: Wiley, 1968.

Douglas, William O. *The Three Hundred Year War: A Chronicle of Ecological Disaster.* New York: Random House, 1972.

Dubos, René. *A God Within.* New York: Scribner, 1972.

Ehrlich, Paul R. *The Population Bomb.* New York: Ballantine, 1968.

Gray, Elizabeth Dodson, and David Dodson Gray. *Growth and Its Implications for the Future.* Branford, Conn.: Dinosaur Press, 1975.

Leonard, Jeffrey H., J. Clarence Davies III, and Gordon Binder (eds.). *Business and Environment: Toward Common Ground.* Washington, D.C.: Conservation Foundation, 1977.

Leopold, Aldo. *A Sand County Almanac with Essays on Conservation from Round River.* San Francisco: Sierra Club/Ballantine, 1974.

Lundborg, Louis B. *Future Without Shock.* New York: Norton, 1975.

McHarg, Ian L. *Design With Nature.* New York: Natural History Press, 1969.

Marsh, George Perkins. *Man and Nature,* ed. by David Lowenthal. Cambridge, Mass.: Belknap Press of Harvard University Press, 1965.

Meadows, Donella H., Dennis L. Meadows, Jørgen Randers, and William W. Behrens III. *The Limits to Growth.* 2nd ed. New York: Universe, 1974.

Miller, G. Tyler, Jr. *Living in the Environment: Concepts, Problems, and Alternatives.* Belmont, Calif.: Wadsworth, 1975.

Mumford, Lewis. *The Pentagon of Power.* New York: Harcourt Brace Jovanovich, 1970.

Nash, Roderick. *Wilderness and the American Mind.* New Haven: Yale University Press, 1973.

Nash, Roderick (ed.). *The American Environment: Readings in the History of Conservation.* Reading, Mass.: Addison-Wesley, 1968.

National Parks for the Future: An Appraisal of the National Parks as They Begin the Second Century in a Changing America. Washington, D.C.: Conservation Foundation, 1972.

Passmore, John. *Man's Responsibility for Nature: Ecological Problems and Western Traditions.* New York: Scribner, 1974.

Progress as if Survival Mattered: A Handbook for a Conserver Society. San Francisco: Friends of the Earth, 1977.

Osborn, Fairfield. *Our Plundered Planet.* Boston: Little, Brown, 1948.

Reilly, William K. (ed.). *The Use of Land: A Citizens' Policy Guide to Urban Growth.* New York: Harper & Row, 1973.

Rivers, Patrick. *The Survivalists.* New York: Universe, 1975.

Santmire, H. Paul. *Brother Earth.* Nashville: Nelson, 1970.

Schumacher, E. F. *Small is Beautiful: Economics as if People Mattered.* New York: Harper & Row, 1973.

Seuss, Dr. *The Lorax.* New York: Random House, 1971.

Simon, John G., Charles W. Powers, and Jon P. Gunnemann. *The Ethical Investor.* New Haven: Yale University Press, 1972.

Stone, Christopher. *Should Trees Have Standing? Toward Legal Rights for Natural Objects.* Los Altos, Calif.: Kaufmann; New York: Avon, 1975.

Taking Charge: A Process Packet for Simple Living, Personal and Social Change. San Francisco: American Friends Service Committee, 1974; New York: Bantam Books, 1977.

Teale, Edwin Way. *The Wilderness World of John Muir.* Boston: Houghton Mifflin, 1954.

Ward, Barbara, and René Dubos. *Only One Earth: The Care and Maintenance of a Small Planet.* New York: Norton, 1972.

INDEX

ACKNOWLEDGMENTS

It is customary for an author to end the acknowledgment section with a tribute to a spouse for care, feeding, and support during the travail of authorship. I find it a requirement of honesty, however, to place the efforts of my wife Pat at the top of the list of those to whom I am deeply indebted. Even while working as director of public affairs for the U.S. Environmental Protection Agency before devoting full time to helping me with the book, she carried much of the load of organizing, editing, and rewriting the material as it progressed through several revisions. I was also assisted in research and formulation of concepts for the book by Patricia M. Nesbitt in early stages of the work, and for more than two years by Raymond L. Tretheway, III. A number of individuals at the Conservation Foundation, especially President William K. Reilly and Vice-President Jack Noble, contributed a great deal by reading parts of the manuscript and suggesting ways to make it more readable. John Rosenberg and Jeff Leonard of the Conservation Foundation also contributed editorial help, and Lucy McMichael gave secretarial assistance. I am grateful to Alan Abramson, Wallace Bowman, S. P. R. Charter, David Dodson Gray, Elizabeth Dodson Gray, Charles Little, George Lowe, Gordon J. F. MacDonald, John Rodman, John Waugh, and Dwain Winters for assistance in reviewing chapters and making valuable suggestions for improvement. Among others who gave assistance are Fred Anderson, Hazel Henderson, A. Starker Leopold, Estella Leopold, Dennis and Donella Meadows, Christina Peterson, Russell W. Peterson, Jørgen Randers, David Sive, Lee M. Talbot, Judith Ditmar Tretheway, and Beatrice Willard.

I also wish to express appreciation for financial assistance from the general funds of the Conservation Foundation, as well as to the Rockefeller Brothers Fund and to a family foundation which prefers to remain anonymous, for their grants to the Conservation Foundation in support of early stages of this project.